# Persian Cuisine

A good cookbook belongs in the kitchen,
not on the coffee table!

# Persian Cuisine

## Traditional, Regional, and Modern Foods

By

M. R. Ghanoonparvar

Line Illustrations by
Claudia Kane and Jill Lieber

**Mazda Publishers, Inc.**
Costa Mesa, California 2006

Mazda Publishers, Inc.
*Academic Publishers since 1980*
P.O. Box 2603, Costa Mesa, California 92628 U.S.A.
www.mazdapub.com

**Library of Congress Cataloging-in-Publication Data**
Ghanoonparvar, M. R. ( Mohammad Reza)
Persian Cuisine: Traditional, Regional, and Modern Foods
by M. R. Ghanoonparvar—New Edition.
p.cm.
**ISBN: 1-56859-191-8**
(Hard cover, alk. paper)
1. Cookery, Iranian. I. Title.
TX725.I7G434 2006
641.5955—dc22
2006044953

Printed in Hong Kong.

*For Mina and Trent*
*with love*

# Contents

# *Acknowledgements*

Many friends, acquaintances, and relatives as well as professional chefs in the course of many years have generously shared their knowledge of culinary arts with me. Regarding a number of regional and ethnic recipes, I am particularly indebted to Sadiqeh Abhari, Mina M. Dioun, Shamsi Faraji, Lucinda Farrokh, Guitty Givehchian, Maryam Jabbari, Parsa Jabbari, Shiva Jabbari, Fereshteh Karkouti, Mehrangiz Katanchi, Farideh Mohazzabi, Amineh Nakhshab, Mitra Nakhshab, Janet Noparast, Afsaneh Oskouy, Jaleh Pakpoor, Gazal Rashad, Sayeh Rashad, Shokuh Sharifian, Shahpar Torkian, Farzaneh Zahedani, and Fahimeh Zamani. Many of the photographs in this volume were provided by friends in Iran, the United States, and elsewhere, including Jamshid Bayrami, Farin Farzaneh, Jassem Ghazbanpour, Noosheen Hashemi, A. Kamron Jabbari, Rasoul M. Oskouy, Shabnam Rezaei, Susan Sprachman, and Diane Wilcox.

Mazda Publishers and I are especially grateful to Mahmoud Khossoussi of Maykadeh Restaurant, Mark Bolourchi of Pacific Plaza Imports, Morteza Negahi of Le Piyalet, Inc., and Darioush Khaledi of Darioush Winery for their professional support. In addition, Professor Faegheh Shirazi has kindly contributed many of the religious cultural notes for this volume, for which I am most appreciative. Special thanks to Nargess Yusefzadeh for assisting with many hours of research on new recipes for this collection. And I am most thankful to Professor Rudi Matthee for his contribution of the very informative and scholarly chapter on "Wine and Wine Drinking in Iran." As is the case with other books I have published with Mazda Publishers, the professional dedication of Dr. A. Kamron Jabbari and his editorial and production staff to the completion of this volume has been indispensable and is most appreciated. Finally, as always, I am most indebted and grateful to my wife, Diane, without whose love, dedication, encouragement, and inspiration this project would not have been possible or completed.

# Introduction

The cuisine of every nation is a way of celebrating its culture. It is true that food is a necessity for human survival, but combining various edible ingredients, devising different methods of preparation, and arranging and decorating various dishes for presentation at the table to members of families and guests is an art developed in every culture by many generations that requires not only skill, creativity, and patience, but also care and compassion. Persian cuisine is also the product of the skill, creativity, patience, care, and compassion of many generations of cooks, whether mothers, fathers, wives, or husbands preparing food for their families or professional cooks at royal courts and the homes of the affluent. The recipes presented in this book that comprise Persian cuisine also represent a celebration of several thousand years of Persian culture.

Like all cuisines, the Persian culinary tradition has also evolved throughout the course of centuries, and it is a reflection of the development of indigenous foods as well as adaptations from other cultures.

Given Iran's relatively large size and diversity of climates (from the Persian Gulf in the south to the Caspian Sea in the north), its history of several thousand years, and the numerous ethnic groups populating it, Persia—as it was called internationally less than a century ago—has a rich culinary tradition that differs from region to region and sometimes even season to season. However, Iran's national cuisine, which has spread to and influenced the cuisines of other cultures and countries in South and Central Asia and the Middle East, consists of ethnic and regional foods that have been refined and perfected over the course of many centuries, particularly by the master chefs of the royal courts. To the uninitiated tastes, Iranian food may seem both exotic and familiar: exotic because of the many novel combinations of vegetables, herbs, spices, and fruits; familiar because almost all the ingredients are commonly used in the West. What distinguishes this cuisine is essentially the subtlety of its emphasis on flavors.

Persian foods are categorized in more than a dozen main groups according to their ingredients and preparation methods. They include: *polo* (rice mixed with other ingredients such as legumes, meats, vegetables, or herbs), *khoresh* (stew-type dishes that are usually served over *chelo*, plain rice), *kabab* (generally, grilled meats), *ash* (thick pottage-like dishes), *abgusht* (soups), *dolmeh* (stuffed vegetables and grape leaves), *kufteh* (meat and/or rice balls), and *kuku* (vegetable or other soufflé-type dishes). Rice is one of the most important dietary staples in Iran and often serves as the main dish. Rice dishes are usually decorated with saffron-flavored grains of rice. Traditionally, red meat (usually mutton) and poultry are not consumed in the quantities that are customary in the West. Meats are often used to flavor dishes, as are other ingredients. I should mention here that in most of the red meat dishes in this book, the recipes provide an option of lamb or beef. I have done so for two reasons: firstly, it has been my experience that the taste of Persian lamb differs somewhat from that of American lamb, and secondly because beef is more readily available and of a better quality in the United States and Europe. It should be noted, however, that on the whole the end products of the recipes will not vary drastically in taste whether beef or lamb is used.

Persian foods are by no means bland, but neither are they spicy, as are some other ethnic cuisines. What distinguishes an Iranian table is the subtlety of the combination of flavors. A typical Iranian meal may consist of a rice dish with a meat sauce, yogurt, fresh herbs such as mint, basil, and tarragon, and freshly baked bread, of which there are many varieties available on every street corner.

Cookbook writing has a long tradition in Iranian history. There are extant recipe books by chefs of the royal courts or the homes of the notables, including two cookbooks from the 16th century, one of which is by the chef of the court of Shah Abbas the Great, and another from the 19th century, again by a chef affiliated with the royal court. There is even a cookbook written in verse from the 15<sup>th</sup> century. In recent years, the number of cookbooks published in Iran has increased, and there are now many available that deal with regional and ethnic foods as well as European and other cuisines. The present book, however, is the most comprehensive collection of recipes to date on Iranian cuisine.

In this selection of recipes, which also include those in *Persian Cuisine I, Traditional Foods* (first printing, 1982) and *Persian Cuisine II, Regional and Modern Foods* (first printing, 1984), both published by Mazda Publishers, I have tried to avoid redundancies by excluding hundreds of recipes that often have a slightly different name but are similar to those presented in this book. But I have also added many recipes as well as cultural notes of interest, and moreover simplified and updated the methods of preparation in many instances.

This combined new and totally revised editon, *Persian Cuisine: Traditional, Regional, and Modern Foods,* is a user-friendly cookbook that belongs in the kitchen, not on the coffee table! In keeping with this philosophy, the pictures in the volume for the most part come from the kitchens and tables of average users of these recipes, not from a professional studio using enhanced photography. That means that the user should be able to create the same end products seen in the photographs. Wine historians believe that winemaking originated in ancient Persia and wine has been an indisputably crucial component of Persian culture. Hence, a chapter on the history of wine in Iran has been added to this new edition. The book is divided into chapters according to the type of food, and a comprehensive list of the recipes is available in the Index.

M. R. Ghanoonparvar
University of Texas at Austin

Facing: A pomegranate tree.
*Photo by Kamron.*

# Herbs and Spices

Herbs and spices play an important role in Persian cuisine. Fresh herbs are used in most dishes when in season, and in dried form, generally prepared at home when fresh herbs are not available. While most herbs are grown locally and are cultivated throughout Iran, most spices are imported from India and elsewhere. Herbs and particularly spices in Iranian foods are used for aroma and flavor. They are used in moderation to enhance the flavor of other ingredients in the dish. Generally Persian cuisine does not use large amounts of hot spices, since they are thought to numb the taste buds and prevent enjoyment of the natural flavors in a dish. An exception to this rule consists of dishes that are indigenous to the coastal areas, especially along the coasts of the Persian Gulf, where hot and spicy foods are prevalent. While there are a large number of herbs that are sold fresh in vegetable and herb shops throughout the cities and are also available in dried form in herbalist and spice shops, the number of spices most commonly used in Persian cuisine is relatively limited. Among these, in addition to salt and black pepper, turmeric and saffron are favored. Below are descriptions of the most common herbs and spices used in Persian cuisine.

## Herbs

**Basil (*Reyhan*):** Fresh basil is a favorite at every table and is an important ingredient in *Sabzikhordan*, even though it is not used as much as other herbs in cooking. Nevertheless, it is used in a variety of dishes in Persian cuisine. There are several types of basil, most of which originate in Asia. The variety used in Iran has a stronger flavor than most common basils sold in supermarkets in the United States. Basil is a very delicate herb and should be used very soon after harvesting; otherwise the leaves will turn black.

Spice rack in an Iranian supermarket
in California.
*Photo by Kamron*

**Coriander (*Geshniz*):** This herb, which is also known as Chinese parsley and cilantro in United States, has a unique flavor which, unlike some other herbs, does not disappear after cooking. It is used in a wide variety of dishes and is a good substitute for parsley. Coriander seeds are also used to flavor many dishes in seasons when fresh coriander is not available.

**Dill (*Shevid*):** Chopped fresh dill or dried dill weed is used in a variety of dishes, including rice with fava or, as a substitute, lima beans and in *kufteh* (rice meatballs), among others. Dill can be cultivated in most climates and grows rather rapidly after harvesting. The unique flavor of dill sets it apart from other herbs, and its aroma enhances the flavor of other ingredients in a dish. In ancient times, dill was thought to be a remedy for a variety of physical ailments and discomforts, including hiccups. Dill seed is also used in some dishes, often as a substitute for fresh or dried dill.

**Fenugreek (*Shanbalileh*):** Unlike the fenugreek that is found in supermarkets in the United States in powder form and is actually from the seeds of this herb, *shanbalileh* has an intense flavor and is an indispensable herb for one of the most popular Iranian dishes, *Qormehsabzi*. Because of its strong aroma, this herb can be used to flavor other dishes as well.

**Leeks (*Tareh*):** In any dish in which a variety of herbs are used as the main ingredient, leeks often make up the bulk and one of its most important components. Leeks that grow in Iran are much more tender and can cook more easily than the thick stocks of leek available in the United States. For this reason, green onions are generally suggested as a substitute for leeks in this book.

**Marjoram (*Avishan-e Shirazi*):** Marjoram is often regarded as the domesticated version of oregano, which has a stronger flavor. It has, however, a flavor of its own and can be substituted for oregano or thyme.

**Oregano (*Avishan*):** This herb is used in many dishes, especially *Adasi*, a lentil paste which is served in wintertime for breakfast. It is from the same general family of marjoram and thyme, and it is often mistaken for one or the other, especially in bilingual dictionaries. This herb is usually used in dry form.

**Parsley (*Ja'fari*):** This is a widely used herb in many dishes. Even though parsley does not have the flavor and aroma of coriander, it is perhaps more utilized in Persian cuisine than coriander, given the fact that fresh green herbs make up the majority of the ingredients in dishes such as *Qormehsabzi* and *Ash-e Reshteh*, as well as many other kinds of *ash* and in stews.

**Pennyroyal (*Puneh*):** This wild herb, a member of the mint family, that grows in the mountains is only used to flavor yogurt and yogurt beverage. It can, however, be used to flavor thick soups and other dishes.

**Savory (*Marzeh*):** An herb in the mint family with a flavor similar to thyme and sage; although not as widely used as mint, tarragon, and basil, this herb is sometimes included in *Sabzikhordan* (see page 187) and can used in dishes that call for mint.

**Spearmint (*Na'na*):** This herb is not only used in fresh and dry forms in many Iranian dishes and summer beverages, but in fresh form as an indispensable part of *Sabzikhordan*, a combination of various fresh herbs, which is served at every Iranian table. Peppermint is rarely available or used in Iran, because of its overpowering flavor. Fresh or dried spearmint is also added to sautéed onions both as a decoration and as flavor in many *ash* recipes.

**Tarragon (*Tarkhun*):** Fresh tarragon is an important ingredient in *Sabzikhordan* and is also added to yogurt for flavoring. It is also used in several varieties of *ash* and *khoresh* in both fresh and dried forms.

**Watercress, Iranian variety (*Shahi*):** An herb often used in *sabzikhordan*.

# Spices

**Black Pepper (*Felfel-e Siyah*):** A mixture of this popular spice with turmeric and salt, which is generally referred to as *adviyeh* or seasoning, is the most indispensable ingredient in Persian cooking. With this mixture and in the absence of other spices, you can prepare most Persian cuisine recipes.

**Cardamom (*Hel*):** Powdered cardamom is used mostly in deserts, but its very aromatic flavor makes a great substitute for the much more expensive saffron. When saffron is not available, a blend of cardamom and turmeric can be used instead.

**Cinnamon (*Darchin*):** Cinnamon in powdered form plays an important role in many meat dishes. Great cooks sprinkle meat with cinnamon before browning it for *khoresh*, a secret that they rarely share with others. Cinnamon is the spice that lends its flavor to *Beryan*, the famous dish from Isfahan. It is also used in a wide variety of deserts.

**Cloves (*Mikhak*):** This spice that has a pungent but pleasant taste and aroma can add a unique flavor to many dishes, if used sparingly. Traditionally, cloves were prescribed by apothecaries for toothache, because it has a numbing quality.

**Ginger (*Zanjabil*):** This spice, which is used sparingly in certain regional dishes because it is too hot for the average Persian palate, is made of the ground up roots of the plant. It is the important ingredient in *Zanjabil-e Parvardeh* and *Zanjabil-e Parvardeh-ye Shekari*, which were traditionally prescribed by herbalists for rheumatic arthritis.

**Nutmeg (*Jowz-e Hendi*):** Although rarely used, this spice can add a unique flavor to many sauces as well as deserts. Fresh nutmeg is crushed for use in a variety of dishes when available. In Iran, however, it is not available in fresh form. Traditionally, nutmeg was prescribed for stomach upsets and also as an aphrodisiac.

**Paprika (*Felfel-e Sorkh*):** This spice is mostly used in Persian cuisine for decorating the tops of dishes such as *Halim Badenjan* and *Ash*.

**Saffron (*Za'faran*):** Regarded as the spice of kings, saffron is the most expensive spice in the world. The best saffron is cultivated in a relatively small area in the province of Khorasan, in northeastern Iran. The reason for its high price is that its cultivation and harvesting require great care. When it is ready to be

Saffron from Mashhad, Iran

picked, this must be done within a very short period of time. Saffron is also cultivated in other areas of Iran and other parts of the world, but the quality is far inferior to that of Khorasan saffron. It is used to give its pleasing aromatic flavor and color to *chelo* and all varieties of *polo* as well as many other dishes. In fact, there are few dishes in which saffron cannot be used. It is the flavor of the sought-after Iranian ice cream. Like many other spices, saffron can lose its flavor if it is heated in a microwave oven. Because it was so dear, parents often warned their children against eating too much saffron, telling them that it would make them laugh uncontrollably, and they could laugh themselves to death.

**Sumac (*Somaq*):** Sumac in powdered form, which has nothing in common with "poison sumac," is a dark brown spice that is sprinkled on all forms of *Kabab*. It has a tart, almost citric taste and brings out the flavor of all sorts of barbequed meat. It is also said to have medicinal qualities and to aid in digestion.

**Turmeric (*Zardchubeh*):** Other than salt and black pepper, turmeric may be the most important and most widely used spice in Persian cuisine. There are few *khorsh*es and *ash*es in which this spice is not used. Turmeric has a subtle flavor and gives an appetizing color to foods. When fried in cooking oil with other ingredients, the color of turmeric turns red. It is also the main ingredient in curry powder. Recent research classifies turmeric as an antioxidant that can help prevent cancer.

## Seeds

**Caraway Seeds (*Zireh-ye Kermani*):** This is a very popular ingredient in many *ash*es and soups. It is most widely used, however, mixed with plain rice, called *Zireh Polo*. As its name in Persian indicates, in Iran it is cultivated in the eastern province of Kerman.

**Celery Seeds (*Tokhm-e Karafs*):** These seeds are usually used, especially in winter when fresh celery was previously not available, to flavor soups, *ash*es, and other dishes.

**Cumin (*Zireh-ye Sabz*):** Cumin can be used in most *ash*es for additional flavoring. It can also be mixed with plain rice. On the whole, however, most people prefer its relative, caraway seed, which is more flavorful.

**Nigella Seeds (*Siyahdaneh*):** Next to sesame seeds, nigella seeds are the most popular seeds for decorating the tops of flatbreads. This seed is also used for pickling eggplants as well as in other *Torshi*s.

**Poppy Seed (*Khashkhash*):** Poppy seed is popular for sprinkling on Iranian flatbreads. The natural color of poppy seeds is a light creamy color. The poppy seed that is available in the United States is generally dyed black or different colors. In Iran, however, dried poppy seed is used in its natural form.

**Sesame Seed (*Konjed*):** This seed is mainly used to decorate various Iranian flatbreads and is also used in some sweets. Although other seeds are also used for this purpose, sesame is more popular than others. In fact, most families often recommend to the person who is given the responsibility of buying bread from specialized bakeries to buy *Nan-e Konjedi*.

# Mixed Spices

**Curry Powder (*Pudr-e Kari*):** This spice mixture has become more popular in recent decades. In Iran, spice merchants usually mix their own curry powder, about 50 percent of which is turmeric. The Iranian version is a milder form than what is generally used in Indian restaurants.

## Azerbaijan-Style Seasoning
### (Adviyeh-ye Makhlut):

*about ½ cup*

**Ingredients:**
*2 cup dried crushed fragrant pink rose petals*
*1 cup cinnamon*
*1 Tbs. cardamom*
*½ tsp black pepper*
*1 Tbs. marjoram*
*1 tsp nutmeg*
*½ tsp caraway seeds*

### DIRECTIONS FOR PREPARATION

Mix together all ingredients except caraway seeds and store in an airtight container. Add caraway seeds when using, unless recipe omits them.

## Seasoning for Rice Dishes
### (Adviyeh-ye Polo)

### DIRECTIONS FOR PREPARATION

Mix the ingredients for Azerbaijan-Style Seasoning, omitting caraway seeds.

# Rice and Rice Dishes
## *(Chelo, Polo and Tahchin)*

Rice is certainly one of the most important staples in the Iranian diet. In fact, rice for most Iranians is not necessarily a side dish but a main dish. Other foods or ingredients are put in rice, over rice, or around rice, but rice is the main feature.

The Iranian way of making rice is quite different from that of most other cuisines. The recipes that follow for *chelo* and *polo* will result in fluffy, separated grains of rice. Most of the dishes in this section can be served as whole meals accompanied perhaps with a salad. Since rice is a major part of Persian cuisine, naturally Iranians are often adamantly particular about the quality of rice they choose, especially for *chelo* and *polo*. The best rice available in Iran is grown around the coast of the Caspian Sea, in Mazandaran Province. *Sadri* and *dom siyah* (literally "blacktailed") are two of the best quality extra-long grain rice that are favorites of Iranians, both of which have a distinctive flavor and aroma.

In the United States, "basmati" rice, available in most Iranian, Middle Eastern, and South Asian grocery stores, offers perhaps the closest substitute in flavor, but using imported rice is not crucial. In choosing rice, select a good quality hard, long or extra-long grain rice for *chelo* and *polo*.

As rice plays a very important part in Iranian cooking, naturally, there is an abundant array of recipes, both traditional and modern. The variety of rice dishes is still further enriched by the special regional touches and variations on traditional dishes found in various parts of Iran.

*Chelo* is the term used for plain cooked rice, which is generally served with meats or topped with stew-like dishes (*khoresh*). Then there are *polo* (fluffy rice dishes), *kateh* and *dampokht* (simple, one-step rice dishes), and *tahchin* (literally 'arranged on the bottom' crusted rice dishes), which are most often mixed with a variety of meats, vegetables, fruits, seeds, and/or herbs, and, much like a casserole, are generally considered meals by themselves. They are served accompanied by salads, yogurt, pickles, or relishes, for both lunch and dinner.

A note of interest regarding the use of butter or margarine in these recipes: In Iran, ghee, or clarified butter, is considered to add the ultimate aroma and flavor to rice dishes. However, in recent years, ghee has been commonly replaced in many families with various kinds of vegetable oil.

# Chelo
## (Steamed plain rice)

*6 servings*

**Ingredients:**
*3 cups long or extra-long grain rice*
*¼ cup butter, melted*
**Spices:**
*4 Tbs. salt*
*1/8 tsp saffron, dissolved in 2 Tbs. warm water (optional)*

### DIRECTIONS FOR COOKING

**1.** Rinse the rice several times in warm water to remove the starch

**2.** Bring 8 cups or more water and 2 Tbs. salt to a boil in a large pot. (The pot should be large enough to allow the rice to roll around freely as the water boils.)

**3.** Drain the water from the soaked rice and add the rice to the boiling water. Boil 5 to 10 minutes (boiling time differs according to the quality of rice and the amount of soaking time) or until the kernels are no longer crunchy but still quite firm. Stir occasionally to prevent the grains from sticking together.

**4.** Drain the rice in a colander. (At this point other ingredients may be added to the rice for *polo*.)

**5.** Cover the bottom of the pot with some of the melted butter.

**6.** Sprinkle the rice into the pot a large spoonful at a time, heaping at center of pot so as not to touch the sides of the pot.

**7.** With the handle of a cooking tool, perforate the rice in several places all the way to the bottom of the pot and evenly pour over the rest of the melted butter. (More butter can be added.)

**8.** Cover the underside of the pot lid with a dish towel (which absorbs the moisture that would otherwise accumulate on the lid and drip back into the rice making it soggy) and place the lid tightly on the pot.

**9.** Cook the rice approximately 10 minutes over medium heat, then reduce the heat and allow the rice to steam for another 30 minutes or so. The heat can then be turned very low and the rice kept warm until serving time. Rice can also be steamed in a moderate oven for 30 minutes, then turned low until serving time.

**10.** Rice cooked atop the stove will form a golden crust, the *tahdig* (see following recipe) which can be loosened to be removed and served in one piece by soaking the bottom of the pot, lid closed, in cold water a few minutes. (A good *tahdig* is savored as proof of one's culinary abilities!) If you use a non-stick pot, soaking the pot is not necessary.

**11.** For decoration, take about 2/3 cup of the cooked rice and mix it well with the dissolved saffron so that the rice picks up the color evenly. When the plain rice has been placed on a serving platter, sprinkle the saffron-flavored rice over the top and serve.

# Tahdig
## (golden crust)

*Tahdig* can be made with virtually any rice recipe. For variety, try placing one of the following at the bottom of the pot after melting the butter (Step 5 of the *chelo* recipe) and before adding the rice:

*1 raw potato, peeled and thinly sliced*
*1 loaf thin flat bread\**

\* See bread recipes, especially *taftun,* or substitute one flour tortilla or half a loaf of pita bread.

Prepared by Fahimeh Z.

**Four types of *Tahdig*.**
Above, from left to right: plain rice;
rice under fava bean.
Top right: rice under sour cherry.
Right: potato under plain rice.
Prepared by Afsaneh O.

### *Tahdig* Appetizer

*Tahdig* can also be made separately from *chelo* or *polo* and served as an appetizer. Melt 2 Tbs. butter in a frying pan. Spread 2 cups *chelo* in the pan and fry until golden. Then turn the crust over and fry the other side. Transfer *tahdig* to a platter, break into several pieces, and top with *Qeymeh* or *Qormeh Sabzi*. (See pages 48 and 51 for recipes.)

## Adas Polo ba Gusht
(rice and lentils with meat)

*5 to 6 servings*

**Ingredients:**
*2 Tbs. butter*

*2 medium onions, sliced*
*1 ½ lb. beef or lamb cubes or pieces of chicken*
*1 cup lentils*
*3 cups uncooked rice and other ingredients in* chelo *recipe*
*¼ cup raisins or chopped dates (optional)*
**Spices:**
*½ tsp. salt*
*¼ tsp. cinnamon*
*½ tsp. turmeric*

### DIRECTIONS FOR COOKING

**1.** Sauté onions in butter; remove and set skillet and onions aside.
**2.** Sprinkle meat with spices. Brown on all sides in butter remaining in skillet from sautéing onions and some of the butter allotted in the *chelo* recipe, if necessary.
**3.** Add 2 cups water to meat; bring to a boil, reduce heat to medium and simmer for 1 hour or until meat is quite tender
**4.** Boil the lentils in enough salted water to cover them for about 10 minutes or until tender but not soft. Drain and set aside.
**5.** Cook rice in salted water according to directions for *chelo* through Step 4.
**6.** Mix together the lentils and rice (and raisins or dates, if desired).
**7.** Place some of the melted butter allotted in the *chelo* recipe on the bottom of the pot or casserole dish. Sprinkle half of the rice mixture in the pot or casserole; top with meat and cover meat with onions; cover meat and onions with remaining rice mixture. Pour over the top any juices remaining from having cooked the meat.
**8.** Continue steaming as in *chelo* recipe (Steps 7 to 11).

## Adas Polo
(rice with lentils)

*4 to 6 servings*

**Ingredients:**
*1 cup lentils*
*3 cups uncooked rice and other ingredients in* chelo *recipe*
*¼ cup raisins, currants, dates, or toasted slivered almonds (optional)*

### DIRECTIONS FOR COOKING

**1.** Boil the lentils in enough salted water to cover them for about 10 minutes or until tender but not soft. Drain and set aside.
**2.** Cook rice in salted water according to directions for *chelo* through Step 4.
**3.** Resume steps for *chelo*. alternating layers of rice and cooked lentils with other optional ingredients, or mixing all ingredients, except butter, before putting in pot to steam.
**4.** Follow Steps 7 to 11 of *chelo* recipe for steaming and serving.

Prepared by Diane W.

Prepared by Sayeh R.

# Albalu Polo
### (Rice with tart cherries)

*6 to 8 servings*

**Ingredients:**
*3 cups uncooked rice and other ingredients in*
      chelo *recipe*
*2 cups fresh pitted or 1 can tart pitted cherries*
*2 to 3 Tbs. sugar*
**Spices:**
*1 tsp. cinnamon (optional)*

**DIRECTIONS FOR COOKING**

**1.** Follow directions for *chelo* through Step 4.
**2.** Drain cherries (if using canned) and mix cherries with rice.
**3.** Follow Steps 5 through 10 for *chelo*. To serve, place rice on a platter and sprinkle with sugar and (if desired) cinnamon.

# Zereshk Polo
(rice with *zereshk*)

*6 to 8 servings*

**Ingredients:**
*1 cup dried* zereshk
*3 cups uncooked rice and other ingredients in* chelo *recipe*
*1 cup sugar (optional)*
**Spices:**
*¼ tsp. saffron dissolved in 2 Tbs. hot water*

### Zereshk
### (Barberry)

*Zereshk* is a tart wild berry that is now available in dried form in virtually all Iranian grocery stores. To clean, generously cover with water and soak for several minutes. Remove from water carefully, making sure that any grains of sand contained in the dried *zereshk* have settled on the bottom of the container. *Zereshk* is used in many of the recipes throughout this book.

### DIRECTIONS FOR COOKING

**1.** Soak *zereshk* in water for an hour and rinse thoroughly.
**2.** Cook rice according to recipe for *chelo* through Step 4.
**3.** Drain *zereshk* and mix with rice.
**4.** Continue Steps 5 through 10 in *chelo* recipe.
**5.** To serve, take ½ cup of the cooked rice and mix well with dissolved saffron; sprinkle over the rice in the serving dish. Also sprinkle top with sugar, if desired.

NOTE:This dish is an excellent accompaniment to any kind of baked chicken and goes very well with *Kuku Qandi* (see recipe in "Kuku..." section). See also *Morgh-o Polo.*

Prepared by Shahpar K.

# Kalam Polo
(rice with cabbage)

*9 to 10 servings*

**Ingredients:**
*¾ lb. ground beef or lamb*
*1 large onion, grated*
*1 medium head of cabbage, shredded*
*¼ cup butter or margarine*
*3 cups uncooked rice and other ingredients in* chelo *recipe*
*1 Tbs. butter*
**Spices:**
*1½ tsp. salt*
*¼ tsp. pepper*
*¼ tsp. turmeric*

**DIRECTIONS FOR COOKING**

**1.** Mix together meat, spices, and onion and press flat into frying pan; brown over medium heat, then turn over to cook other side. Break into small strips and keep warm over very low heat.
**2.** Sauté cabbage in butter or margarine for 10 minutes; add to meat.
**3.** Prepare rice as in *chelo* through Step 4.
**4.** Melt butter in bottom of large pot; spread evenly. Alternate 2-3 layers each of rice and cabbage-meat mixture in pot and follow Steps 7 through 10 of *chelo* recipe.

# Baqali Polo
(rice with fava beans and dill weed)

*4 to 6 servings*

**Ingredients:**
*1 lb. fresh or 1 10-12 oz. can of fava beans\**
*3 cups uncooked rice and other ingredients in* chelo *recipe*
*½ cup dried or ¾ cup fresh dill weed*

**DIRECTIONS FOR COOKING**

**1.** If using fresh beans, bring to a boil in 3-4 cups lightly salted water; reduce heat to medium and simmer for about 20 minutes or until beans are tender but not soft. If using canned beans, drain and set aside.
**2.** Remove beans from outer membrane; set aside.
**3.** Prepare rice according to *chelo* recipe through Step 4.
**4.** Combine the beans and dill weed with the rice.
**5.** Follow Steps 5 through 11 of *chelo* recipe for steaming and serving.

*Dried fava beans may be substituted for fresh or canned beans. These are available in Iranian, Italian and Greek grocery stores. If dried beans are used, soak them in water for several hours until tender. Cook over moderate heat and then follow the directions above. Fresh or frozen lima beans, which are more readily available, can be substituted for fava beans.

Prepared by Afsaneh O.

# Baqali Polo ba Gusht
(rice with fava beans, dill weed and meat)

*6 to 8 servings*

## Ingredients:
*2 medium onions, sliced*
*¼ cup butter or margarine*
*1 ½ lb. shoulder of lamb or beef, cut in chunks*
*3 cups uncooked rice and other ingredients in* chelo *recipe*
*¼ to 1/3 cup dried or ½ cup fresh chopped dill weed*
*1 lb. fresh or 1 10-12-oz. can fava beans*
## Spices:
*½ tsp. salt*
*½ tsp. pepper*
*¼ tsp. cinnamon*

### DIRECTIONS FOR COOKING

**1.** Sauté onions in butter or margarine. Remove from skillet and set aside.

**2.** Sprinkle seasonings over meat and brown meat on all sides in butter remaining from sautéed onions. Then add 2 cups water, cover, and let simmer 30 to 40 minutes or until meat is tender.

**3.** If using fresh beans, bring to a boil in 3 to 4 cups lightly salted water; reduce heat to medium and simmer for about 20 minutes or until beans are tender but not soft. Remove beans from outer membrane; set aside. If using canned beans, drain and set aside.

**4.** Follow recipe for *chelo* through Step 4.

**5.** Combine the beans and dill weed with the cooked rice.

**6.** Cover the bottom of the pot or casserole dish with about 1 ½ Tbs. of the melted butter allotted in the *chelo* recipe. Add half the rice mixture.

**7.** When the meat is quite tender (with about ¼ cup of water remaining), arrange it on top of the rice mixture in the pot. Place sautéed onions over the meat and top that with the remaining rice mixture.

**8.** Follow remaining steps for *chelo.*

*See *Baqali Polo* recipe for substitutes.

Prepared by Fereshteh K.

## Havij Polo ba Gusht
(rice with meat and carrots)

*6 to 8 servings*

| Ingredients: | Spices: |
| --- | --- |
| *1 onion, thinly sliced* | *½ Tsp. cinnamon* |
| *½ cup butter* | *½ tsp. salt* |
| *1 lb. beef or lamb, cut in cubes* | |
| *8 medium carrots, peeled and* | |
| *    cut into thin strips (1" × 1/8")* | |
| *3 cups uncooked rice and other* | |
| *    ingredients in* chelo *recipe* | |
| *3 Tbs. sugar* | |

### DIRECTIONS FOR COOKING

**1.** In a skillet, sauté onion in butter. Remove from butter and set aside both onions and skillet (for browning meat).

**2.** Sprinkle meat with seasonings and brown in butter remaining from the sautéed onions. Transfer meat to a small pot. Set aside butter and skillet (for browning carrots).

**3.** Add 2 cups water to pot with meat and bring to a boil; reduce heat and simmer for 30 to 40 minutes or until meat is tender.

**4.** Lightly brown carrots in butter (saved from browning meat). Remove carrots from butter and set aside both carrots and skillet (for making sauce).

**5.** When meat is tender, remove from water; mix meat with onions and set aside; also set juices aside for making sauce.

**6.** Follow recipe for *chelo* through Step 4. After buttering the bottom of pot or casserole dish, arrange layers of rice, topped with meat and onion mixture, topped with carrots.

**7.** Pour juices from cooking meat (about 1 cup) into skillet that was set aside from browning carrots and add sugar, mixing well until sugar is dissolved. Pour over layered rice, meat, and carrots.

**8.** Follow Steps 7 through 10 of *chelo* recipe for steaming.

## Sabzi Polo va Mahi
(vegetable rice with fish)

*6 to 8 servings*

Ingredients:
*3 cups uncooked rice and other ingredients in* chelo *recipe*
*2 bunches green onions, chopped*
*1 bunch parsley, chopped*
*1 bunch coriander, chopped*
*3 Tbs. butter or margarine*
*2 ½ lbs. fish filets*
Spices:
*1½ tsp salt*
*½ tsp pepper*
*1 tsp turmeric*

### DIRECTIONS FOR COOKING

**1.** Prepare rice as in *chelo* recipe through Step 4.
**2.** Sauté green onions, parsley, and coriander in 5 Tbs. of the butter from the *chelo* recipe.
**3.** Combine rice and greens.
**4.** Follow Steps 5 through 9 of the *chelo* recipe.
**5.** Sprinkle the fish with salt, pepper, and turmeric. In a skillet brown the fish on both sides in butter. Place fish on top of rice to steam during the final 10 to 15 minutes.
**6.** To serve: Remove the fish from the pot and proceed with Step 10 for *chelo*. Arrange the rice on a large platter; arrange the fish on top. Serve the *tahdig* in a separate dish. Serve with slices of fresh lemon or yogurt.

NOTE: This dish is traditionally served for the Persian New Year, which corresponds with the first day of spring. Before refrigerated transport was common in Iran, fish used in most inland cities was smoked. The smoked fish was marinated in lemon juice, herbs, and yogurt overnight, then fried and served with *sabzi polo.*

# Shirin Polo
(sweet, saffron-flavored rice with chicken)

*5 to 6 servings*

**Ingredients:**
*Peel of 2 oranges,\* cut into strips (1" x 1/8")*
*½ cup butter*
*3 large carrots, cut into strips (1" x 1/8")*
*1 cup slivered almonds*
*¾ cup sugar*
*¼ cup chopped, unsalted pistachio nuts*
*2 ½-3 lbs. boneless chicken thighs or breasts*
*¼ olive oil*
*2 medium onions, quartered*
*2 cups uncooked rice*
**Spices:**
*4 ½ Tbs. salt*
*1 tsp ground saffron, dissolved in ½ cup warm water*

## DIRECTIONS FOR COOKING

**1.** Place the orange peels into a small pan of cold water; bring to a boil; then drain the peels and run cold water over them. Repeat this step several times until the orange peeling is no longer bitter.
**2.** Melt the butter over medium heat in a heavy skillet. Add the carrots, stirring occasionally, and cook for 5 minutes, or until the carrots are semi-cooked. Add the orange peel, almonds, sugar, and saffron to the carrots. Reduce heat to low and stir constantly until the sugar dissolves; cover and simmer for 20 to 30 minutes. Add the pistachios and cook a few minutes more. Set aside.
**3.** Heat the oil in a heavy skillet. Pat the chicken dry with paper towels and brown on all sides in the oil. Remove the pieces to a plate; pour off and discard the fat in the skillet and return the chicken to the pan. Sprinkle with salt and arrange the onions on top. Add 4 cups water; bring to a boil over high heat; cover and reduce heat to low and simmer 30 minutes or until chicken is tender. Discard the juices. Let cool, then cut into bite-sized pieces. Set aside.
**4.** Preheat the oven to 350°.
**5.** Cook the rice following directions for *chelo* through Step 4.
**6.** Butter the bottom and sides of a 3- to 4-quart casserole. Spread half the rice evenly in the bottom of the casserole dish, top with half the chicken, and then layer with half the carrot, orange peel, and nut mixture. Repeat layers of rice, chicken, and carrot, orange peel, nut mixture. Cover tightly and bake for 30 minutes.

\*Remove the pulp from the orange peels to make them tastier and less bitter.

Prepared by Gazal R.

# Morqh-o Polo ba Zereshk
### (chicken with rice and *zereshk*)

*6 to 8 servings*

**Ingredients:**
*1 cup* zereshk
*2 lbs. chicken thighs or breasts*
*2 Tbs. butter or margarine*
*3 cups uncooked rice and other ingredients in* chelo *recipe*
**Spices:**
*½ tsp salt*

## DIRECTIONS FOR COOKING

**1.** Soak *zereshk* in water for an hour and rinse thoroughly to remove all sand.
**2.** Sprinkle chicken with cinnamon and salt; brown in butter on all sides and set aside.
**3.** Follow recipe for *chelo* through Step 4. Spread some of the butter allotted in the *chelo* recipe on the bottom of a large pot and sprinkle several spoonfuls of the cooked rice on the bottom of the pot and arrange chicken on top of it.
**4.** Drain *zereshk*. Sprinkle several spoonfuls over the chicken.
**5.** Mix the remaining *zereshk* with the rice and pile the mixture over the chicken.
**6.** Follow Steps 7 through 11 of *chelo* recipe.

Prepared by Fereshteh K.

## Estamboli Polo
### (rice with meat, tomatoes, and green beans)

*6 to 8 servings*

Ingredients:
*2 medium onions, sliced*
*1/3 cup butter or margarine*
*1 ½ lbs. beef or lamb tenderloin, cut in 1" x ¼" strips*
*5 large tomatoes, cut in ½" slices*
*3 Tbs. lemon juice*
*3 cups uncooked rice and other ingredients in*
  *chelo recipe (except saffron)*
*1 lb. fresh or frozen green beans*
Spices:
*1 tsp salt*
*1 tsp tumeric*
*½ tsp black pepper*

### DIRECTIONS FOR COOKING

**1.** Sauté onions in a skillet, using all but 1 Tbs. of the butter, which will be set aside. Add meat and seasonings and sauté until meat is tender, 10-15 minutes.
**2.** Wash, snip ends off green beans and cut into 1½" pieces. Boil in slightly salted water 10-15 minutes or until slightly undercooked; set aside. If using frozen beans, thaw and set aside.
**3.** Add remaining ingredients with ½ cup water and simmer over low heat for 20 minutes. Add fresh cooked or frozen green beans; simmer another 10 minutes or until beans are tender.
**4.** Follow recipe for *chelo* through Step 4; set rice aside.
**5.** Melt remaining butter, pour in bottom of pot or casserole dish.
**6.** Gently mix together rice and sauce in mixing bowl, then, transfer to buttered pot or casserole. If using a pot, cover with a dish towel and steam over medium-low heat for 30 minutes. If using a casserole dish, cover and bake in moderate, 350°, oven for 30 minutes.

## Reshteh Polo
### (rice with noodles and meat)

*8 to 10 servings*

Ingredients:
*2 medium onions, chopped*
*¼ cup butter*
*¾ cup raisins or chopped dates*
*2 lbs. lean lamb or beef, cut in ½" cubes*
*2-3 Tbs. lemon juice*
*½ lb. vermicelli noodles*
*3 cups uncooked rice and other ingredients in* chelo *recipe*
Spices:
*1 tsp salt*
*½ tsp turmeric*
*½ tsp cinnamon*
*¼ tsp black pepper*

### DIRECTIONS FOR COOKING

**1.** In a skillet, sauté onions in butter. Stir in raisins or dates, then remove from butter and set skillet aside.
**2.** Sprinkle seasonings over meat and brown in the skillet. Add 2 cups water and lemon juice, simmer for 30-40 minutes or until meat is tender.
**3.** Cook noodles according to package instructions; drain, rinse, and set aside.
**4.** Cook rice according to the directions for *chelo* through Step 4 and set aside.
**5.** Use some of the butter allotted in *chelo* recipe to cover the bottom of a large pot. Arrange layers of rice, onion and raisin (or date) mixture, noodles, and meat. Pour over remaining butter and continue steps for *chelo*.

# Keshmesh Polo
### (rice with raisins)

**Ingredients:**
*2 cups rice*
*1½ cups raisins*
*½ cup butter or margarine*
*1 loaf taftun (Persian flat) bread, or 2 loaves pita bread*
*3 Tbs. sugar*
**Spices:**
*2 Tbs. salt*
*1 tsp turmeric*
*1 tsp cinnamon*
*½ tsp ground ginger*

## DIRECTIONS FOR COOKING

**1.** Prepare rice as in *chelo* recipe through Step 4.

**2.** Sauté raisins in 3 Tbs. of the butter or margarine over low heat; sprinkle with seasonings and stir for 2 more minutes.

**3.** Melt 2 Tbs. of the butter in the bottom of a large pot (preferably non-stick). Cover bottom of pot with flat bread.

**4.** Spread 1 cup of the cooked rice on top of bread; sprinkle 2 Tbs. raisins evenly over rice; cover with half the remaining rice; top with remaining raisins, and cover with remaining rice.

**5.** Perforate rice with a spatula handle. Pour 3 Tbs. melted butter evenly over top. Cover lid of pot with a towel; cover pot, and steam over medium heat for 10 minutes. Then, reduce heat to low and steam for an additional 30 minutes. To serve: If using a non-stick pot, when ready to serve, dish out the rice and raisin mixture on a serving platter. Remove the crust (*tahdig*) from the bottom of the pot, break into serving size pieces, and serve on a separate dish. Sugar may be sprinkled on individual servings, if desired. If using a pot without a non-stick coating, before removing the lid, soak the bottom of the pot in cold water for a few minutes to loosen the bottom crust.

# Polo Kari
### (curried rice)

*6 to 8 servings*

**Ingredients:**
*1½ lbs boneless chicken breasts or thighs,*
   *cut in 1" pieces*
*1 lb fresh or frozen green peas*
*2 cups rice*
*5 Tbs. butter*
*2 large potatoes, grated*
**Spices:**
*2 tsp salt*
*1 Tbs. curry powder*

## DIRECTIONS FOR COOKING

**1.** Place chicken in 1½ cups water, ½ tsp salt, and curry powder and simmer for 30 minutes. Set aside.

**2.** Simmer fresh peas in water and ½ tsp salt for 15 minutes or just until tender. If using frozen peas, follow package directions. Drain and set aside.

**3.** Bring rice, 2 cups water, 2 Tbs. butter, and 1 tsp salt to a boil. Reduce heat and simmer for 20 minutes. Set aside.

**4.** Preheat oven to 350°. Mix together rice and chicken with stock. Grease a casserole dish with 1 Tbs. melted butter. Pour the chicken and rice mixture in the casserole dish and spread out evenly. Spread the grated potatoes evenly over the chicken and rice mixture. Cover and bake for 35-40 minutes.

**5.** Melt 2 Tbs. butter. Remove cover of casserole and pour melted butter evenly over top; then place under broiler for about 5 minutes or until potatoes are golden brown.

# Morassa Polo
## ('bejeweled rice': rice with chicken, orange peel, nuts, raisins and *zereshk*)

*6 to 8 servings*

**Ingredients:**
*1½ lbs. boneless chicken breasts*
*1 small onion, quartered*
*2 cups rice*
*1 cup orange peeling,\* slivered*
*½ cup slivered almonds*
*½ cup pistachio nuts, chopped*
*1 cup raisins*
*1 cup* zereshk
*2 Tbs. olive oil*
*10 Tbs. butter or margarine, melted*
**Spices:**
*2¼ Tbs. salt*
*¼ tsp saffron, dissolved in 2 Tbs. hot water*

### DIRECTIONS FOR COOKING

**1.** Place chicken, onion, and 1 tsp of the salt in 2 cups water in pot and simmer 30-40 minutes; remove, cool, and set aside.

**2.** Rinse rice several times in warm tap water; drain. Meanwhile, bring 8 cups of water and 2 Tbs. of salt to a boil in a large pot. Add rice to boiling water and boil rapidly for 5-10 minutes or until kernels are no longer crunchy but still quite firm. Drain and set aside.

**3.** Boil orange peeling in several cups of water for 15 minutes. Drain and set aside.

**4.** Mix together orange peelings, almonds, pistachios, raisins and *zereshk*.

**5.** Melt 2 Tbs. of the butter in a large pot (preferably nonstick), and evenly spread 1/3 of the cooked rice on the bottom of the pot. Arrange chicken pieces on top of rice.

**6.** Mix together remaining rice, orange peeling, nuts, raisins, *zereshk*, and cardamom and spread out evenly on top of chicken pieces. Perforate rice to the bottom of the pot with the handle of a spatula.

**7.** Mix together ½ cup hot water and butter or margarine and pour over the rice mixture.

**8.** Cover lid with a towel and secure on top of pot. Steam rice and chicken over medium heat for 15 minutes, reduce heat to low and steam for an additional 30-40 minutes.

**9.** Mix together 2 cups of the cooked rice with the saffron solution. Dish out the rice on a large platter in a mound; arrange the pieces of chicken with the crust (*tahdig*) around the bottom of the mound. Sprinkle the saffron-rice mixture on top.

\*Make sure to remove the pulp from the peelings. See NOTE to *Shirin Polo*.

# Lubiya Polo
## (rice with green beans and meat)

*6 to 8 servings*

**Ingredients:**
*1 lb. stew beef or lamb, cut in ½" cubes*
*½ cup butter or margarine*
*1 large onion, sliced*
*1½ lbs. fresh or frozen green beans*
*2 cups rice*
*1 cup tomato sauce*
**Spices:**
*2¼ Tbs. salt*
*½ tsp cinnamon*
*¼ tsp black pepper*

### DIRECTIONS FOR COOKING

**1.** Sprinkle meat with cinnamon and pepper; brown in ¼ cup butter. Add sliced onions, stirring occasionally for 5 minutes. Set aside.

**2.** Snap or cut off ends of green beans (if using fresh). Bring 2 cups water and 1 tsp. salt to a boil; add beans and reduce heat; simmer for 20 minutes or just until tender. (If using frozen beans, follow package directions.) Drain and set aside.

**3.** Rinse rice several times in warm tap water. Meanwhile, bring 8 cups water and 2 Tbs. salt to a boil. Add rice and boil rapidly for 5-10 minutes or until kernels are no longer crunchy but still firm. Drain and set aside.

**4.** Melt 4 Tbs. butter or margarine in the bottom of a large pot (preferably nonstick). Add 2/3 of the cooked rice. Top with the meat, then the green beans, spreading out evenly. Cover with remaining rice. Melt 4 Tbs. butter or margarine, mix in tomato sauce and pour mixture over top of rice.

**5.** Cover lid of pot with a towel and steam rice mixture over medium heat for 20 minutes, then reduce heat and steam an additional 45 minutes.

To Serve: Dish out the rice mixture and place on a serving platter; decorate the rice with the crusted rice (*tahdig*) from the bottom of the pot. If not using a nonstick pot, after dishing out the rice, cover the pot again with the lid and place the bottom of the pot in a few inches of cold water to loosen the crusted rice.

Variation: Ground beef may be substituted for stew beef.

With ground beef.
Prepared by Sayeh R.

With lamb cubes, garnished with chopped cooked tomatoes.
Prepared by Shamsi F.

# Qeymeh Polo
(rice with meat and yellow split peas)

*6 to 8 servings*

**Ingredients:**
*1 large onion, sliced*
*3 Tbs. butter or margarine*
*1½ lb stew beef or lamb, cut in 1" cubes*
*1 cup yellow split peas*
*3 large tomatoes, quartered*
*2 cups rice*
*2 medium potatoes, peeled and sliced*
*2 Tbs. lemon juice*
**Spices:**
*½ tsp cinnamon*
*1¼ Tbs. salt*
*½ tsp turmeric*
*¼ tsp black pepper*

**DIRECTIONS FOR COOKING**

**1.** Sauté onion in butter or margarine.
**2.** Sprinkle meat with cinnamon and add to onions. Brown about 5 minutes.
**3.** Place meat, onions, split peas, tomatoes, remaining seasonings, and 3 cups water in a large pot and simmer for 35-40 minutes or until meat is tender. Set aside.
**4.** Bring 6 cups water and 1 Tbs. salt to a boil. Meanwhile, rinse rice thoroughly in hot tap water several times. Drain and add to boiling water; boil rapidly, stirring occasionally, for 5-10 minutes or until rice is no longer crunchy but still very firm. Drain and set aside.
**5.** Melt 1 Tbs. butter or margarine in a large pot (preferably nonstick). Arrange sliced potatoes on the bottom.
**6.** Stir in lemon juice to meat and split pea mixture.
**7.** Place half the rice on top of the potatoes in the pot; remove meat and split pea mixture from broth (save the broth) and spread evenly over the rice; cover with remaining rice.
**8.** Perforate the rice in several places down to the potato layer with the handle of a spatula; pour over the broth; cover the lid of the pot with a cloth or paper towel and cover the pot tightly with it. Cook over medium heat for 10 minutes, then reduce heat to low and steam for an additional 40-45 minutes.

To serve: Place rice mixture on a platter and decorate with the potatoes from the bottom of the pot (which should be a golden brown).

# Qormeh Sabzi Polo
### (rice with meat and green vegetables)

*6 to 8 servings*

Ingredients:
*1½ lbs stew beef or lamb, cut in 1" cubes*
*¼ cup butter or margarine*
*2 bunches parsley, chopped*
*2 bunches scallions (or leeks, or green onions), chopped*
*2 dried limes, crushed, or 2 Tbs. lemon juice*
*1 onion, quartered*
*2 cups rice*
Spices:
*½ tsp cinnamon*
*2¼ Tbs. salt*
*¼ tsp black pepper*
*1 tsp turmeric*

### DIRECTIONS FOR COOKING

**1.** Sprinkle meat with cinnamon and brown in 6 Tbs. butter or margarine. Stir in parsley and scallions (leeks or onions) for 2 minutes.
**2.** Put 2 cups water in a pot; add meat, vegetable mixture, ½ tsp of the salt and remaining seasonings, and dried limes or lemon juice; cook for 40-50 minutes or until the meat is tender.
**3.** Meanwhile, rinse rice in warm water several times while bringing 6 cups water and 2 Tbs. salt to a boil; add rice to boiling water; boil rapidly for 5-10 minutes or until the rice kernels are no longer crunchy but still quite firm. Drain and set aside.
**4.** Melt 2 Tbs. butter or margarine in a large (preferably nonstick) pot. Pour in half the cooked rice.
**5.** Remove meat and vegetable mixture from the pot (save the juices); spread over rice in pot.
**6.** Pour the remaining rice over this mixture and spread out; pour the juices evenly over the top. Cover lid of the pot with a cloth or paper towel; place tightly on top of pot. Cook on top of the stove over medium heat for 10 minutes; then reduce heat and cook an additional 30-40 minutes.

# Qonabid Polo (Qom)
### (rice with meat and kohlrabi)

*6 to 8 servings*

Ingredients:
*1½ lb ground meat*
*2 onions, sliced*
*10 Tbs. butter or margarine*
*1½ lb kohlrabi*
*1 cup yellow split peas*
*2 cups rice*
*2 cups tomato sauce*
Spices:
*2 tsp cinnamon*
*½ tsp black pepper*
*3 Tbs. salt*

### DIRECTIONS FOR COOKING

**1.** Sprinkle meat with cinnamon and pepper and brown in its own fat in a skillet; set aside.
**2.** Sauté onions in ¼ cup butter or margarine in a large skillet; add kohlrabi and stir for 5 minutes; set aside.
**3.** Simmer yellow split peas in water for 20 minutes, or until cooked, but not soft; drain and set aside.
**4.** Rinse rice several times in hot tap water to remove starch; drain. Bring 8 cups water and salt to a rapid boil in a large pot. Gradually add rice to boiling water and boil rapidly for 5-10 minutes or until kernels are no longer crunchy but still quite firm. Drain rice in a colander. Set aside.
**5.** Melt 2 Tbs. butter in a large pot. Mix together rice, meat, onion, kohlrabi mixture, and tomato sauce and pour into the pot. With the handle of a spatula, perforate rice mixture to bottom of pot several times. Wrap lid of pot with a towel; cover pot and steam the mixture over low heat for 30 minutes.

# Polo-ye Qalebi-ye Shirazi
(rice with chicken, eggplants, and *zereshk*, Shiraz style)

*6-8 servings*

**Ingredients:**
½ *cup dried* zereshk
*1½ lbs. boneless chicken breasts or thighs*
*1 medium onion, quartered*
*2 cups rice*
*2 medium eggplants*
*¼ cup olive oil*
*1½ cup plain yogurt*
*2 eggs*
*1 Tbs. sugar*
*4 Tbs. melted butter or margarine*
**Spices:**
*3 Tbs. salt*
*¼ tsp saffron, dissolved in 2 Tbs. hot water*

## DIRECTIONS FOR COOKING

**1.** Thoroughly wash and soak *zereshk* in warm water and set aside.

**2.** Cook chicken with onion, ½ tsp salt and 2 cups water in a pot for 30-40 minutes over medium heat or until chicken is tender (add more water, if necessary) Remove chicken from broth, cool and set aside. Also set aside the broth and keep warm.

**3.** Peel eggplants and slice into rings about 1 inch (2 ½ cm) thick. Sprinkle with salt and set aside for 30 minutes. Then wipe off salt and moisture with paper towel and brown on both sides in oil, adding more oil gradually as needed (use additional oil if necessary).

**4.** Bring 8 cups water and 2 Tbs. salt to a boil in a large pot. Rinse rice several times in warm water and add gradually to the boiling water; allow to boil rapidly for 5-10 minutes or until the kernels are no longer crunchy but still firm. Drain and set aside.

**5.** Preheat oven to 350°.

**6.** Beat together yogurt, eggs, and sugar. Mix in 1½ cups of the cooked rice.

**7.** Drain water from *zereshk* and mix in with remaining rice.

**8.** Spread 2 Tbs. melted butter or margarine over the bottom of a large casserole and spread the yogurt-rice mixture evenly in the bottom of the casserole.

**9.** Arrange the chicken in a layer on top of the yogurt-rice mixture and top that with the eggplants.

**10.** Top that with the rice and *zereshk* mixture and even out the surface.

**11.** Stir in the dissolved saffron in the warm chicken broth (set aside in Step 2) and pour evenly over the top of the rice mixture; bake for 30 minutes, then reduce heat to low (200°) and bake an additional 30 minutes. Cut in squares to serve.

# Polo Meygu
(rice with shrimp)

*6 to 8 servings*

**Ingredients:**

*1 ½ lb medium-sized fresh or frozen shrimp, shelled and de-veined*
*¼ cup chopped fresh celery leaves*
*1 medium onion, chopped*
*10 Tbs. butter or margarine*
*1 bunch parsley, chopped*
*3 tomatoes, quartered*
*2 Tbs. lemon juice*
*2 cups rice*

**Spices:**
*2¼ Tbs. salt*
*¼ tsp black pepper*
*1 tsp cinnamon*

## DIRECTIONS FOR COOKING

**1.** Bring 3 cups water to a boil; drop shrimp along with celery leaves into boiling water; reduce heat and simmer 3 to 4 minutes; drain. If using frozen shrimp, drop into boiling water, bring to a boil again, reduce heat and simmer 3 to 4 minutes; drain. Cut off tails and set aside.

**2.** Sauté onions in ¼ cup (8 Tbs.) butter or margarine. Stir in parsley for one minute.

**3.** Add seasonings, tomatoes, lemon juice, and ½ cup water to onions and parsley and simmer over medium heat for 15 minutes.

**4.** Rinse rice in warm tap water several times; drain. Bring 6 cups water and 2 Tbs. salt to boil in a large pot. Gradually add rice and boil rapidly for 5-10 minutes or until kernels are no longer crunchy but still quite firm. Drain and set aside.

**5.** Melt 2 Tbs. butter or margarine in a large pot (preferably non-stick). Sprinkle cinnamon evenly over the butter or margarine in the bottom of the pot. Add half the rice and spread out evenly.

**6.** Mix together shrimp and tomato-onion-parsley mixture. Top rice in pot with this mixture and add remaining rice, spreading out evenly. Cover lid of pot with a towel and secure lid to pot. Steam rice over medium heat for 10 minutes; reduce heat to low and steam an additional 30 minutes.

# Polo Meygu-ye Kari
## (curried rice with shrimp)

*8 servings*

**Ingredients:**
*1½ lb fresh or frozen baby shrimp, shelled and de-veined*
*¼ cup chopped fresh celery leaves*
*2 cups rice*
*¼ cup butter or margarine*
**Spices:**
*2½ Tbs. salt*
*2 Tbs. curry powder*

### DIRECTIONS FOR COOKING

**1.** Bring 3 cups water and 2 Tsp. salt to a boil; drop shrimp and celery leaves into boiling water, reduce heat and simmer 3 to 4 minutes; drain, cut off tails, and set aside.
**2.** Rinse rice in warm tap water several times; drain. Bring 6 cups water and 2 Tbs. salt to a boil; gradually add rice and bring to a rapid boil for 5-10 minutes or until kernels are no longer crunchy but still quite firm; drain and set aside.
**3.** Preheat oven to 350°.
**4.** Melt the butter or margarine and use 2 Tbs. of it to grease a casserole dish. Pour the rice into the casserole dish and smooth out the surface. Arrange the shrimp evenly on top of the rice.
**5.** Mix the curry powder into the remaining melted butter or margarine and pour evenly over the shrimp. Cover the casserole dish and bake for 35-40 minutes.

# Polo Torki
## ('Turkish rice': tomato-flavored rice with meat and onions)

*5 to 6 servings*

**Ingredients:**
*1 lb lamb or beef, cut in ¼" cubes*
*½ cup butter or margarine*
*2 onions, sliced*
*2 cups rice*
*2 cups tomato sauce*
**Spices:**
*1½ tsp salt*

### DIRECTIONS FOR COOKING

**1.** Sprinkle meat with ¼ tsp salt, then brown in ¼ cup butter or margarine.
**2.** Add onions and sauté over medium heat for 5 minutes.
**3.** Transfer to a saucepan; add 1½ cups water and simmer for 30 minutes.
**4.** Melt ¼ cup butter over medium heat and stir in uncooked rice for 5 minutes.
**5.** Add all ingredients in addition to 2 cups water to meat mixture and bring to a boil; reduce heat to low and simmer for 25-30 minutes.

# Polo Rubiyun I

(rice with shrimp, Khuzestan style)

*5 to 6 servings*

## Ingredients:
*1 onion, chopped*
*3 Tbs. olive oil*
*2 cloves garlic, minced*
*1½ lb shrimp*
*2 cups chopped parsley*
*2 Tbs. tamarind paste*
*3 cups rice*
*½ cup butter, melted*
## Spices:
*2 Tbs. salt*
*½ tsp black pepper*
*1 tsp turmeric*
*2 tsp powdered cumin*
*1 Tbs. coriander seeds*
*1 tsp fenugreek*

### DIRECTIONS FOR COOKING

**1.** Sauté onion in olive oil. Stir in garlic.
**2.** Add shrimp and stir over medium heat for a few minutes.
**3.** Mix in parsley, tamarind paste, ½ tsp of the salt, and other spices; remove from heat.
**4.** In a large pot, bring 8 cups of water and remaining salt to a boil. Add rice and boil for 10 minutes. Drain the rice in a colander.
**5.** Grease the bottom of a casserole dish with some of the butter. Cover the bottom of the dish with half the cooked rice. Then cover with half the shrimp mixture and top with remaining rice and the remaining shrimp mixture. Pour remaining melted butter on top. Cover and bake in a 350° oven for 35 to 40 minutes.

# Polo Rubiyun II

(rice with shrimp, Khuzestan style)

*5 to 6 servings*

## Ingredients:
*1 onion, chopped*
*3 Tbs. olive oil*
*2 cloves garlic, minced*
*2 Tbs. chopped chili pepper*
*1 lb shrimp*
*2 cups chopped parsley*
*1 cup* zereshk
*1 cup chopped walnuts*
*2 Tbs. tamarind paste*
*3 cups rice*
*½ cup butter, melted*

## Spices:
*2 Tbs. salt*
*½ tsp black pepper*
*1 tsp turmeric*
*2 tsp powdered cumin*
*1 Tbs. coriander seeds*
*1 tsp fenugreek*
*½ tsp saffron, dissolved*
*   in ¼ cup hot water*

### DIRECTIONS FOR COOKING

**1.** Sauté onion in olive oil. Stir in garlic and chili pepper.
**2.** Add shrimp and stir over medium heat for a few minutes.
**3.** Mix in parsley, *zereshk*, walnuts, tamarind paste, ½ tsp of the salt, and other spices, except for saffron, and remove from heat.
**4.** In a large pot, bring 8 cups of water and remaining salt to a boil. Add rice and boil for 10 minutes. Drain the rice in a colander.
**5.** Grease the bottom of a pot with some of the butter. Mix the rice with the shrimp mixture and transfer to the pot. Pour remaining melted butter over top. Cover and simmer over low heat for 40 to 50 minutes.
**6.** To serve, mix about 1 cup of the rice mixture with the saffron solution. Dish out the rice (without the crust) on a platter. Break off pieces of the crust and place around the rim of the platter. Sprinkle saffron rice mixture on top.

# Tahchin-e Morgh
(chicken in a crust of saffron-flavored rice)

*6 to 8 servings*

**Ingredients:**
*3 cups uncooked rice*
*1½ cups plain yogurt*
*2 eggs*
*¾ cup butter*
*3 lbs. chicken thighs or breasts*
**Spices:**
*4 Tbs. salt*
*1 tsp saffron, dissolved in ¼ cup hot water*

## DIRECTIONS FOR COOKING

**1.** Cook rice according to recipe for *chelo* through Step 4.

**2.** Mix 3 cups of the cooked rice in a separate bowl with yogurt.

**3.** Add dissolved saffron to rice and yogurt mixture. Add eggs and stir.

**4.** Melt butter in a large, wide-bottomed (preferably nonstick) pot. Arrange pieces of chicken at the bottom of the pot; pour rice and yogurt mixture over chicken and smooth the top. Add the remaining plain rice on top and pour melted butter evenly over it. Cover the pot lid, as in Step 8 of the *chelo* recipe, with a dish towel and place tightly on the pot. Cook over medium heat for 10 to 15 minutes, then reduce to low heat and cook 40 to 50 minutes more.

**5.** If using a nonstick pot, when ready to serve, place serving dish over the pot and turn pot upside down and carefully remove the pot. The *tahchin* will then sit on the serving dish like a cake. With other pots, before removing the lid, soak the bottom of the pot in cold water for a few minutes. This will help loosen the crust. Then, remove the loose, white rice from the top and arrange on serving platter. Next, break the saffron rice with chicken into pieces and position around and on top of the loose rice or on a separate serving dish.

**6.** This dish can also be prepared without the plain rice and baked, covered, in a large, oblong Pyrex baking dish, in which case the chicken should be browned lightly on both sides in butter or margarine and arranged evenly in the bottom of the lightly greased baking dish. Follow the steps above for the rice and yogurt mixture and pour over the chicken. Bake in a moderate 350° oven for 1 hour. In this case, the remaining white rice can be steamed according to Steps 5 through 10 of the *chelo* recipe.

Prepared by Sayeh R.

# Tahchin-e Esfenaj
(rice with a crust of spinach)

*8 to 10 servings*

**Ingredients:**
*1½ lbs beef or lamb, cut in 1" cubes*
*½ cup butter or margarine*
*2 lbs fresh spinach*
*3 cups rice*
*1 onion, sliced*
*2 eggs*
*1 cup plain yogurt*
*½ lb pitted prunes*
**Spices:**
*1 tsp cinnamon*
*3 Tbs. salt*
*¼ tsp saffron, dissolved in 2 Tbs. hot water*

## DIRECTIONS FOR COOKING

**1.** Sprinkle meat with cinnamon and brown in 3 Tbs. butter or margarine. Set aside.

**2.** Cook spinach in 2 cups water and 1 tsp salt just until tender. Drain and set aside.

**3.** Bring 8 cups water and remaining salt to a boil in a large pot. Meanwhile, rinse rice several times in warm tap water; drain. Gradually add rice to boiling water and boil for 5-10 minutes or until kernels are no longer crunchy but still firm. Drain and set aside.

**4.** Preheat oven to 350°.

**5.** Sauté onions in 2 Tbs. butter or margarine. Set aside.

**6.** Mix together eggs, yogurt, saffron, spinach and 1 cup of the cooked rice.

**7.** Transfer sautéed onions to a deep casserole or a large nonstick pot and spread evenly over the bottom.

**8.** Spread half the spinach-rice mixture on top of the onions, then layer with meat, prunes, and the remaining spinach-rice mixture. Then sprinkle over the remaining rice.

**9.** With a spatula handle, perforate rice to the bottom of the dish or pot to facilitate the steaming process; pour 3 Tbs. melted butter evenly over the rice.

**10.** Bake in preheated oven for 30 minutes, then reduce heat to low (200°) and bake another hour. If using a pot and cooking on the stove, cover the lid with a towel and put lid on the pot. Cook over medium heat for 10-15 minutes, then reduce heat and let cook for another hour.

# Tahchin-e Barreh
(lamb and orange peel in a crust of saffron-flavored rice)

*5 to 6 servings*

**Ingredients:**
*3 lbs shoulder of lamb*
*1 onion, quartered*
*peelings of 2 oranges, cut into narrow strips (1" x 1/8")*
*2 cups rice*
*3 cups plain yogurt*
*2 eggs, beaten*
*¼ cup slivered almonds*
*¼ cup pistachio nuts, chopped*
*¼ cup butter or margarine, melted*
**Spices:**
*3 Tbs. salt*
*½ tsp saffron, dissolved in 2 Tbs. hot water*

## DIRECTIONS FOR COOKING

**1.** Place meat, onion, 3 cups water and ½ tsp salt in a medium-size pot and simmer over medium heat for 40 minutes.

**2.** Boil orange peelings in a generous amount of water for 15 minutes. Drain and set aside.

**3.** Rinse rice several times in warm tap water. Bring 8 cups water and 2½ Tbs. salt to a boil; gradually add rice and boil for 5-10 minutes or until kernels are no longer crunchy but still quite firm. Drain and set aside.

**4.** Mix together saffron solution, yogurt, and eggs. Mix together orange peeling, almonds, pistachios and cooked rice.

**5.** Pour 2 Tbs. of the butter or margarine in a wide-bottomed (preferably nonstick) pot. Arrange pieces of lamb on the bottom of the pot; top with rice mixture. Spread out surface and perforate several times with the handle of a spatula.

**6.** Pour remaining butter or margarine evenly over top. Cover the pot lid with a dishtowel (to absorb moisture) and place tightly over pot. Steam over medium heat for 15 minutes; reduce heat to low and continue steaming for 40-50 minutes. This dish can also be baked, covered, in a moderate oven (350°) for 40-50 minutes.

To Serve: If using a nonstick pot, when ready to serve, remove the lid and place a serving dish over the pot and turn pot upside down while holding the platter. The pot will then be sitting upside down on the platter. When it is carefully removed, the *tahchin* will sit on the serving dish like a cake. If not using a nonstick pot, before removing the lid, soak the bottom of the pot in cold water for a few minutes to help loosen the crust. Then, remove the rice from the top and arrange on a serving platter. Next, break the crust into serving-size pieces and arrange around and on top of the rice on the serving platter or on a separate serving dish.

# Tahchin-e Badenjan

(eggplants and meat in a crust of
saffron-flavored rice)

*6 to 8 servings*

Ingredients:
*1 lb stew beef or lamb*
*¼ cup butter or margarine*
*5 medium eggplants*
*¼ cup olive oil*
*2 cups rice*
*1 medium onion, sliced*
Spices:
*2½ Tbs. salt*
*1 tsp turmeric*
*¼ tsp saffron, dissolved in 2 Tbs. hot water*

### DIRECTIONS FOR COOKING

**1.** Sprinkle meat with ½ tsp salt and the turmeric and brown in butter or margarine. Add 1½ cups water and simmer over medium heat for 30 minutes. Set aside both meat and broth.

**2.** Peel and slice eggplants lengthwise; sprinkle with 1 tsp salt and set aside for 15-20 minutes. Then, wipe off salt and excess moisture with paper towel and brown on both sides in small amounts of olive oil, adding more when necessary. Set aside.

**3.** Rinse rice several times in warm tap water; drain. Bring 6 cups water and 2 Tbs. salt to a boil; slowly add rice and boil rapidly for 5-10 minutes or until kernels are no longer crunchy but still quite firm. Drain and set aside.

**4.** Melt 2 Tbs. butter in the bottom of a large pot. Spread onion evenly over the bottom of the pot; top with 1 cup of the cooked rice. Place meat on top of the rice, then layer with eggplants and remaining rice.

**5.** Mix saffron solution into broth from cooking meat and pour evenly over rice. Cover lid of the pot with a towel; place on pot and steam over medium heat for 10 minutes; then, reduce heat and steam for an additional 35-40 minutes. Serve with yogurt.

# Tahchin-e Gusht-o Sibzamini

(a crust of potatoes and meat with cinnamon-
flavored rice)

*5 to 6 servings*

Ingredients:
*1 lb ground beef or lamb*
*1 onion, grated*
*2 cups rice*
*½ cup butter or margarine*
*3 large potatoes, peeled and grated*
Spices:
*3 tsp cinnamon*
*2¼ Tbs. salt*
*¼ tsp. black pepper*

### DIRECTIONS FOR COOKING

**1.** Mix together meat, onions, 1 tsp. cinnamon, ½ tsp of the salt, and pepper, in the meat's own fat over medium-low heat. Set aside.

**2.** Rinse rice several times in warm tap water; drain. Bring 6 cups water and 2 Tbs. salt to a boil; add rice slowly and boil rapidly for 5-10 minutes or until kernels are no longer crunchy but still quite firm. Drain and set aside.

**3.** Melt ¼ cup butter or margarine in a wide-bottomed pot. Spread grated potatoes evenly at the bottom of the pot. Top with meat, then half the cooked rice. Sprinkle with 1 tsp cinnamon; add the remaining rice and sprinkle with 1 tsp cinnamon.

**4.** Perforate with a spatula handle; pour melted butter evenly over top. Cover the lid of the pot with a dishtowel and place securely over pot. Steam over medium heat for 10-15 minutes; reduce heat and steam an additional 30 minutes.

## Tahchin-e Morgh-o Kadu
(chicken and zucchini in a crust of
saffron-flavored rice)

*6 to 8 servings*

**Ingredients:**
*2½ lb. skinless chicken thighs*
*2 Tbs. olive oil*
*¾ cup butter or margarine*
*8 medium-size zucchinis*
*2 cups rice*
*2 cups yogurt*
*2 eggs, beaten*
**Spices:**
*2¼ Tbs. salt*
*¼ tsp pepper*
*¼ tsp saffron, dissolved in 2 Tbs. hot water*

### DIRECTIONS FOR COOKING

1. Sprinkle chicken with ½ tsp salt and pepper and brown in olive oil on all sides.
2. Melt 2 Tbs. butter in a large pot (preferably non-stick). Arrange chicken in the bottom. Set aside.
3. Peel and cut zucchini lengthwise. Brown on both sides in ¼ cup butter or margarine.
4. Rinse rice several times in warm tap water; drain. Bring 6 cups water and 2 Tbs. salt to a boil. Slowly add rice and boil rapidly for 5-10 minutes or until kernels are no longer crunchy but still firm. Drain and set aside.
5. Mix 2 cups of the cooked rice with yogurt, eggs and saffron solution and spread evenly over chicken in the pot.
6. Top with zucchini and then cover with remaining rice. Melt remaining butter and pour evenly over top of rice. Cover lid of pot with a towel; place on pot. Steam rice over medium heat for 20-25 minutes; reduce heat and steam for another 30 minutes.

To loosen crust, follow serving directions for *Tahchin-e Barreh.*

## Tahchin-e Gusht-o Gowjeh Farangi
(meat and tomato in a crust of
saffron-flavored rice)

*4 to 5 servings*

**Ingredients:**
*1 lb stew beef or lamb*
*6 Tbs. butter or margarine*
*5 medium tomatoes, quartered*
*2 cups rice*
*1 medium onion, sliced*
*2 eggs, beaten*
**Spices:**
*1 tsp cinnamon*
*2¼ Tbs. salt*
*¼ tsp pepper*
*¼ tsp saffron, dissolved in 2 Tbs. hot water*

### DIRECTIONS FOR COOKING

1. Sprinkle meat with cinnamon, ½ tsp salt and pepper and brown in 2 Tbs. butter or margarine. Add 1 cup water and tomatoes and simmer for 30 minutes.
2. Rinse rice several times in warm tap water; drain. Bring 6 cups water and 2 Tbs. salt to a boil; add rice slowly and boil rapidly for 5-10 minutes or until kernels are no longer crunchy but still firm. Drain and set aside.
3. Melt 2 Tbs. butter or margarine in the bottom of a medium pot (preferably non-stick). Arrange onions evenly on bottom of pot and cover with 2 cups of the cooked rice.
4. Stir eggs thoroughly into meat sauce. Spread this mixture evenly over the rice in the pot. Top with remaining rice.
5. Mix together dissolved saffron and 2 Tbs. melted butter or margarine and pour evenly over rice. Cover the lid of the pot with a towel and cover the pot. Steam rice for 20 minutes over medium heat; reduce heat to low and steam 30 minutes more.

# Tahchin-e Buqalamun

(turkey breasts in a rice crust)

*6 to 8 servings*

**Ingredients:**
*3 lbs. turkey breasts*
*2 cups plain yogurt*
*3 cups uncooked rice*
*3 eggs*
*¾ cup butter*
**Spices:**
*4 Tbs. salt*
*1 tsp saffron, dissolved in ¼ cup hot water*

### DIRECTIONS FOR COOKING

**1.** Soak turkey in yogurt overnight in refrigerator.

**2.** Remove turkey from yogurt (save the yogurt), and cook in 3 cups of water for 45 minutes or until tender.

**3.** Cook rice according to recipe for *chelo* through step 4.

**4.** Mix 3 cups of the cooked rice in a separate bowl with yogurt. Add eggs and stir.

**5.** Melt butter in a large, nonstick baking pan. Arrange pieces of turkey in the pan; pour rice and yogurt mixture over chicken and smooth the top. Add the remaining plain rice on top and pour melted butter evenly over it. Cover the pot lid, as in step 8 of the *chelo* recipe, with a dishtowel and place tightly on the pot. Cook over medium heat for 10 to 15 minutes, then reduce to low heat and cook 40 to 50 minutes more.

**6.** If using a nonstick pot, when ready to serve, place serving dish over the pot and turn pot upside down and carefully remove the pot. The *tahchin* will then sit on the serving dish like a cake. With other pots, before removing the lid, soak the bottom of the pot in cold water for a few minutes. This will help loosen the crust. Then, remove the loose, white rice from the top and arrange on a serving platter. Next, break the saffron rice with chicken into pieces and position around and on top of the loose rice or on a separate serving dish.

**7.** This dish can also be prepared without the plain rice and baked, covered, in a large, oblong Pyrex baking dish, in which case the chicken should be browned lightly on both sides in butter or margarine and arranged evenly in the bottom of the lightly greased baking dish. Follow the steps above for the rice and yogurt mixture and pour over the chicken. Bake in a moderate 350° oven for 1 hour. In this case, the remaining white rice can be steamed according to steps 5 through 10 of the *chelo* recipe.

**8.** To serve, dish out the additional rice on top of turkey. Turn pan over a large platter. Mix 1 cup cooked rice with saffron thoroughly. Place plain rice on top of *Tahchin-e Morq*. Decorate with saffron and rice mixture.

## Sholeh Beriyan-e Zireh

(rice with caraway seeds, Isfahan style)

5 to 6 servings

| Ingredients: | Spices: |
|---|---|
| 1 lb. stew beef or lamb | 1½ tsp salt |
| 2 cups rice | ½ tsp turmeric |
| ½ cup caraway seeds | |
| ¾ cup butter or margarine | |

### DIRECTIONS FOR COOKING

**1.** Simmer meat in 6 cups water and salt for 40 minutes or until meat is quite tender. Remove meat from broth (set broth aside) and mash well. (A food processor can be used for this purpose.)

**2.** Add rice and turmeric to broth and simmer for 30 minutes, or until rice is quite soft.

**3.** Add meat, caraway seeds, and butter or margarine; mix well; cover and simmer over very low heat for 15 additional minutes. Serve with yogurt.

## Kateh

(boiled "sticky" rice)

5 to 6 servings

| Ingredients: | Spices: |
|---|---|
| 2 cups rice | 1½ tsp salt |
| 3 Tbs. butter or margarine | |

### DIRECTIONS FOR COOKING

**1.** Combine all ingredients with 4 cups water in a medium-size pot.

**2.** Bring to a boil; reduce heat to medium-low and simmer lightly for 30-40 minutes. Serve with yogurt at the side.

NOTE: For variety, this rice can also be made with the addition of one of the following ingredients, added along with the above ingredients, and served with yogurt as either a main or side dish:

2 Tbs. caraway seeds (Kateh-ye Kermani)
2 Tbs. dill weed (Kateh-ye Shevid)
1 cup cooked lentils (Kateh-ye Adas, 6-8 servings)
1 cup cooked mung beans (Kateh-ye Mash, 6-8 servings)

## Kateh-ye Morgh-o Zireh

(rice with chicken and caraway seeds,
Isfahan style)

6 to 8 servings

Ingredients:
1½ lbs boneless, skinless chicken breasts
1 onion, quartered
2 cups rice
1 Tbs. caraway seed
¼ cup butter or margarine
Spices:
2 tsp salt

### DIRECTIONS FOR COOKING

**1.** Simmer chicken with onion and salt in 4 cups water for 30 minutes. Set aside chicken and broth separately.

**2.** Rinse rice several times in warm tap water; drain. Add to chicken broth.

**3.** Stir caraway seeds and butter or margarine into rice and broth and stir over medium heat until butter or margarine is melted.

**4.** Place chicken on top of rice, cover and simmer over medium heat for 15-20 minutes or until the broth has been absorbed by the rice. Then, reduce heat and steam an additional 30 minutes.

# Yarma Qablisi

(saffron-flavored cakes of bulgur, rice, fruit and nuts, Azerbaijan style)

*8 to 10 servings*

**Ingredients:**
*2 cups bulgur*
*1 cup rice*
*½ cup butter*
*½ cup slivered almonds*
*½ cup chopped pistachios*
*½ lb dried apricots*
*½ lb fresh plums*
*5 prunes*
**Spices:**
*1 tsp salt*
*¼ tsp saffron, dissolved in ¼ cup hot water*

## DIRECTIONS FOR COOKING

**1.** Simmer bulgur and rice in 3 cups water and salt, stirring occasionally to prevent sticking, until the mixture becomes a thick paste.

**2.** Grease a non-stick pot or deep casserole dish with 2 Tbs. butter. Set aside three dried apricots, 1 Tbs. slivered almonds, and 1 Tbs. of pistachios for decoration later. Spread out evenly 1/3 of the bulgur-rice mixture in the pot or casserole dish; top evenly with 1/3 of the almonds, pistachios, apricots, and plums. Repeat layering until all these ingredients are used up.

**3.** With the handle of a spatula, perforate rice to the bottom of the pot or dish. Mix together saffron solution and 3 Tbs. melted butter; pour evenly over top of the mixture in the pot or dish. Cover and steam over low heat or bake in moderate (350°) oven for 30 minutes.

**4.** Melt 3 Tbs. butter in a skillet and stir in previously set-aside fruits and nuts as well as prunes. Keep warm.

**5.** To serve, if using a non-stick pot, place a large platter over the top of the pot, turn over platter and pot and remove the pot. Then decorate with fruit and nut topping and slice in wedges to serve. If using a casserole dish, cut in squares and decorate with fruit and nut topping.

# Kateh-ye (Dami) Shirazi
(rice with parsley, scallions, cabbage and meat,
Shiraz style)

*5 to 6 servings*

## Ingredients:
*1 lb stew beef or lamb, cut into thin strips*
*6 Tbs. butter or margarine*
*½ cup lentils*
*1 bunch parsley, rinsed and chopped*
*1 bunch scallions, rinsed and chopped*
*1 lb cabbage, shredded*
*1½ cups rice*
## Spices:
*1 ½ tsp salt*
*2 tsp dried fenugreek leaves*

### DIRECTIONS FOR COOKING

**1.** Brown meat in 2 Tbs. butter or margarine. Transfer to a medium-size pot; add 4½ cups water and salt and simmer over medium heat for 20 minutes or until meat is tender.
**2.** Add lentils and simmer an additional 15 minutes.
**3.** Sauté parsley, scallions, and cabbage in remaining butter over medium heat.
**4.** Add parsley-scallion-cabbage mixture, rice, and fenugreek to meat and lentil mixture and simmer over medium heat for 10-15 minutes or until liquid has been absorbed by rice. Then, reduce heat, cover and steam an additional 20 minutes.

Different brands of Basmati rice from India and Dom-siyah rice from Mazandaran province in Iran.
*Photo by Kamron.*

# Meat and Poultry Entrees in Sauce
## *(Khoresh and Khorak)*

A *khoresh* is simply a stew-type dish that generally is served over rice. In Iran, such dishes are often quite time consuming to make in terms of cleaning and readying the various ingredients. But, thanks to modern technology, which affords the customer relatively clean vegetables as well as machines that handle chopping with great speed, not to mention a few shortcuts, most of the following *khoresh* recipes are quite simple and quick to prepare. They have been selected, for the most part, because they are among the most popular dishes in Iran and because their ingredients are readily available.

This section also features dishes called *khorak*. Whereas a *khoresh*, as mentioned, is generally served over rice, a *khorak* is not, but is, rather, considered a meal in itself and is usually served with bread and pickled vegetables or salad.

The different names given to the class of Iranian dishes in this chapter, including *qelyeh*, *qateq*, and *qeymeh*, which were in the past names of particular variations on this type of dish, are now often indistinguishable to the average Iranian.

In addition to traditional entrées, this section also includes dishes from various regions throughout Iran.

## Qormeh-ye Sib va Albalu
(apple and tart cherry stew)

*5 to 6 servings*

**Ingredients:**
*1 lb beef or lamb, cut in cubes*
*1 Tbs. butter*
*1 onion, quartered*
*8 tart cooking apples, cut into ½" wedges*
*1 cup fresh or 1 can pitted tart cherries*
*2 Tbs. sugar*
**Spices:**
*2 tsp cinnamon*
*1 tsp salt*
*1 tsp turmeric*

### DIRECTIONS FOR COOKING

**1.** Sprinkle meat with cinnamon; brown in butter.  Place in a medium pot.
**2.** Add onions and water and simmer over medium heat for 40 minutes or until meat is tender.
**3.** Add apples and spices and simmer for another 20 minutes.
**4.** Add cherries and sugar and simmer for 5-10 minutes more.

Serve over plain rice.

## Khoresh-e Na'na Jafari
(mint and parsley stew**)**

*6 to 8 servings*

**Ingredients:**
*1 lb beef or lamb, cut in 1" cubes*
*3 Tbs. butter*
*1 cup fresh mint, chopped*
*2 cups fresh parsley, chopped*
*1½ lb green plums or 1 lb sour grapes (if not available, substitute 2 cups fresh or frozen cranberries)*
*4 Tbs. sugar*
**Spices:**
*1 tsp salt*
*1 tsp cinnamon*
*2 tsp turmeric*

### DIRECTIONS FOR COOKING

**1.** Lightly brown meat in butter, salt, and cinnamon over medium heat.
**2.** Add mint and parsley and stir in for 2 minutes; remove skillet from heat.
**3.** Transfer meat and mint-parsley mixture to a medium-size pot along with all remaining ingredients (excluding cranberries, if used) and 2 cups water; bring to a boil, then reduce heat to medium-low and simmer for 40 minutes.  If using cranberries, add in the last few minutes, just before serving.
Serve over plain rice.

NOTE: The end product should be a pleasant blend of sweet and sour; sugar may be adjusted to taste.

# Fesenjan

## (Braised Poultry in Walnut and Pomegranate Sauce)

*8 to 10 servings*

### Ingredients:

2½ cups walnuts, coarsely ground
2 medium onions, grated
¼ cup olive oil
4 lbs boneless, skinless chicken
    thighs or breasts*
2 Tbs. butter
5 Tbs. tomato paste
2 Tbs. lemon juice
3 Tbs. sugar
½ cup pomegranate syrup or molasses**

### Spices:

½ tsp cinnamon
¼ tsp ground black pepper
2 tsp salt

### DIRECTIONS FOR COOKING

**1.** Brown walnuts lightly in heavy skillet, stirring constantly to prevent burning. Transfer walnuts to a 5-6 quart pot.

**2.** Sauté onions lightly in oil. Remove onions with slotted spoon and add to walnuts. Set skillet aside.

**3.** Add all remaining ingredients except chicken to walnut and onion mixture, along with 2½ cups water. Mix well. Simmer over low heat for 10 minutes.

**4.** Brown poultry in butter in a skillet. Add chicken to sauce, cover, simmer for approximately 1 hour more, stirring occasionally to prevent sticking.

Serve over plain rice.

NOTE: The *Fesanjun* sauce should be sweet-and-sour. Because pomegranate syrup or molasses can vary in sweetness, before adding sugar or lemon juice, taste and adjust these ingredients accordingly.

*Duck can be substituted for chicken, in which case, use 5 lbs duck and increase the simmering time (Step 4) until the duck is tender. Make sure to add water, if necessary.

**If pomegranate syrup or molasses is not available, cranberry jelly can be substituted, in which case the sugar should be eliminated altogether or at least reduced.

Prepared by Fahimeh Z.

# Fesenjan-e Shomali

(meatballs in pomegranate sauce, Northern Provinces style)

*8 to 10 servings*

**Ingredients:**
*2½ cups walnuts, coarsely ground*
*2 medium onions, grated*
*¼ cup olive oil*
*2 lbs lean ground beef or lamb*
*¼ cup lemon juice*
*½ cup pomegranate syrup or molasses*
**Spices:**
*½ tsp cinnamon*
*¼ tsp ground black pepper*
*3 tsp salt*

### DIRECTIONS FOR COOKING

**1.** Brown walnuts lightly in heavy skillet, stirring constantly to prevent burning. Transfer walnuts to a 5-6 quart pot.

**2.** Sauté onions lightly in oil. Remove onions with slotted spoon and add all but 2 Tbs. to walnuts. Set skillet aside. Set onions aside.

**3.** Add all remaining ingredients, except for the meat and 1 tsp of the salt, to the walnut and onion mixture, along with 2½ cups water. Mix well. Simmer over low heat for 10 minutes.

**4.** In a bowl mix together ground meat, ½ tsp salt, and the remaining grated onion. Make meatballs the size of small walnuts and drop in the pomegranate sauce; cover and simmer for approximately 30 minutes, stirring occasionally to prevent sticking.

Serve over plain rice.

NOTE: This dish is supposed to be rather tart.

## Khoresh-e Sabzi Fesenjan
### (meatballs and herbs in pomegranate sauce)

*8 to 10 servings*

**Ingredients:**
*2½ cups walnuts, coarsely ground*
*2 medium onions, grated*
*¼ cup olive oil*
*1 bunch parsley, finely chopped*
*1 bunch fresh corriander, finely chopped*
*2 lbs lean ground beef or lamb*
*¼ cup lemon juice*
*½ cup pomegranate syrup or molasses*
**Spices:**
*1 tsp turmeric*
*¼ tsp ground black pepper*
*3 tsp salt*

### DIRECTIONS FOR COOKING

**1.** Brown walnuts lightly in heavy skillet, stirring constantly to prevent burning. Transfer walnuts to a 5-6 quart pot.
**2.** Sauté onions lightly in oil. Remove onions with slotted spoon and add to walnuts. Set skillet aside.
**3.** Add all remaining ingredients, except for the meat and 1 tsp of the salt, to the walnut-onion-herb mixture, along with 2½ cups water. Mix well. Simmer over low heat for 10 minutes.
**4.** In a bowl mix together ground meat, remaining salt, and turmeric and black pepper. Make meatballs the size of small walnuts and drop in the pomegranate sauce; cover and simmer for approximately 30 minutes, stirring occasionally to prevent sticking.
Serve over plain rice.

NOTE: This dish is supposed to be rather tart.

## Khoresh-e Morqh-o Alu
### (chicken and prune stew)

*4 to 6 servings*

**Ingredients:**
*2 lb boneless, skinless chicken thighs*
*2 Tbs. olive oil*
*1 medium onion, quartered*
*2 large potatoes*
*1 lb dried prunes, pitted*
*¼ cup sugar*
*¼ cup lemon juice*
**Spices:**
*2 tsp salt*
*2 tsp turmeric*

### DIRECTIONS FOR COOKING

**1.** Cut chicken into serving-size pieces. Brown in oil.
**2.** Put chicken, onion, salt, and turmeric along with 4 cups water in a 4-5 quart pot. Bring to a boil; reduce heat to medium and simmer 30-40 minutes or until chicken is well cooked.
**3.** Peel potatoes; halve and slice about ½" thick. Add to chicken mixture along with prunes and sugar. Simmer 15 minutes more.
**4.** Add lemon juice; stir.

Serve with rice.

NOTE: Sugar and lemon juice can be adjusted according to taste. The end product should be a mild blend of sweet and sour.

# Khoresh-e Karafs
## (celery stew)

*4 to 5 servings*

**Ingredients:**
*½ cup butter*
*1 lb stew beef, cut in 1" cubes*
*1 large onion, finely chopped*
*5 cups celery, sliced in ½-inch pieces*
*1 cup chopped parsley*
*1 Tbs. dried or 2 Tbs. fresh chopped mint*
*½ cup lemon juice*
**Spices:**
*½ tsp pepper*
*1 tsp salt*
*1 tsp cinnamon*
*¼ tsp nutmeg*
*1 tsp turmeric*

### DIRECTIONS FOR COOKING

**1.** Sauté onion in ¼ cup of the butter.
**2.** Add meat and seasoning and brown.
**3.** Add 2 cups water to the meat, cover, and let cook for about 30 minutes or until the meat is tender.
**4.** Melt ¼ cup of the butter in a skillet and add celery, parsley and mint, and sauté lightly.
**5.** Add the sautéed celery mixture and lemon juice to the meat and let simmer for another 15-20 minutes.

Serve over plain rice.

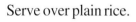

Prepared by Shahpar T.

# Khoresh-e Kadu
## (zucchini stew)

*4 to 5 servings*

**Ingredients:**
*8 small zucchinis*
*5 Tbs. butter*
*1 medium onion, sliced*
*4 medium tomatoes, halved*
**Spices:**
*1 tsp salt*
*¼ tsp pepper*
*1 tsp turmeric*

### DIRECTIONS FOR COOKING

**1.** Heat oven to 360°. Peel zucchini; cut evenly in half lengthwise.
**2.** Melt 3 Tbs. of the butter in skillet. Brown zucchini well on both sides. Add more butter as needed. Arrange with cut sides up in a flat-bottomed casserole dish.
**3.** Sauté onion in skillet in remaining butter; arrange on top of zucchini.
**4.** Arrange tomatoes cut side down on zucchini and onion.
**5.** Combine ¼ cup water, salt, pepper, and turmeric; mix well. Pour over zucchini. Bake for about 20 minutes or until tomatoes are soft.
Serve over plain rice.

Prepared by Diane W.

# Qeymeh

## (Yellow Split Pea Stew)

*4 to 6 servings*

### Ingredients:

*2 Tbs. butter*
*1 large onion, halved and sliced*
*1 lb. lean ground beef (or stew beef cut in 1" cubes)*
*1 cup dried yellow split peas*
*2 or 3 dried lemons (or 4 Tbs. lemon juice)\**
*1 medium potato cut in ½ inch cubes*
*1Tbs. tomato paste*
*2 large or 3 medium tomatoes, quartered*

### Spices:

*1 tsp salt*
*1 tsp turmeric*
*¼ tsp black pepper*

## DIRECTIONS FOR COOKING

**1.** Melt butter in heavy pot and sauté onion. Add 4 cups water and seasonings; bring to a boil.
**2.** Make meatballs about 1" in diameter (if using beef cubes, brown well in 2 Tbs. additional butter) and drop in boiling water and onion mixture.
**3.** Add split peas and dried lemon (*if using lemon juice, add just before serving) and simmer 20 minutes.
**4.** Add potatoes, simmer 10 minutes more.
**5.** Add tomato paste and tomatoes. Mix and simmer over low heat for 15 minutes.
Serve over *chelo* or as a side dish to be mixed with *ash-e reshteh.*

VARIATION: Eliminate potato cubes from the list above and instead garnish the dish with crisp, thin French fries before serving. NOTE: Generally, *Qehmeh* made with cubed meat is served over rice and when it is to be served with *Ash-e Reshteh*, it is made with meatballs. Traditionally, the juice of sour grapes or whole sour grapes are used instead of dried lime or lemon juice.

Prepared by Fahimeh Z.

# Qelyapiti
(chicken livers)

*6 servings*

Ingredients:
*2 large onions, chopped*
*½ cup butter*
*2 lb beef liver, cut in small, 1" pieces (or substitute chicken livers)*
*¼ cup lemon juice*
**Spices:**
*2 tsp salt*
*1 tsp pepper*
*1 tsp turmeric*

### DIRECTIONS FOR COOKING

**1.** Sauté onions in butter.
**2.** Add liver and seasonings. Mix gently. Sauté for 5 minutes or until all sides of liver are lightly browned.
**3.** Add lemon juice and 2 cups water. Cover and let simmer over medium heat for 10-15 minutes.

Serve with flat bread and yogurt or over rice with yogurt.

# Khoresh-e Esfenaj
(spinach stew)

*5 to 6 servings*

Ingredients:
*1 lb lean beef or lamb, cut in 1" cubes*
*2 Tbs. olive oil*
*1 lb dried pitted prunes*
*1 lb fresh spinach, coarsely chopped*
*1 bunch parsley, coarsely chopped*
*3 Tbs. sugar*
*1 large onion, thinly sliced*
*1 Tbs. butter*
*¼ cup fresh mint, chopped (or 2 Tbs. dried)*
*½ cup lemon juice*
**Spices:**
*2 tsp cinnamon*
*1 tsp salt*
*2 tsp turmeric*
*½ tsp black pepper*

### DIRECTIONS FOR COOKING

**1.** Sprinkle meat with cinnamon and salt and lightly brown in olive oil over medium heat.
**2.** Place in a 3-quart pot with 3 cups water. Bring to a boil; reduce heat to medium and simmer for 20-30 minutes or until meat is well cooked.
**3.** Add prunes, spinach, parsley, sugar, turmeric, and pepper. Simmer an additional 10 minutes.
**4.** Sauté onions in butter. Remove from heat, add mint and stir together.
**5.** Remove stew from heat and stir in the onion-mint mixture and lemon juice.
Serve over plain rice.

## Khoresh-e Rivas
### (rhubarb stew)

*4 to 6 servings*

**Ingredients:**
*1 lb lean beef or lamb, cut in 1" cubes*
*¼ cup butter*
*1 large onion, thinly sliced*
*1 bunch coriander, coarsely chopped*
*1 lb rhubarb, fresh or frozen*
**Spices:**
*½ tsp cinnamon*
*1 tsp salt*
*½ tsp black pepper*
*1 tsp turmeric*

**DIRECTIONS FOR COOKING**

**1.** Sprinkle meat with cinnamon and brown lightly in 2 Tbs. of the butter in a skillet.
**2.** Put meat and remaining spices with 2 cups water in a medium-size pot; bring to a boil; reduce heat to medium and simmer 30-40 minutes or until meat is tender.
**3.** Sauté onions in butter; remove from heat. S t i r coriander into onion and set aside.
**4.** If using fresh rhubarb, wash and cut in 1" pieces. Add along with onion-coriander mixture to meat. Simmer 20 minutes, or until rhubarb is tender. If using frozen rhubarb, add onion-coriander mixture to meat and simmer 10 minutes. Then add frozen rhubarb and simmer 5 minutes more.
Serve over plain rice.

## Khoresh-e Bamiyeh
### (okra stew)

*6 to 8 servings*

**Ingredients:**
*2 large onions, chopped*
*¼ cup butter*
*1 lb stew beef or lamb, cubed*
*1 lb fresh okra*
*2 medium potatoes, diced*
*4 medium tomatoes, quartered*
*¼ cup lemon juice*
**Spices:**
*2 tsp salt*
*1 tsp turmeric*

**DIRECTIONS FOR COOKING**

**1.** Sauté onions in butter.
**2.** Add meat, salt, and turmeric and brown over medium heat for 10 minutes.
**3.** Cut off both ends of washed and dried okra and slice into 4-5 pieces.
**4.** Place meat and onion mixture, okra, potatoes, tomatoes, and 2 cups water in a pot. Bring to a boil; reduce heat to medium-low; cover and simmer over medium-low heat 30-40 minutes or until meat is tender
**5.** Add lemon juice. Simmer 5 more minutes.
Serve over plain rice.

Prepared by Kamron J.

# Qormeh Sabzi

## (Green Vegetable Stew)

*6 to 8 servings*

### Ingredients:
*1 large onion, sliced*
*1/3 cup butter*
*1½ lb stew beef or lamb, cut in 1" cubes*
*3 bunches scallions (or green onions), chopped*
*2 bunches parsley, chopped*
*½ cup fresh fenugreek, chopped (or 3 Tbs. dried)*
*1 cup cooked kidney beans*
*(optional: 2 medium potatoes, cubed)*
*2 Tbs. dried lemon, or 2 whole dried limes*
*¼ cup lemon juice*

### Spices:
*1 tsp turmeric*
*1½ tsp salt*
*½ tsp black pepper*

### DIRECTIONS FOR COOKING

**1.** Sauté onion in butter.
**2.** Add meat and lightly brown on all sides.
**3.** Stir in scallions, parsley, and fenugreek and remove from heat.
**4.** Transfer to a medium-size pot. Add seasonings, beans, and 1½ cups water. Bring to a boil; reduce heat and simmer over medium heat for 40-50 minutes or until meat is tender.
**5.** If using optional potatoes, add here and simmer another 10 minutes.
**6.** Add dried lemon or limes; simmer 15 minutes more.
**7.** Add lemon juice. Keep on very low heat until ready to serve.
Serve over plain rice.

Prepared by Fahimeh Z.

# Khoresh-e Badenjan ba Gusht
(eggplant stew with meat)

*6 to 8 servings*

**Ingredients:**
*3 medium eggplants*
*1 lb stew beef or 1½ lb lamb shanks*
*2 Tbs. butter*
*1 large onion, halved and sliced*
*¼ cup olive oil*
*4 large tomatoes, halved*
*2 Tbs. tomato paste dissolved in ¼ cup water*

**Spices:**
*1 tsp cinnamon*
*2 tsp salt*
*½ tsp black pepper*
*1 tsp turmeric*

## DIRECTIONS FOR COOKING

**1.** Peel eggplants; cut lengthwise in ½" slices. Sprinkle both sides of each slice lightly with half the salt (to prevent eggplants from soaking up too much oil while browning). Set aside.

**2.** Sprinkle meat with cinnamon; brown in butter. Add onion and sauté with meat

**3.** Transfer meat and onion mixture to a 3-quart pot. Add 2½ cups water and spices; bring to a boil; lower heat to medium-low and simmer until meat is tender, about 30 minutes.

**4.** Meanwhile, pat eggplants dry with paper towel. Brown on both sides in 1 Tbs. of the olive oil at a time. (Add more oil as needed, since eggplants vary in amount of oil they absorb.)

**5.** Add eggplants to pot with meat, onion, and broth.

**6.** Arrange tomatoes skin side up on top of eggplants.

**7.** Pour dissolved tomato paste over eggplants; cover and simmer over medium-low heat for 30 minutes. Serve over plain rice with plain yogurt as a side dish.

NOTE: Two Lamb shanks may be substituted for meat.

# Khoresh-e Badenjan
(vegetarian eggplant stew)

*5 to 6 servings*

**Ingredients:**
*3 medium eggplants*
*1 Tbs. butter*
*1 large onion, halved and sliced*
*¼ cup olive oil*
*4 large tomatoes, halved*
*2 Tbs. tomato paste dissolved in 2 cups water*
**Spices:**
*2 tsp salt*
*½ tsp black pepper*
*1 tsp turmeric*

### DIRECTIONS FOR COOKING

**1.** Peel eggplants; cut lengthwise in ½" slices. Sprinkle both sides of each slice lightly with half the salt (to prevent eggplants from soaking up too much oil while browning). Set aside.

**2.** Sauté onion in butter; set aside.
**3.** Pat eggplants dry with paper towel. Brown on both sides in 1 Tbs. of the olive oil at a time. (Add more oil as needed, since eggplants vary in amount of oil they absorb).
**4.** Arrange eggplants in a baking dish, arrange tomatoes, skin side up, on top of eggplants.
**5.** Stir spices into diluted tomato paste and pour the mixture over the eggplants; cover and simmer over medium-low heat for 30 minutes.

Serve over plain rice with plain yogurt as a side dish or pour over the top 1 cup liquid whey (*kashk*\*).
\*Available at Iranian and Middle Eastern grocery stores.

Prepared by Gazal R.

## Qormeh-ye Beh
### (quince stew)

*6 to 8 servings*

Ingredients:
*2 medium onions, sliced*
*¼ cup butter*
*1 lb lamb or beef, cut in cubes*
*3 medium quinces*
*2 Tbs. flour*
*3 Tbs. sugar*
*¼ cup lemon juice*
**Spices:**
*1 tsp cinnamon*
*1 tsp salt*
*¼ tsp black pepper*

### DIRECTIONS FOR COOKING

**1.** Sauté onions in butter in a large skillet.
**2.** Sprinkle meat with cinnamon; add to onions and brown lightly.
**3.** Stir in salt and pepper.
**4.** Wash quinces; cut in quarters and remove the seed and core of each. Then, slice them in ½" wedges and stir in with meat and onions until they are lightly browned.
**5.** Transfer meat, onion, and quince mixture to a medium-size pot; add 2½ cups water, flour, and sugar. Bring to a boil; reduce heat and simmer for 1 hour. Add additional water if the mixture seems to be getting too dry or thick.
**6.** Stir in lemon juice and simmer an additional 10 minutes.

NOTE: Since quince is not readily available in all parts of the United States, for a similar dish, substitute 6 large baking apples for quinces, in which case, cooking time in Step 5 should be reduced to 35-40 minutes.

## Khoresh-e Turshehkabab
### (tart chicken, Gilan style)

*3 to 4 servings*

Ingredients:
*One whole chicken*
*1 cup olive oil*
*½ cup lemon juice*
*4 medium potatoes, peeled and sliced*
*6 small tomatoes*
**Spices:**
*1 tsp cinnamon*
*1 tsp turmeric*
*1 tsp salt*
*½ tsp black pepper*

### DIRECTIONS FOR COOKING

**1.** Wash chicken in cold water, pat dry with paper towel, and brown in olive oil in a skillet on all sides. Transfer chicken into a deep pot, and set the oil and skillet aside.
**2.** Add 4 cups of water along with spices and the lemon juice to the chicken in the pot and simmer for 45 minutes.
**3.** Brown potatoes on both sides in olive oil in the skillet; remove with a slotted spoon and add to chicken.
**4.** Brown tomatoes in olive oil on all sides, then remove with a slotted spoon and add to chicken. Let simmer for an additional 15 minutes.

To serve, transfer the chicken to a platter, arrange potatoes and tomatoes around it, and pour the soup over the chicken.

# Khorak-e Havij va Lubiya Sabz
(carrot and green bean stew)

*6 to 8 servings*

**Ingredients:**
*1 lb beef or lamb, cut in cubes*
*¼ cup butter*
*1 lb green beans, cut in 1" pieces*
*1 cup tomato paste*
*1 lb carrots, cut in 1" slices*
*2 large potatoes, peeled and cut in 1" cubes*
**Spices:**
*½ tsp cinnamon*
*1 tsp salt*
*¼ tsp black pepper*
*1 tsp turmeric*

### DIRECTIONS FOR COOKING

**1.** Sprinkle meat with cinnamon and brown in butter in a skillet. Transfer meat to a 5-quart pot.
**2.** Add 2 cups water to meat in the pot, bring to a boil, reduce heat to medium-low and simmer 30-40 minutes or until meat is well cooked
**3.** Add green beans, tomato paste, carrots, potatoes, and remaining seasoning. Stir together and simmer over medium-low heat for 30 minutes.

Serve as a main dish with flat bread or over plain rice.

# Qur Avij
(meatballs in sour grape juice,
Gilan-Mazandaran style)

*4 to 5 servings*

**Ingredients:**
*1 lb ground beef or lamb*
*1 small onion, grated*
*1 Tbs. flour*
*1 Tbs. butter*
*2 bunches parsley, chopped*
*½ cup fresh mint, chopped*
*1 tsp sugar*
*1 large potato, diced*
*½ cup sour grape juice*
**Spices:**
*1¼ tsp salt*
*1 tsp turmeric*
*¼ tsp black pepper*

### DIRECTIONS FOR COOKING

**1.** Mix together meat, onion, ¼ tsp salt, and flour. Form into meatballs the size of small walnuts. Brown on all sides in butter.
**2.** Bring 2 cups water and seasonings to a boil; drop in meatballs and boil for 5 minutes.
**3.** Add parsley, mint, sugar, and potato; reduce heat and simmer for 30 minutes.
**4.** Add sour grape juice and simmer for 2 minutes more. Serve over rice.

# Khoresh-e Hendi

(stew with chicken, green peppers, tomatoes, and coriander, Indian style)

*3 to 4 servings*

**Ingredients:**
*1½ lb skinless chicken thighs*
*2 Tbs. olive oil*
*1 medium onion, chopped*
*2 Tbs. butter*
*2 green peppers, diced*
*3 tomatoes, diced*
*1 bunch coriander, chopped*
*1 clove garlic, crushed*
*1 Tbs. dried mint*
*2 Tbs. roasted chickpea flour*
**Spices:**
*1 tsp salt*
*1 tsp turmeric*
*½ tsp black pepper*
*1 tsp powdered caraway seeds*
*1 tsp cinnamon*
*1 tsp cardamom*
*½ tsp powdered cloves*

### DIRECTIONS FOR COOKING

**1.** Brown chicken in olive oil. Add salt and 2 cups water and simmer over medium heat for 25 minutes.
**2.** Sauté onions in butter.
**3.** Add green peppers, tomatoes, coriander, garlic, and seasonings to chicken and simmer over medium heat for 30 minutes.
**4.** Dissolve chickpea powder in ¼ cup water and stir into above mixture. Simmer for 5 more minutes, stirring occasionally. Serve over rice.

# Khoresh-e Havij-o Alu

(prune and carrot stew)

*4 to 5 servings*

**Ingredients:**
*1 lb beef or lamb, cut in 1" cubes*
*3 Tbs. butter*
*1 onion, sliced*
*6 carrots, sliced*
*¼ lb pitted prunes*
*2 Tbs. brown sugar*
**Spices:**
*½ tsp cinnamon*
*1 tsp salt*
*½ tsp turmeric*
*½ tsp cardamom*

### DIRECTIONS FOR COOKING

**1.** Sprinkle meat with cinnamon and brown in butter in a large saucepan.
**2.** Add onions to meat and sauté for 5 minutes.
**3.** Add carrots to onion-meat mixture and stir in for 2 minutes.
**4.** Add all remaining ingredients along with 2½ cups water and simmer over low heat for 1 hour, adding additional water if necessary. Serve over rice.

## Khoresh-e Lubiya Sabz
(green bean stew with meat, tomatoes,
and almonds)

*5 to 6 servings*

Ingredients:
*1 lb beef or lamb, cut in 1" cubes*
*5 Tbs. butter*
*1 onion, sliced*
*1½ lb fresh green beans*
*¼ cup slivered almonds*
*3 medium tomatoes, quartered*
*1 Tbs. lemon juice*
Spices:
*1 tsp cinnamon*
*1 tsp salt*
*½ tsp black pepper*
*1 tsp turmeric*

### DIRECTIONS FOR COOKING

**1.** Sprinkle meat with seasonings and brown in 2 Tbs. butter.
**2.** Transfer meat to saucepan; add 2 cups water and simmer for 30 minutes.
**3.** Sauté onions in 3 Tbs. butter.
**4.** Rinse and drain green beans; snap off ends. Add to onions and stir over medium heat for 10 minutes. Add almonds and stir for 2 minutes.
**5.** Preheat oven to 350° F.
**6.** Transfer bean mixture, meat, and broth to a deep casserole dish. Arrange tomatoes on top and pour over lemon juice. Cover and bake for 30 minutes.

## Khoresh-e Baqala
(fava or lima bean stew with meat)

*4 to 5 servings*

Ingredients:
*1½ lb fresh fava beans (or 1 lb dried fava beans, or 1 lb frozen lima beans)*
*1 lb beef or lamb, cut in 1" cubes*
*5 Tbs. butter*
*1 large onion, sliced*
*½ cup chopped fresh or ¼ cup dried dill weed*
Spices:
*2 tsp salt*
*1 tsp turmeric*
*¼ tsp black pepper*

### DIRECTIONS FOR COOKING

**1.** If using dried beans, soak in a generous amount of water for several hours.
**2.** Sprinkle meat with 1 tsp of the salt and the other spices and brown in 2 Tbs. butter.
**3.** Add onions and sauté over medium heat for 5 minutes. Transfer to a saucepan, add 2½ cups water, and simmer 40 minutes.
**4.** Simmer beans for 10 minutes in 5 cups water and 1 tsp salt; drain.
**5.** Melt butter in a skillet. Add beans and dill weed and stir for 5 minutes. Add to meat and onion mixture; simmer for 20 additional minutes.

## Khoresh-e Kadu Tanbal
(pumpkin stew with meat and yogurt)

*5 to 6 servings*

Ingredients:
*1 lb beef or lamb, cut in 1" cubes*
*4 Tbs. butter*
*1 onion, chopped*
*1½ lb fresh pumpkin*
*2 cups yogurt*
*1 Tbs. brown sugar*
Spices:
*1 tsp cinnamon*
*1 tsp salt*

**DIRECTIONS FOR COOKING**

**1.** Sprinkle meat with cinnamon and brown in 2 Tbs. butter; transfer to large saucepan.
**2.** Sauté onion in 2 Tbs. butter. Add to meat in saucepan.
**3.** Cut away the shell from the pumpkin and cut pulp into 1" cubes. Add to meat and onion mixture along with 1 cup water; simmer over medium heat for 5 minutes.
**4.** Add yogurt and salt to the meat and pumpkin mixture and simmer for 1 hour.
**5.** A few minutes before serving, stir in brown sugar; serve over rice.

## Khoresh-e Kari ba Gusht
(curried lamb or beef)

*6 to 8 servings*

Ingredients:
*1 lb beef or lamb, cut in 1" cubes*
*¼ cup butter*
*2 medium onions, chopped*
*1 bunch parsley, chopped*
*2 cups ground almonds*
*1½ Tbs. sugar*
*¼ cup lemon juice*
Spices:
*1 tsp salt*
*1 Tbs. curry powder*

**DIRECTIONS FOR COOKING**

**1.** Brown meat in butter.
**2.** Add onions and sauté, stirring occasionally, for 5 minutes.
**3.** Stir in chopped parsley.
**4.** Place meat-onion-parsley mixture, seasonings, almonds, and 2½ cups water in a pot and simmer for 1 hour.
**5.** Add sugar and stir for 2 minutes.
**6.** Stir in lemon juice. Serve over rice.

# Khoresh-e Qarch
### (mushroom stew with meat)

*6 to 8 servings*

**Ingredients:**
*1½ lb skinless chicken thighs, or 1 lb beef or*
*    lamb cut in 1" cubes*
*¼ cup butter*
*1 medium onion, sliced*
*1½ lb mushrooms, sliced*
*2 Tbs. chopped fresh or 1 Tbs. dried tarragon*
*2 Tbs. flour*
*2 Tbs. lemon juice*

**Spices:**
*½ tsp nutmeg*
*1 tsp salt*
*¼ tsp black pepper*

### DIRECTIONS FOR COOKING

**1.** Brown meat in 2 Tbs. butter.  Set aside.
**2.** Sauté onions in 2 Tbs. butter.
**3.** Wash mushrooms and pat dry; add to onions and sprinkle with nutmeg.  Stir for 5 minutes or until mushrooms begin to turn a golden brown.
**4.** Place meat, onion-mushroom mixture, seasoning, tarragon, and water in a large pot with 2 cups water and simmer for 1 hour.  Add additional water if necessary.
**5.** Dissolve flour in 1 cup water and add along with lemon juice to meat-onion-mushroom mixture; simmer for an additional 10 minutes, stirring occasionally to prevent sticking.  Serve over rice.

# Khoresh-e Qeymeh Badenjan
### (yellow split pea and eggplant stew)

*5 to 6 servings*

**Ingredients:**
*1 lb beef or lamb, cut in 1" cubes*
*1 Tbs. butter*
*1 large onion, chopped*
*3 Tbs. tomato paste*
*½ cup yellow split peas*
*3 medium eggplants*
*¼ cup olive oil*
*2 Tbs. lemon juice or 3 dried limes*

**Spices:**
*1 tsp turmeric*
*1 tsp salt*
*¼ tsp black pepper*

### DIRECTIONS FOR COOKING

**1.** Brown meat in butter.
**2.** Add onion; sauté over medium heat for 5 minutes.
**3.** Dissolve tomato paste in 2 cups water; mix together with meat, seasoning and split peas in a medium-size pot; simmer for 45 minutes.
**4.** Preheat oven to 350° F.
**5.** Meanwhile, peel and cut eggplants lengthwise into slices 1" thick.  Sprinkle with salt and set aside for 5 minutes.  Then, with a paper towel, pat off excess moisture and brown on both sides in olive oil, adding oil gradually (increase amount of oil if necessary, as eggplants absorb varied amounts).
**6.** Arrange eggplants in a casserole dish. Add lemon juice or dried lime to meat and split pea mixture and pour on top of eggplants. Bake for 30 minutes. Serve over rice.

## Khoresh-e Kari ba Morgh
### (curried chicken)

*6 to 8 servings*

**Ingredients:**
*2 lb skinless chicken thighs or breast*
*¼ cup butter*
*2 medium onions, chopped*
*2 cups ground almonds*
*1½ Tbs. brown sugar*
*¼ cup lemon juice*
**Spices:**
*1 tsp salt*
*1 Tbs. curry powder*

### DIRECTIONS FOR COOKING

**1.** Brown chicken in butter.
**2.** Add onion and sauté, stirring occasionally for about 5 minutes.
**3.** Place meat and onion mixture, seasonings, almonds, and 3 cups water in a pot and simmer for 1 hour.
**4.** Add sugar and stir for 2 minutes.
**5.** Stir in lemon juice.
Serve over rice.

## Khoresh-e Kari ba Morgh-o Mowz
### (curried chicken with bananas)

*5 to 6 servings*

**Ingredients:**
*1½ lb. boneless, skinless chicken thighs*
*½ cup olive oil*
*5 firm bananas*
*1 cup flour*
*2 Tbs. lemon juice*
*2 Tbs. brown sugar*
**Spices:**
*1½ tsp salt*
*1 Tbs. curry powder*
*½ tsp ground ginger*

### DIRECTIONS FOR COOKING

**1.** Brown chicken lightly in 2 Tbs. of the olive oil.
**2.** Place chicken in a pot with 2 cups water and simmer for 30 minutes or until chicken is tender, adding more water if necessary. You should have about 1½ cups of broth when chicken is cooked.
**3.** Peel bananas and cut into 1" slices.
**4.** Dissolve flour in 1 cup water, making sure all lumps disappear. Add curry powder, ½ tsp salt, and ginger and mix well.
**5.** Dip banana slices into flour batter and lightly brown on all sides in the remaining olive oil.
**6.** Add lemon juice and sugar to chicken broth and bring to a boil.
**7.** Add bananas to chicken; reduce heat and simmer over medium-low heat for 20-30 minutes more. Serve over plain rice.

## Khoresh-e Kari ba Gusht-o Mowz
### (curried lamb with bananas)

*6 servings*

**Ingredients:**
*1 lb stew lamb or beef*
*6 Tbs. butter*
*¼ cup flour*
*1 Tbs. lemon juice*
*1 egg, beaten*
*4 firm bananas, sliced in 1" pieces*
*1 Tbs. brown sugar*

**Spices:**
*1¼ Tbs. curry powder*
*1 tsp salt*
*½ tsp baking soda*

### DIRECTIONS FOR COOKING

**1.** Lightly brown meat in 2 Tbs. butter. Add 2 cups water and 1 tsp of the curry powder and simmer over medium heat for 30-40 minutes or until meat is thoroughly cooked. Set aside.
**2.** Dissolve flour in ¼ cup water to form a smooth paste; mix in lemon juice, seasonings, baking soda, and beaten egg.
**3.** Dip bananas in this mixture and brown on both sides in remaining butter. Add more butter if needed.
**4.** Place meat, broth, and bananas in a medium-size pot and mix brown sugar into broth. Cook over low heat for 30 minutes.
Serve over rice.

## Khoresh-e Anar Avij  I
### (meat, vegetables, and nuts stewed in pomegranate juice, Gilan-Mazandaran style)

*4 to 5 servings*

**Ingredients:**
*1 lb stew beef or lamb*
*2 Tbs. butter*
*1 medium onion, chopped*
*1 ½ cups  walnuts, minced*
*1 bunch parsley, chopped*
*½ lb spinach, chopped*
*¼ cup coriander, chopped*
*1 Tbs. dried mint*
*2 cloves garlic, crushed*
*¼ cup rice flour*
*2 cups pomegranate juice*
*2 eggs, beaten*

**Spices:**
*1 tsp salt*
*¼ tsp pepper*
*¼ tsp cinnamon*

### DIRECTIONS FOR COOKING

**1.** Brown meat in butter.
**2.** Add onion and sauté for 5 minutes.
**3.** Stir in walnuts for 2 more minutes.
**4.** Stir in parsley, spinach, coriander, mint and garlic for 2 minutes.
**5.** Transfer to a medium-size pot; add water and seasonings and simmer over medium heat for 45 minutes.
**6.** Dissolve rice flour in pomegranate juice and stir into above mixture; simmer for 10 minutes, stirring occasionally to prevent stickir~
**7.** Stir in eggs.
Serve over rice.

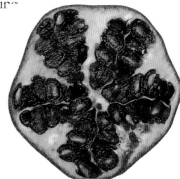

# Khoresh-e Anar Avij II

(meatballs, vegetables, and nuts stewed in pomegranate juice, Gilan-Mazandaran style)

*4 to 5 servings*

**Ingredients:**
*1 lb ground beef or lamb*
*2 Tbs. butter*
*1 bunch fresh coriander, chopped*
*½ cup cooked beets, diced*
*½ lb spinach, chopped*
*¼ cup chopped fresh mint*
*1 small onion, chopped*
*3½ cup walnuts, minced*
*3 Tbs. lemon juice*
*1 cup pomegranate syrup*
**Spices:**
*1 tsp cinnamon*
*2 tsp salt*
*1 tsp turmeric*
*¼ tsp black pepper*

### DIRECTIONS FOR COOKING

**1.** Mix ground meat with cinnamon and ½ tsp salt. Make meat balls the size of hazel nuts and brown on all sides in butter in a medium-size saucepan. Remove from butter and set aside.
**2.** In the same pan, stir in coriander, beets, spinach, mint, and onions over medium heat for 5 minutes.
**3.** Stir in walnuts for 2 more minutes.
**4.** Add meatballs, 2½ cups water, and remaining ingredients and simmer over medium heat for 20-30 minutes.
Serve over rice.

# Khoresh-e Havij

(carrot stew)

*5 to 6 servings*

**Ingredients:**
*2 large onions, sliced*
*¼ cup butter*
*1 lb stew beef or lamb*
*1 cup wine vinegar*
*1 cup sugar*
*10 carrots, sliced*
**Spices:**
*1 tsp cinnamon*
*1 tsp salt*
*½ tsp black pepper*
*2 tsp turmeric*

### DIRECTIONS FOR COOKING

**1.** Sauté onions in butter.
**2.** Sprinkle meat with cinnamon; add to onions and brown.
**3.** Transfer meat and onions to a saucepan; add 4 cups water along with the remaining spices and simmer for 45 minutes or until the meat is tender.
**4.** Add remaining ingredients and simmer for another 15 minutes.

## Khorak-e Maghz
### (sautéed brain)

*5 to 6 servings*

**Ingredients:**
¾ cup lemon juice
1½ lb lamb or beef brain
2 large onions, quartered
¼ cup vinegar
4 eggs
2 cups flour
1 Tbs. dried mint
½ cup butter
¼ cup fresh parsley, chopped
1 lemon, thinly sliced
**Spices:**
5 tsp salt
1½ tsp black pepper

### DIRECTIONS FOR COOKING

**1.** Mix together 2 quarts cold water, lemon juice, and 2 tsp salt in a glass bowl. In half the water solution, soak the brain for several hours.

**2.** Remove brain from water (discard water solution), gently skin it, and soak it again in the remaining water solution for 30 minutes in refrigerator or other cool place.

**3.** Remove brain from soaking solution and place along with onions, 2 tsp salt, 1 tsp pepper, vinegar, and 4 cups water in a large pot. Bring to a boil and reduce heat to medium and simmer for 10-15 minutes.

**4.** Remove brain gently and set aside to cool; break into bite-size pieces.

**5.** In a mixing bowl, beat together a batter of eggs, flour, 1 tsp salt, ½ tsp pepper, and mint.

**6.** Melt butter in a skillet over low heat.

**7.** Gently take pieces of brain, dip into the batter and sauté on all sides in melted butter.

**8.** Place on a serving dish; garnish with lemon slices and chopped parsley.

## Khorak-e Zaban
### (lamb tongue)

*4 to 5 servings*

**Ingredients:**
6 lamb tongues
1 medium onion, sliced
3 bay leaves
2 Tbs. lime juice or vinegar
**Spices:**
2½ tsp salt
½ tsp black pepper
¼ tsp of saffron dissolved in 2 Tbs. hot water

### DIRECTIONS FOR COOKING

**1.** Scrub tongues in warm water with a brush or the edge of a knife.

**2.** Place in a medium-size pot together with 4 cups water, onion, bay leaves, salt and pepper. Cover pot and bring to a boil; reduce heat and let simmer 2 hours.

**3.** With a sharp knife, remove skin from tongue and return tongue to pot.

**4.** When the tongue is tender, add lemon juice or vinegar; let simmer an additional 20 minutes.

**5.** Place on a platter, pour remaining juice over the tongues and add saffron. Garnish with parsley and lime or lemon.

Serve with flat bread.

## Khorak-e Morgh ba Mast
(chicken with yogurt and raisins)

*6 servings*

**Ingredients:**
*1 whole chicken, about 4-4½ lb*
*1 large onion, sliced*
*3 Tbs. butter*
*2 cups plain yogurt*
*½ cup raisins*
**Spices:**
*1 tsp salt*
*¼ tsp saffron, dissolved in 2 Tbs. hot water*

### DIRECTIONS FOR COOKING

1. Brown chicken on all sides in its own fat.
2. Sauté onion in butter.
3. Mix salt and saffron into yogurt and then stir into sautéed onions. Remove from heat.
4. Preheat oven to 350° F.
5. Place chicken in a deep casserole dish. Pour yogurt sauce over chicken. Cover and bake for 40 minutes.
6. Remove casserole from oven. Sprinkle raisins over the yogurt sauce and bake an additional 20 minutes.
7. To serve, transfer chicken to a serving dish. Remove raisins and onions from sauce with a slotted spoon. Pour sauce over chicken and decorate chicken with raisins and onions.

## Khorak-e Morgh ba Zorrat
(chicken with tomatoes and corn)

*3 to 4 servings*

**Ingredients:**
*1½ lb skinless chicken thighs*
*1 Tbs. olive oil*
*2 cloves garlic, crushed*
*5 tomatoes, quartered*
*2 cups fresh or frozen kernel corn*
*2 Tbs. vinegar or lemon juice*

**Spices:**
*1 tsp salt*
*¼ tsp black pepper*
*1 tsp powdered mustard*

### DIRECTIONS FOR COOKING

1. Brown chicken in olive oil. Stir in garlic for 5 minutes.
2. Transfer chicken to a medium size pot; add all remaining ingredients with 1 cup water and simmer over medium heat for 1 hour.
To Serve: Arrange pieces of chicken on a serving platter and pour sauce and corn around chicken.

## Khorak-e Morgh ba Khameh
(chicken baked in cream)

*4 servings*
**Ingredients:**
*4 boneless chicken breasts*
*¼ cup butter*
*1 medium onion, grated*
*1 cup cream*
*3 Tbs. flour*
*¼ cup lemon juice*

**Spices:**
*1 tsp salt*
*¼ tsp black pepper*

### DIRECTIONS FOR COOKING

1. Preheat oven to 350° F.
2. Sprinkle chicken with ½ tsp salt and pepper and brown lightly in 2 Tbs. of the butter over medium heat.
3. Stir onion in with chicken over medium heat for 5 minutes.
4. Use the remaining butter to grease the bottom and sides of a casserole dish and transfer chicken to the dish. Mix together cream, flour, lemon juice and remaining salt and pour over chicken. Cover and bake for 1 hour.

## Khorak-e Sib-o Anar

(chicken with apples and pomegranates, Isfahan style)

*5 to 6 servings*

**Ingredients:**
*1½ lb skinless, boneless chicken breasts*
*1 Tbs. olive oil*
*7 cooking apples, each cored and cut into 8-10 wedges*
*1 medium onion, sliced*
*2 Tbs. butter*
*½ cup pomegranate syrup*
*2 Tbs. sugar*
*1 6-oz. can tomato paste*
**Spices:**
*1 tsp salt*
*2 tsp cinnamon*

### DIRECTIONS FOR COOKING

**1.** Sprinkle chicken with salt and brown on both sides in olive oil.
**2.** Arrange chicken pieces in a large casserole dish and cover with apple slices.
**3.** Sauté onions in butter and spread over apples.
**4.** Preheat oven to 350° F.
**5.** Mix together well pomegranate syrup, sugar, and tomato paste; spread mixture evenly on top of chicken and apple mixture.
**6.** Evenly pour ½ cup water around sides of casserole dish. Sprinkle cinnamon evenly over top; cover with aluminum foil and bake for 1 hour.

Prepared by Diane W.

## Morgh-e Torsh

(tart chicken, Rasht style)

*6 servings*

**Ingredients:**
*1 whole chicken, 4-4½ lb*
*½ cup dried yellow split peas*
*1 bunch parsley*
*1 bunch scallions*
*1 bunch fresh coriander*
*6 Tbs. fresh chopped mint*
*2 cloves garlic, crushed*
*3 Tbs. butter*
*¼ cup lemon juice*
*2 Tbs. rice flour*
*4 eggs, beaten*
**Spices:**
*2 tsp salt*

### DIRECTIONS FOR COOKING

**1.** Brown chicken in its own fat on all sides over low heat. Place in a deep baking dish.
**2.** Simmer split peas in 2 cups water and salt over medium heat for 20 minutes. Set aside; do not drain.
**3.** Mince parsley, scallions, coriander, mint and garlic as fine as possible. (A food processor would be ideal for this purpose.) Squeeze out extra juice (set aside) and brown vegetables and garlic in butter for 5 minutes.
**4.** Preheat oven to 350° F.
**5.** Mix together a solution of lemon or lime juice and ½ cup water; dissolve rice flour in this solution.
**6.** Mix together browned vegetable-garlic mixture, the juice squeezed from mixture, cooked split peas, and rice flour solution and pour over chicken. Cover and bake for 1 hour.
**7.** Stir eggs into the sauce around the chicken. Bake an additional 5 minutes.

## Lavangi-ye Morgh
### (stuffed chicken, Astara style)

*5 to 6 servings*

**Ingredients:**
*2 cups chopped walnuts*
*½ cup olive oil*
*1 large onion, grated*
*¼ cup pomegranate concentrate*
*¼ cup lime juice*
*1 Tbs chopped fresh mint*
*¼ cup chopped coriander*
*1 whole chicken*
*¼ cup melted butter*
**Spices:**
*1 tsp salt*
*¼ tsp black pepper*
*1 tsp turmeric*

### DIRECTIONS FOR COOKING

**1.** Lightly brown walnuts in olive oil over medium heat.
**2.** Add onion and sauté lightly. Add pomegranate concentrate, lime juice, mint, coriander, and spices and simmer for three to five minutes. Remove from heat.
**3.** Brush chicken with half of melted butter; brush a baking dish with remaining butter.
**4.** Stuff chicken with the prepared ingredients, secure with toothpicks, and bake in a 350° oven for one hour.

Serve with bread or plain rice.

## Qelyeh-ye Kadu-ye Rashti
### (yellow squash and lentil sauce, Rasht style)

*5 to 6 servings*

**Ingredients:**
*1 cup lentils*
*1 medium onion, sliced*
*¼ cup butter*
*6 summer squash*
*2 Tbs. chopped parsley*
**Spices:**
*1 tsp salt*
*¼ tsp black pepper*

### DIRECTIONS FOR COOKING

**1.** Cook lentils in 2 cups water and ½ tsp of the salt for 20 minutes.
**2.** Sauté onion in butter. Remove from butter with a slotted spoon and add to lentils. Set butter in pan aside.
**3.** Rinse squash and pat dry; cut off both ends and slice into 1-inch rings. Brown in butter left over from sautéing onions.
**4.** Add squash to lentils along with seasonings and simmer for 30 minutes.
**5.** Partially mash squash into a paste-like mixture with small chunks of squash. Transfer to serving dish; decorate with parsley. Serve over rice.

## Qelyeh-ye Esfenaj

(sauce of spinach, meat, and black-eyed peas)

*4 to 6 servings*

**Ingredients:**
*1 lb ground beef or lamb*
*1 large onion, grated*
*2 Tbs. flour*
*2 Tbs. butter*
*½ cup black-eyed peas*
*½ cup lentils*
*2 lb spinach, chopped*
*1 cup liquid whey, or plain yogurt*
**Spices:**
*2½ tsp salt*
*½ tsp black pepper*
*paprika*

### DIRECTIONS FOR COOKING

**1.** Mix together meat, onion, ½ tsp of the salt and flour; form into meatballs the size of hazel nuts and brown on all sides in butter. Set aside in saucepan.
**2.** Cook black-eyed peas in 3 cups water and 1 tsp of the salt for 30 minutes or until tender. Drain and add to meatballs.
**3.** Cook lentils in 3 cups water and remaining salt for 20 minutes or until tender. Drain and add to meatball and black-eyed pea mixture.
**4.** Place all ingredients except whey or yogurt and paprika in a saucepan. Simmer for 20 minutes. Transfer to a serving bowl or tureen.
**5.** Beat whey or yogurt well to make it smooth and decorate top with it. Sprinkle with paprika. Serve over rice or with flat bread.

## Bozqormeh

(sauce of meat, yellow split peas, and herbs atop flat bread, Yazd style)

*5 to 6 servings*

**Ingredients:**
*¼ cup fresh chopped tarragon*
*½ cup chopped mint*
*3 onions, sliced*
*½ cup vinegar*
*1½ lb goat or lamb shanks*
*3 Tbs. butter*
*1 cup yellow split peas*
*1 loaf flat Persian-style bread, or 4 loaves pita bread*
**Spices:**
*1 tsp salt*
*½ tsp black pepper*
*1 tsp turmeric*
*1 tsp cinnamon*

### DIRECTIONS FOR COOKING

**1.** Soak tarragon, mint, and 2/3 of the sliced onions in vinegar for several hours.
**2.** Brown meat and remaining onions in butter in a skillet. Transfer to a large pot; add 2 cups water and seasonings and simmer for 35-40 minutes or until meat is tender and the soup has almost evaporated.
**3.** Boil yellow split peas in 3 cups water for 20 minutes or until tender; drain and add split peas to meat mixture.
**4.** Add half the onion-mint-tarragon mixture to meat mixture and simmer for 2-3 minutes.
**5.** Arrange bread on a platter; spread the *Bozqormeh* on top of the bread.
**6.** Decorate top with remaining onion-mint-tarragon mixture. Serve with yogurt.

# Talakuleh Ghurabeh

(chicken in a tart sauce with walnuts, Northern Provinces style)

*5 to 6 servings*

**Ingredients:**
*2 lb skinless chicken thighs*
*¼ cup walnuts, minced*
*3 Tbs. butter*
*1 bunch parsley, chopped*
*1 bunch scallions, chopped*
*3 Tbs. dried coriander*
*2 eggs, beaten*
*½ cup sour grape juice*
*1 Tbs. sugar*
**Spices:**
*1 tsp salt*
*½ tsp cinnamon*

**DIRECTIONS FOR COOKING**

**1.** Brown chicken lightly in its own fat. Add salt and 4 cups water and simmer over medium heat for 45 minutes. Transfer to a medium-size pot.
**2.** Brown walnuts in a heavy skillet, stirring constantly to prevent burning. Remove from skillet immediately and set aside.
**3.** Melt butter in skillet and stir in parsley, scallions, and coriander over medium heat for 5 minutes.
**4.** Add all ingredients to chicken and simmer over medium heat for 30 minutes. Serve over rice.

# Tursheh Shami

(ground veal patty stew, Gilan style)

*3 to 4 servings*

**Ingredients:**
*1 lb ground veal*
*1 large onion, grated*
*1 egg*
*½ cup olive oil*
*1 cup tomato sauce*
*1 cup lemon juice*
*4 potatoes, peeled and sliced*
**Spices:**
*1 tsp salt*
*½ tsp black pepper*

**DIRECTIONS FOR COOKING**

**1.** In a mixing bowl, mix veal, onion, egg, salt, and pepper.
**2.** Divide mixture into eight parts and make round patties.
**3.** Brown both sides of patties in olive oil; transfer to a saucepan.
**4.** Brown both sides of the potato slices; place on the top of patties in the saucepan.
**5.** Add tomato sauce and lemon juice to the saucepan, bring to a boil, and simmer over low heat for 15 to 20 minutes.
Serve over plain rice.

# Tas Kabab

(lamb or beef stew)

*6 to 8 servings*

**Ingredients:**
*1 large onion, sliced*
*3 Tbs. butter*
*1 lb stew beef or lamb, cubed*
*water*
*3 large potatoes, peeled and sliced*
*2 large tomatoes, quartered*
*2 Tbs. tomato paste*
*2 Tbs. lemon juice (or 2 dried limes)*
**Spices:**
*1½ tsp salt*
*½ tsp black pepper*
*1 tsp turmeric*

### DIRECTIONS FOR COOKING

**1.** Sauté onion lightly in butter.
**2.** Add meat and brown on all sides.
**3.** Add 2 cups water and seasonings and simmer over medium heat for 30 minutes or until meat is tender. Remove meat from broth and set both aside.
**4.** Add lemon juice or dried limes to the broth and simmer slowly over medium heat while completing the next step.
**5.** Arrange half the potatoes on the bottom of a baking dish or medium-size pot; top with the meat and onion mixture; top that with the tomatoes; finally, top with the remaining potatoes.
**6.** Dissolve tomato paste in broth and pour broth over the ingredients in the baking dish or pot.
**7.** Bake in preheated moderate (350°) oven or cook over medium heat on top of the stove for 30 minutes.
Serve with bread.

# Kashk-o Badenjan

(eggplants with whey, Isfahan style)

*5 to 6 servings*

**Ingredients:**
*1 lb stew beef or lamb, cut in 1" cubes*
*3 Tbs. butter*
*2 onions, sliced*
*3 medium eggplants*
*¼ cup olive oil*
*½ cup powdered whey, or 1 cup whey paste*
**Spices:**
*1 tsp salt*
*1 tsp turmeric*
*¼ tsp black pepper*

### DIRECTIONS FOR COOKING

**1.** Brown meat in 1 Tbs. of the butter. Add 1½ cup water and simmer for 30 minutes.
**2.** Sauté onion in 2 Tbs. of the butter. Set aside.
**3.** Peel eggplants, cut off tops, and slice lengthwise in ½-inch slices. Sprinkle with salt and set aside for 20 minutes. Then, wipe off salt and excess moisture and brown on both sides in modest amounts of olive oil, adding more if necessary.
**4.** Preheat oven to 350° F.
**5.** In a casserole dish, place a layer of half the eggplants; arrange half the meat on top of that; and top with half the onions; repeat layers using up remaining eggplants, meat, and onions.
**6.** Mix into whey the turmeric, remaining salt, and pepper; pour over eggplants and bake for 35-40 minutes. Serve with rice or bread.

# Grilled Meats
# and Cutlets
## *(Kabab, Shami, and Kotlet)*

*K*abab is a meat dish that is prepared over charcoal; however, a few of the *kabab* recipes that follow are cooked in a pot on top of the stove or fried in a skillet. Some of them, such as *kabab kubideh* and *kabab barg,* are sold in specialty shops and served either on flat bread or on rice.

Some of the *kabab* recipes in this section might defy the general conception of *kabab* with which most people are probably familiar because they are more like stews or patties, but as they are known as *kabab* in Iran, they have been included here. The best *kabab* is made with a tender cut of beef or lamb.

While in the average Iranian meal, meat does not play a dominant role—most dishes using meat, for example, feature such ingredients as vegetables, fruits, and herbs—*kabab* is an exception to this rule. In fact, *chelo kabab,* or rice and kabob, is considered by some as the Iranian national dish. *Kabab* is usually seasoned and marinated in a variety of mixtures, including yogurt and saffron. *Kabab* of red meat is usually sprinkled with powdered sumac. In recent decades, various kinds of *biftek* (beefsteak) have become popular. These are prepared for the most part much like western-style beefsteaks, and, therefore, have not been included here. *Shami* is a traditional group of foods which have modern variants. *Shami* is a patty which usually contains meat that has been finely pounded with a stone mortar and wooden pestle (or, today, finely ground) and is held together with eggs. *Shami* is also served as a side dish, but may also be used for sandwiches. Most of the dishes in this chapter can be served as sandwiches with flat bread and fresh herbs (such as mint, basil, and tarragon) and green onions and radishes accompanied by plain yogurt.

The term *kotlet,* basically a meat dish, is a Persian rendition of the Western term 'cutlet,' which suggests that most types of *kotlet* are relatively modern innovations. However, as some of these recipes reveal, Iranian cooks have been rather creative with their *kotlet,* often using traditional or regional concepts in preparing these dishes. *Kotlet* dishes are often served in modern sandwich shops as a form of Iranian fast food.

# Jujeh Kabab I
### (broiled skewered chicken)

*4 to 5 servings*

**Ingredients:**
*1 cup finely grated onion*
*½ cup lemon juice*
*2 lbs boneless, skinless chicken thighs, each cut into*
*      two or three pieces*
*4 Tbs. olive oil*
**Spices:**
*2 tsp salt*
*¼ tsp ground saffron, dissolved in 1 Tbs. hot water*
*1 tsp ground black pepper*

**DIRECTIONS FOR COOKING**

**1.** In a stainless steel or glass bowl combine the onion, lemon juice and spices, stirring until they are
thoroughly blended.

**2 .**Add the chicken and mix well.  Marinate at room
temperature for at least 1 hour or in the refrigerator
for at least 2 hours.

**3.** Add olive oil to the marinated chicken and mix
well.  Using bamboo skewers, place two side-by-side
(to make it easier to turn on the grill and to prevent
the chicken from falling off one skewer) and skewer
chicken (¼-inch metal skewers can also be used, in
which case, they do not need to be doubled).

**4.**Grill slowly over glowing charcoal for 10-15 minutes, turning the skewers occasionally to prevent burning.

Serve with *chelo* and garnish with grilled tomatoes.

# Jujeh Kabab II
(broiled skewered chicken, marinated in yogurt)

*4 to 5 servings*

Ingredients:
*1 cup finely grated onion*
*1 cup plain yogurt*
*2 lbs boneless, skinless chicken thighs,*
*    each cut into two or three pieces*
*4 Tbs. olive oil*
Spices:
*2 tsp salt*
*1 tsp ground black pepper*
*2 tsp turmeric*

### DIRECTIONS FOR COOKING

**1.** In a stainless steel or glass bowl combine the onion, yogurt and spices, stirring until they are thoroughly blended.
**2.** Add the chicken and mix well. Marinate at room temperature for at least 1 hour or in the refrigerator for at least 2 hours.
**3.** Add olive oil to the marinated chicken and mix well. Using bamboo skewers, place two side-by-side (to make it easier to turn on the grill and to prevent the chicken from falling off one skewer) and skewer chicken (¼-inch metal skewers can also be used, in which case, they do not need to be doubled).
**4.** Grill slowly over glowing charcoal for 10-15 minutes, turning the skewers occasionally to prevent burning.
Serve with *chelo* and garnish with grilled tomatoes.

# Kabab Bakhtiari
(Bakhtiari-tribe-style kabob)

*3 to 4 servings*

Ingredients:
*1 lb lean beef or lamb, cut in 1" x 2" strips*
*meat tenderizer*
*1 lb boneless chicken breast*
*1 onion, finely grated*
*2 Tbs. lemon juice*
*¼ cup butter, melted*
Spices:
*½ tsp salt*
*¼ tsp black pepper*
*¼ tsp saffron, dissolved in 2 Tbs. hot water*

### DIRECTIONS FOR COOKING

**1.** Sprinkle meat with tenderizer; pound the pieces once or twice with a meat hammer.
**2.** Mix onion, lemon juice, saffron, and salt and pepper together in a bowl. Add meat and chicken and turn so that all pieces are covered with mixture. Marinate at room temperature for one to two hours or leave in refrigerator for several hours or over night.
**3.** Remove meat and chicken from marinade; skewer 2 or 3 pieces lengthwise on flat, ½" wide stainless steel skewers; alternate beef or lamb and chicken on each skewer.
**4.** Grill over glowing charcoal, turning and basting frequently. If needed brush with melted butter.
NOTE: Bakhtiari-style kabob is served with flat bread or plain rice.

**Tips and things**
*meat tenderizer*
Kiwi fruit is a natural meat tenderizer. Peal the skin off, mash, and marinate the meat in its juices for no more than 10 minutes.

# Kabab-e Kubideh
(grilled ground kabob)

*4 to 6 servings*

**Ingredients:**
*1 lb ground beef or lamb*
*1 medium onion, grated*
**Spices:**
*1 tsp salt*
*½ tsp ground black pepper*
*1 tsp turmeric*

### DIRECTIONS FOR COOKING

**1.** Mix all ingredients in mixing bowl.  For a more authentic texture and to prevent the mixture from falling off the skewers (see Steps 2 and 3), place about half the mixture at a time in a food processor and turn on high speed for about 30 seconds, empty into bowl and repeat this step with remaining mixture. (This will stretch the meat fibers and thus help hold the meat on the skewers.) Cover and let mixture marinate for 1 hour at room temperature or several hours in refrigerator.

**2.** This kabob is traditionally grilled over hot coals out-of-doors, wrapped around long, wide, thin, flat (approximately 14" x 1¼ " x 1/8") stainless steel skewers.  To prepare the dish in this way, divide the meat mixture into 10 - 12 portions.  Press each portion around a stainless steel skewer and shape evenly.

Firmly press both ends of the meat to the metal. Using the index and middle fingers, make 2 or 3 indentations across the meat to ensure that the meat is secured to the metal skewers.

**3.** Grill over glowing charcoal, turning constantly for about 2 minutes to help secure the meat to the skewers.  Then, let the meat cook on each side for 3 - 4 additional minutes.

**4.** Remove from the grill and, to serve, gently push the meat off the sticks and onto a platter or individual plates.

Serve with hot plain rice.

### ALTERNATE METHOD

**1.** If no skewers are available, place aluminum foil over the grill; perforate.

**2.** Form the meat into oblong patties, about 8" x 1½" x ½", and place on foil-covered grill.

**3.** Cook over hot coals for about 5 minutes on each side, or until meat is cooked to taste.  Or, broil in the oven about 5 minutes on each side.

Traditionally, *kabab* is served sprinkled with powdered sumac accompanied by a mound of steaming hot plain rice.  Each portion of rice is accompanied by a pat of butter and an egg yolk, which are mixed in with the rice.  The rice should be hot enough to cook the egg and melt the butter.  *Kabab* can also be served accompanied by a large piece of flat bread in place of rice.

# Kabab-e Soltani
(broiled skewered "royal" kabob)

*3 to 4 servings*

Ingredients:
*1 lb lean beef or lamb, cut in 1" x 2" strips*
*meat tenderizer*
*1 onion, finely grated*
*½ cup plain yogurt*
*1 tsp lemon juice*
*¼ cup butter, melted*
**Spices:**
*1 tsp turmeric*
*½ tsp salt*
*¼ tsp black pepper*
*¼ tsp saffron, dissolved in 2 Tbs. hot water*

### DIRECTIONS FOR COOKING

**1.** Sprinkle meat with tenderizer; pound the pieces once or twice with a meat hammer.
**2.** Mix onion, yogurt, lemon juice, turmeric, salt and pepper together in a bowl.  Add meat and turn so that all pieces are covered with mixture.  Marinate at room temperature for an hour and a half or leave in refrigerator for several hours or over night.
**3.** Remove meat from marinade; skewer 2 or 3 pieces lengthwise on flat, ½"-wide stainless steel skewers.
**4.** Mix together dissolved saffron and melted butter. Baste meat on both sides with this mixture.
**5.** Grill over glowing charcoal, turning and basting frequently.
Serve with *chelo* or flat bread.
NOTE:  Some restaurants serve as *kabab-e soltani* one skewer of *kabab-e soltani* along with one skewer of *kabab-e kubideh*.

# Kabab-e Barg
(broiled skewered kabob)

*3 to 4 servings*

Ingredients:
*1 lb lamb or beef with some fat, cut in 1½" cubes*
*meat tenderizer*
*1 onion, finely grated*
**Spices:**
*1 tsp turmeric*
*½  tsp salt*
*½ tsp black pepper*

### DIRECTIONS FOR COOKING

**1.** Lightly sprinkle meat with tenderizer.
**2.** Mix onion and seasonings in a bowl. Mix in meat and marinate at room temperature for 1½ hours or in refrigerator overnight.
**3.** Remove meat from the marinade.  Place 5 - 6 pieces on each skewer.
**4.** Grill over glowing charcoal, turning frequently. Serve sprinkled with powdered sumac with *chelo* or flat bread.

Kabab-e Soltani and grilled tomatoes.
Prepared by Janet N.

Kabab-e Soltani servd with rice

Kabab-e Barg servd with rice.

# Beryan
(meat patty with chicken livers)

*5 to 6 servings*

**Ingredients:**
*1 lb beef or lamb (choose meat with some fat)*
*water*
*5-10 chicken livers*
*5-6 pieces of flat bread*
**Spices:**
*1½ tsp salt*
*1 tsp turmeric*
*4 Tbs. cinnamon*
*2 tsp black pepper*

### DIRECTIONS FOR COOKING

**1.** Place meat, 2½ cups water, and 1 tsp salt in a medium-size pot; boil 15-20 minutes or until meat is almost cooked.  Remove from heat.

**2.** Remove meat from the broth; add turmeric to the broth and keep warm over low heat.

**3.** Grind meat in a meat grinder twice (or use a food processor, making sure meat is completely pulverized).

**4.** Boil chicken livers in 1½ cups water and ½ tsp salt for 5-10 minutes or until cooked.

**5.** Remove liver from its broth and slice thinly.  Replace sliced liver in its  broth and keep warm.

**6.** Divide the ground meat into 5-6 portions.  Sprinkle a very small frying pan (no larger than 6" in diameter) heavily with cinnamon and some pepper.  Flatten out 1 portion of meat in pan and cook over medium heat.

**7.** On a large platter, place 1 piece at a time of flat bread (or open up large loaf of pita bread); pour some of the broth from cooking the meat over the bread to moisten it.

**8.** Remove the frying pan from the heat and turn it over on the moistened piece of bread, scraping out any stuck portions of meat from the pan (at this point, more cinnamon can be sprinkled over the meat, if desired). Place 2 or 3 pieces of the chicken liver slices at the side of the "patty" of meat and fold the bread over the "patty" or replace the top of the pita bread. Keep in a warm place while the process is repeated for each patty.  When all patties are ready to be served, moisten the bread again with more of the juice from cooking the meat, if desired.

Serve with plain yogurt, *dough* beverage (see recipe in this book), green onions, fresh mint, fresh basil and radishes.

NOTE: This dish is a specialty of the city of Isfahan, where it is made in special shops called *"beryani,"* which is the name given to the dish itself in Tehran

Prepared by Diane W.

and other places outside Isfahan.  It is meant to be eaten with the fingers.

## Kabab Hoseyni
### (skillet kabob)

*4 to 6 servings*

**Ingredients:**
*½ cup lemon juice*
*1 ½ tender filet of beef or lamb, cut in 1" x ½" pieces*
*2 medium onions, quartered and separated*
*3 Tbs. butter*
*water*
**Spices:**
*1 tsp salt*
*½ tsp black pepper*
*¼ tsp saffron, dissolved in ¼ cup hot water*
*½ tsp cinnamon*

### DIRECTIONS FOR COOKING

**1.** Mix lemon juice and seasonings in a bowl.
**2.** Add meat and onions to lemon juice mixture, making sure all pieces are covered with juice; marinade several hours at room temperature or overnight in the refrigerator.
**3.** Remove meat and onions from marinade and set marinade aside.
**4.** Alternate layers of meat and onion on 8" wooden skewers.
**5.** In a skillet, melt butter and brown meat and onions (on skewers) over medium heat. Repeat this process until all the meat on skewers has been browned.
**6.** Return all browned, skewered meat to skillet.
**7.** Add 2 cups water to remaining marinade and pour over the skewered meat in the skillet. Cover and simmer over medium heat for 30 minutes.
Serve over rice.

## Shish Kabab
### (shish kabob)

*3 to 4 servings*

**Ingredients:**
*1 lb beef or lamb, cut in 1" cubes*
*meat tenderizer*
*1 onion, finely grated*
*½ cup plain yogurt*
*1 tsp lemon juice*
*½ lb cherry tomatoes*
*1 green peppers, cut in 2" square pieces*
*2 medium onions, quartered and separated*
*¼ cup butter*
**Spices:**
*1 tsp turmeric*
*½ tsp salt*
*¼ tsp black pepper*

### DIRECTIONS FOR COOKING

**1.** Sprinkle meat with meat tenderizer.
**2.** Mix together grated onion, yogurt, lemon juice, and seasonings; add meat and marinate over night or for several hours.
**3.** Alternate layers of meat, cherry tomatoes, green peppers, and onions on skewers.
**4.** Melt butter; brush over skewered meat and vegetables; grill slowly over glowing charcoal until meat is cooked to taste.
Serve over steaming hot rice.

Prepared by Maryam J.

## Kabab-e Qafqazi
(kabob, Caucasian style)

*3 to 4 servings*

**Ingredients:**
*1 lb ground beef or lamb*
*1 medium onion, grated*
*2 eggs, beaten*
*2 Tbs. flour*
*2 Tbs. butter, melted*
*2 Tbs. lemon juice*
**Spices:**
*½ tsp salt*
*¼ tsp black pepper*
*¼ tsp saffron, dissolved in 4 Tbs. hot water*

### DIRECTIONS FOR COOKING

**1.** Mix together meat, onions, eggs, salt and pepper.
**2.** On a large piece of aluminum foil (about 10" x 14") on a flat surface, spread meat mixture evenly over foil about ½" thick, leaving about 2" of the edges uncovered.
**3.** Place another piece of aluminum foil evenly over top; secure edges.  With a fork, perforate aluminum foil in several places on both sides.
**4.** Grill over glowing charcoal for 5 minutes.
**5.** Slide two large spatulas under the *kabab* in foil and turn carefully to grill on the second side.
**6.** Stir flour in butter over medium heat until the color turns golden.  Immediately mix in lemon juice and saffron solution.
**7.** Remove *kabab* from foil and place on platter. Spread flour mixture evenly over top.
Serve with rice or fried potatoes.

## Kabab Digi
(roasted beef with saffron)

*5 to 6 servings*

**Ingredients:**
*2 lb. fillet steaks, sliced ¼" thick*
*½ cup butter, melted*
*2 large onions, sliced*
**Spices:**
*½ tsp saffron, dissolved in 2 Tbs. hot water*
*1 tsp salt*
*½ tsp black pepper*
*½ tsp turmeric*

### DIRECTIONS FOR COOKING

**1.** Select a roasting pan with a cover and place a wire rack on the bottom.
**2.** Combine saffron solution with melted butter and mix.
**3.** Place a layer of half of the steak slices on the rack. Brush with butter and saffron solution.  Cover with half the slices of onions, and sprinkle with half of the remaining spices.  Repeat this step with the remaining meat, onions, and spices.
**4.** Cover the roasting pan and bake in 350° oven for 45 minutes.
This *kabab* can be served with plain rice or roasted potatoes.

## Kabab-e Morghabi
### (kabob of duck)

*6 servings*

**Ingredients:**
*3½-4 lb duck*
*water*
*1 onion, quartered*
*2 Tbs. chopped parsley*
*¼ cup butter, melted*
*2 fresh lemons*
*¼ cup honey*
**Spices:**
*1 tsp salt*
*½ tsp turmeric*

#### DIRECTIONS FOR COOKING

**1.** Place duck with 1 cup water, seasonings, onion, and parsley in a pressure cooker and cook for 30 minutes (or increase water to 3 cups and simmer over medium heat for 50-60 minutes), or until duck is rather tender; drain water and set duck aside to cool.
**2.** De-bone duck, and cut meat into 2 inch sections. Place several pieces on kabob skewer.
**3.** Brush duck on skewers thoroughly with melted butter and grill slowly over glowing charcoal. Brush more butter on pieces if they are getting dry. Remove duck and place on a serving platter.
**4.** Squeeze juice from lemons into a small saucepan and mix in honey. Warm over low heat. Pour over duck just before serving.

## Kabab-e Tanuri
### (oven-baked kabob)

*3 to 4 servings*

**Ingredients:**
*1 large onion, finely chopped*
*1 lb. ground beef or lamb*
**Spices:**
*1 tsp salt*
*1 tsp turmeric*
*½ tsp black pepper*
*2 tsp powdered sumac*

#### DIRECTIONS FOR COOKING

**1.** In mixing bowl, mix together onions, meat, salt, turmeric, and pepper.
**2.** Transfer the mixture onto a large flat iron griddle. Flatten the mixture with the back of a spatula to ¼" thick.
**3.** Cook for 20 minutes in a 350° oven.
**4.** Sprinkle with powdered sumac before serving. Serve with flat bread and roasted tomatoes.

## Jegarak
### (grilled liver)

*3 to 4 servings*

| **Ingredients:** | **Spices:** |
|---|---|
| *1 lb calf liver, cut in* | *salt* |
| *1"x2" strips* | *pepper* |

#### DIRECTIONS FOR COOKING

**1.** Skewer 2 or 3 pieces of liver lengthwise on each skewer.
**2.** Grill over glowing charcoal, turning occasionally, for 5 minutes.
**3.** Sprinkle with salt and pepper.
Serve with flat bread, plain yogurt, and green onions.
NOTE: *Jegarak* is usually sold in specialty shops or by street vendors. In Iran, it is a favorite late afternoon or early evening snack.

## Dastpich-e Kabab-e Morgh
### (grilled chicken wrap)

*1 sandwich*

Ingredients:
*¼ cup chopped cucumbers*
*¼ cup chopped onions*
*2 Tbs. chopped fresh parsley*
*1 tbs. dried mint or dried dill weed*
*2 Tbs. plain yogurt*
*2 Tbs. lemon juice*
*½ loaf* Lavash *bread, or 1 large wheat tortilla*
*¼ lb. grilled boneless, skinless chicken breast,*
   *cut in strips*
Spices:
*salt*
*black pepper*

**DIRECTIONS FOR PREPARATION**

**1.** Combine plain yogurt and dried mint or dill weed; mix thoroughly and set aside.
**2.** Place cucumbers, onions, and parsley in a small bowl.  Add lemon juice and salt and pepper to taste; mix and set aside.
**3.**  Place bread on a plate; place chicken strips on top.
**4.** Top chicken with the cucumber-onion-parsley and yogurt mixture.
**5.** Roll into a wrap and serve.

## Dastpich-e Kabab-e Barg
### (grilled meat wrap)

*1 sandwich*

Ingredients:
*¼ cup chopped cucumbers*
*¼ cup chopped onions*
*2 Tbs. chopped fresh parsley*
*1 tbs. dried mint or dried dill weed*
*2 Tbs. plain yogurt*
*2 Tbs. lemon juice*
*½ loaf* Lavash *bread, or 1 large wheat tortilla*
*¼ lb. grilled beef or lamb, cut in strips*
Spices:
*salt*
*black pepper*
*1 tsp. sumac*

**DIRECTIONS FOR PREPARATION**

**1.** Combine plain yogurt and dried mint or dill weed; mix thoroughly and set aside.
**2.** Place cucumbers, onions, and parsley in a small bowl.  Add lemon juice and salt and pepper to taste; mix and set aside.
**3.**  Place bread on a plate.  Place meat strips on top.
**4.** Top meat with the cucumber-onion-parsley and yogurt mixture, sprinkle with sumac.
**5.** Roll into a wrap and serve.

Prepared by Kamron J.

# Shami Kabab

(chickpea and meat patties)

*5 to 6 servings*

**Ingredients:**
*1 lb finely ground beef or lamb*
*1 cup roasted chickpea flour*
*1 large onion, minced*
*warm water*
*½ cup olive oil*
**Spices:**
*2 tsp salt*
*½ tsp black pepper*
*½ tsp turmeric*

### DIRECTIONS FOR COOKING

**1.** Mix together all ingredients except for the oil.
**2.** Pour the oil in a skillet.
**3.** Shape meat mixture into round, thin patties; fry over medium heat until one side is golden brown; turn over, adding more oil if necessary, and brown the other side. Repeat until all the meat mixture is used up.

Serve with bread, green onions, fresh mint, fresh basil, radishes, and yogurt.

# Shami-ye Lapeh

(patties with yellow split peas and meat)

*8 to 10 patties*

**Ingredients:**
*1 cup dried yellow split peas*
*1 medium onion, grated*
*1 lb ground beef or lamb*
*1 Tbs. dried coriander*
*2 eggs, beaten*
*¼ cup olive oil*
**Spices:**
*1 tsp salt*
*¼ tsp black pepper*
*1 tsp cinnamon*

### DIRECTIONS FOR COOKING

**1.** Cook peas over medium heat in 2 cups water for 30-40 minutes or until tender. Add additional water if necessary. Drain and mash well.
**2.** Mix together well all remaining ingredients except olive oil.
**3.** Form patties by hand to the size of small pancakes and brown on both sides in oil. Use additional oil if necessary.

Prepared by Shamsi F.

# Shami-ye Sibzamini
## (stuffed meat and potato patties, Azerbaijan style)

*5 to 6 servings*

**Ingredients:**
*½ lb ground beef or lamb*
*1 cup parsley, chopped*
*1 hard-boiled egg, chopped*
*5 large potatoes*
*2 eggs, beaten*
*2/3 cup olive oil*
*sprigs of parsley*
**Spices:**
*1 tsp Azerbaijan-style seasoning (see recipe in*
 *"Spices" section)*
*½ tsp turmeric*
*1 tsp salt*

### DIRECTIONS FOR COOKING

**1.** Lightly brown meat in its own fat in a skillet.
**2.** Stir in parsley, boiled eggs, ½ tsp of the salt, and the remaining spices; remove from heat.
**3.** Cook potatoes, peel and mash. Mix in eggs and remaining salt.
**4.** Wet the palms of your hands with water; take a handful of potato mixture and flatten in the palm of your hand. Place a spoonful of meat mixture on top of that and fold potato over meat so that meat stuffing is secure inside potato mixture; continue until mixture is completely used.
**5.** Brown each patty on both sides in oil over medium heat. Arrange on a platter and decorate with parsley.

# Torsh Shami
## (tart meat patties)

*8 to 10 servings*

**Ingredients:**
*1 tsp baking soda*
*½ cup milk*
*1 cup dried bread crumbs*
*1 lb ground beef or lamb*
*1 medium onion, grated*
*2 eggs*
*1 cup olive oil*
*2 Tbs. lemon juice*
*2 cups tomato juice*
**Spices:**
*½ tsp cinnamon*
*1 tsp salt*
*¼ tsp black pepper*

### DIRECTIONS FOR COOKING

**1.** In a mixing bowl, dissolve baking soda in milk; then soak bread crumbs in milk mixture while preparing meat.
**2.** Sprinkle meat with cinnamon and mix in with bread crumbs; add grated onions and eggs and mix together into a paste.
**3.** Form patties the shape and size of small doughnuts and brown on both sides in oil.
**4.** Place patties in a flat saucepan; mix in lemon juice, tomato juice, and seasonings; simmer for 1 hour or until the juice has thickened. Serve with flat bread.

# Shami-ye Tukhali
(doughnut-shaped meat patties with
yellow split peas)

*5 to 6 patties*

**Ingredients:**
*1 cup dried yellow split peas*
*1 medium onion, chopped*
*2 Tbs. butter*
*½ lb lean ground beef or lamb*
*1 Tbs. flour*
*4 eggs*
*1 cup olive oil*
*parsley*

**Spices:**
*1 tsp salt*
*¼ tsp black pepper*
*¼ tsp turmeric*
*¼ tsp saffron dissolved in 2 Tbs. hot water*

## DIRECTIONS FOR COOKING

**1.** Cook split peas in 2 cups water; drain and set aside to cool.

**2.** Meanwhile, sauté onions in butter for 5 minutes. Set aside to cool.

**3.** Mix together all remaining ingredients except for oil and parsley and blend in a food processor or mash into a paste.

**4.** Grease the palm of your hand with some olive oil and make patties the size and shape of small doughnuts (about 2½ inches in diameter).

**5.** Brown on both sides in oil.

**6.** Drain on paper towels, taking care not to break the patties.  Arrange on a platter and garnish with parsley.  Serve with flat bread and yogurt.

# Shami-ye Mowz
(banana patties)

*15 to 20 patties*

**Ingredients:**
*5 ripe bananas*
*½ cup flour*
*½ cup milk*
*2 eggs*
*¼ cup olive oil*

**Spices:**
*¼ tsp salt*
*½ tsp cardamom*

## DIRECTIONS FOR COOKING

**1.** Peel and mash bananas with potato masher.

**2.** Dissolve flour in milk; add eggs and beat well.

**3.** Mix in spices well.

**4.** In a frying pan or on a griddle, heat 1 or 2 Tbs. of olive oil over medium heat.  Make patties the size of small pancakes.  Brown on both sides.  Continue until all mixture is used up.

# Kotlet
(meat patties)

*4 to 6 servings*

**Ingredients:**
*1 lb ground beef or lamb*
*1 large onion, minced*
*½ cup dried bread crumbs*
*1 egg*
*¾ cup flour*
*¾ cup olive oil*

**Spices:**
*1½ tsp salt*
*¼ tsp black pepper*
*¼ tsp saffron, dissolved in ¼ cup hot water*

## DIRECTIONS FOR COOKING

**1.** Mix together meat, onion, bread crumbs, egg, and seasonings. Shape into oblong patties, 2" x 3½".

**2.** Dip into flour and brown on both sides in oil over medium-low heat.
Serve with flat bread, green vegetables, and yogurt.

Prepared by Farzaneh Z.

## Kotlet-e Tabrizi

(meat patties, Tabriz style)

*10 to 12 patties*

| Ingredients: | Spices: |
|---|---|
| *2 medium potatoes* | *1 tsp salt* |
| *½ cup dried yellow split peas* | *½ tsp* |
| *1 lb lean ground beef or lamb* | *Azerbaijan-* |
| *1 onion, grated* | *style seasoning* |
| *2 eggs, beaten* | |
| *1 cup dried bread crumbs* | |
| *1 cup olive oil* | |

### DIRECTIONS FOR COOKING

**1.** Boil potatoes until very well cooked. Drain, peel, and mash.

**2.** Meanwhile, boil split peas in 2 cups water for 20-30 minutes or until quite tender. Drain and mash well.

**3.** Mix together potatoes, split peas, meat, onion, eggs, and seasonings.

**4.** Heat oil in a skillet; reduce heat to medium. Form meat mixture into oval-shaped patties (about 3" x 5") about ½" thick. Dip both sides of each patty in bread crumbs and fry in oil on both sides.

## Kotlet-e Gusht-o Sibzamini

(meat and potato patties)

*4 to 6 servings*

| Ingredients: | Spices: |
|---|---|
| *¾ lb ground beef or lamb* | *1½ tsp salt* |
| *1 medium onion, grated* | *½ tsp black pepper* |
| *2 medium potatoes, grated* | *½ tsp turmeric* |
| *1 egg* | *½ tsp cinnamon* |
| *¼ cup olive oil* | |

### DIRECTIONS FOR COOKING

**1.** Mix together meat, onion, potatoes, egg, and seasonings.

**2.** Shape into oblong, 2" x 3½" patties and brown on both sides over medium or medium-low heat.

## Kotlet-e Tu Por

(stuffed cutlet, Azerbaijan style)

*5 to 6 servings*

Ingredients:
*½ cup* zereshk
*½ cup slivered almonds*
*2 medium potatoes*
*½ dried yellow split peas*
*1 lb lean ground lamb or beef*
*2 eggs, beaten*
*½ cup parsley, chopped*
*1 cup dried bread crumbs*
*1 cup olive oil*
**Spices:**
*½ tsp saffron, dissolved in ¼ cup hot water*
*1 tsp salt*
*1½ tsp Azerbaijan-style seasoning*

### DIRECTIONS FOR COOKING

**1.** Clean *zereshk* and soak along with almonds in saffron solution.

**2.** Boil potatoes in 2 cups water until well cooked; cool, peal, and mash.

**3.** Boil split peas in water for 20-30 minutes or until quite tender. Drain and mash well.

**4.** Mix together potatoes, split peas, meat, onions, eggs, and seasonings. Shape into patties about 4" in diameter.

**5.** Add parsley to *zereshk*-almond mixture.

**6.** Spread some of the bread crumbs in the middle of a board. Place one patty on bread crumbs; place 1 Tbs. of parsley-*zereshk*-almond mixture in the center of the patty. Cover with another patty and pinch together the edges. Sprinkle bread crumbs evenly over top and set aside. Repeat this step until all meat and stuffing mixtures are used up.

**7.** Fry patties on both sides in oil in a skillet over medium heat. Serve with bread and yogurt.

NOTE: Stuffed cutlets should be served soon after preparation, as they otherwise will become dry.

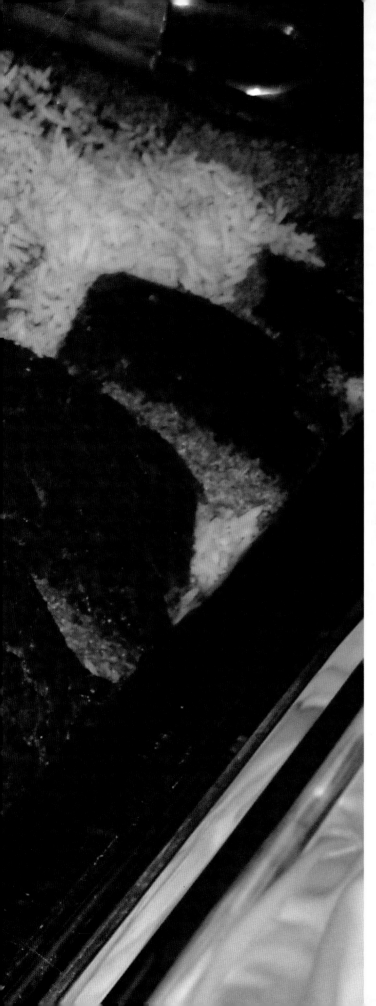

# Quiches, Souffles, and Omelets
## (*Kuku, Nargesi and Sheshandaz*)

The vital ingredient in *kuku, nargesi,* and *sheshandaz* is eggs. *Kuku* dishes are traditional flavorful quiche-like dishes, without the crust, combining herbs, vegetables, and sometimes even meat.

*Nargesi* literally means 'of or like a narcissus.' In classical Persian poetry, the eyes of the beloved are sometimes compared to the narcissus. The reference here is perhaps to the eggs, resembling eyes, which decorate the top of these dishes.

The term *sheshandaz* evokes a variety of meanings, including a juggler and a full moon. *Sheshandaz* dishes are similar in appearance to *nargesi* dishes, with eggs on the top.

The dishes contained in this section may be served as side dishes or light meals.

# Omlet-e Khorma
### (date omelet)

*6 servings*

**Ingredients:**
*3 Tbs. butter*
*¼ lb pitted dates*
*6 eggs*
**Spices:**
*¼ tsp salt*

## DIRECTIONS FOR COOKING

**1.** Melt butter in a skillet; turn heat to low and add dates; sauté lightly for 5 minutes. Spread dates evenly over bottom of skillet.
**2.** Beat eggs together with salt and pour over dates. Cover and cook 3 to 5 minutes or until eggs are set.

NOTE: Generally a breakfast or brunch dish served with bread.

# Khagineh
### (sweet omelet)

*6 to 8 servings*

**Ingredients:**
*6 eggs*
*1½ tsp flour*
*3 Tbs. butter*
*3 Tbs. sugar*
**Spices:**
*¼ tsp salt*
*½ tsp cinnamon (optional)*

## DIRECTIONS FOR COOKING

**1.** Beat together eggs, flour, and salt.
**2.** Melt butter in a skillet and pour in egg mixture. Cover and cook over medium-low heat for 3 to 5 minutes, or until mixture is set.
**3.** Dissolve sugar in ¼ cup hot water to make a thin syrup. Set aside.
**4.** When omelet is browned on bottom, cut into 6 to 8 wedges in skillet and turn each over.
**5.** Pour sugar syrup evenly over the eggs and cook over medium-low heat for 5 minutes more, or until bottom is lightly browned.
**6.** Sprinkle with cinnamon, if desired.

Serve with bread.

NOTE: This dish can be made without sugar, in which case it is referred to as *omlet*.

# Siravij
## (Gilan-style garlic omelet)

*4 servings*

**Ingredients:**
*3 medium cloves of garlic*
*1 cup of chopped leeks*
*3 Tbs. butter*
*5 eggs*
**Spices:**
*½ tsp salt*
*1 tsp turmeric*
*¼ tsp black pepper*

### DIRECTIONS FOR COOKING

**1.** Peel and coarsely chop garlic, mix with chopped leeks.
**2.** Melt butter in a skillet; turn heat to medium and add garlic and leeks; sauté for 5 to 7 minutes. Add salt and turmeric and stir.
**3.** Break the eggs over the garlic and leek mixture and stir until the eggs are set.

This dish must be served immediately after it is cooked. In the northern Province of Gilan, this dish is often served with plain rice.

# Kuku Sabzi
## (green vegetable and herb "quiche")

*4 to 6 servings*

**Ingredients:**
*1½ cups finely chopped parsley*
*½ cup finely chopped leeks*
*¼ cup fresh chopped dill weed*
*¼ cup fresh chopped mint*
*6 eggs, slightly beaten*
*¼ cup butter*
**Spices:**
*1 tsp salt*
*½ tsp black pepper*
*½ tsp saffron, dissolved in 2 Tbs. hot water*

### DIRECTIONS FOR COOKING

**1.** Combine all ingredients except butter in mixing bowl and mix well.
**2.** Melt butter in a non-stick skillet and pour mixture in.
**3.** Cover, cook over medium heat until mixture is set and brown on bottom, 10-15 minutes.
**4.** Cut into pie-shaped wedge, gently turn each piece over and brown the other side.
Serve with bread or with rice.
NOTE: Instead of chopping all the herbs and vegetables, they can be chopped in a food processor; if so, the eggs and other ingredients can be added after chopping.

Prepared by Mitra N.

## Kuku Badenjan I
### (eggplant "quiche")

*4 to 6 servings*

**Ingredients:**
*2 medium eggplants*
*¼ cup olive oil*
*1 medium onion, grated*
*1 tsp crushed garlic*
*3 Tbs. lemon juice*
*6 eggs, slightly beaten*
*1 Tbs. flour*
*¼ cup butter*

**Spices:**
*1 tsp salt*
*½ tsp black pepper*
*1 tsp curry powder*

### DIRECTIONS FOR COOKING

**1.** Peel eggplants; cut lengthwise in thin slices; brown in heavy skillet on both sides; let cool.
**2.** Put eggplants in bowl and mash well.
**3.** Add remaining ingredients, except butter, and beat well.
**4.** Melt butter in skillet. Pour mixture into skillet and cover. Cook over medium heat a few minutes, then turn heat down to low and cook until set and browned on bottom (about 15 minutes).
**5.** Turn over like a pancake and brown the other side. Can also be baked in buttered pyrex dish in 350° oven for 45 minutes, or until browned on bottom and top.

## Kuku Badenjan II
### (eggplant "quiche" with meat)

*6 to 8 servings*

**Ingredients:**
*3 medium eggplants*
*1 cup olive oil*
*3 medium potatoes*
*1 lb ground beef or lamb*
*2 medium onions, chopped*
*2 Tbs. butter*
*½ Tbs. powdered, dried rose petals\**
*2 Tbs. flour*
*5 eggs, beaten*
*½ tsp baking soda*
*2 Tbs. parsley, chopped*

**Spices:**
*1 ½ tsp salt*
*½ tsp black pepper*
*1 ½ tsp cinnamon*

### DIRECTIONS FOR COOKING

**1.** Peel and cut eggplants into ½" cubes; brown in oil; remove from skillet and set aside in a large bowl; also set aside skillet and oil.
**2.** Peel and cut potatoes in ½" cubes; brown in oil remaining from browning eggplants and add to eggplants.
**3.** Brown meat in its own fat and add to the eggplant mixture.
**4.** Sauté onions in butter and add to mixture.
**5.** Add spices, rose petals, flour, eggs, and baking soda to eggplant mixture and mix well.
**6.** Place in a baking dish and bake in a preheated moderate, 350°, oven for 40 minutes.
**7.** Cut the *kuku* in wedges and garnish with chopped parsley.

\* Powdered dried rose petals add a subtle flavor and aroma to a variety of Persian dishes. Aromatic, generally pink roses are the best choice for drying and using in food preparation.

NOTE: A variation of this dish may be made by substituting 5 zucchinis for the eggplants.

## Kuku Sibzamini
(potato patties)

*4 to 6 servings*

**Ingredients:**
*4 medium potatoes, cooked and mashed*
*1 medium onion, grated*
*4 eggs*
*¼ cup butter*
**Spices:**
*½ tsp salt*
*¼ tsp black pepper*
*½ tsp saffron, dissolved in 2 Tbs. hot water*

### DIRECTIONS FOR COOKING

**1.** Combine mashed potatoes with onion, eggs, and spices.
**2.** Shape into small patties, 2½" to 3" in diameter.
**3.** Brown on both sides in butter or oil.

Serve with flat bread, fresh greens (such as mint, basil, tarragon, or green onions; see *Sabzikhordan* in "Miscellaneous" section).

Prepared by Diane W.

## Kuku-ye Golkalam
(cauliflower "quiche")

*6-8 servings*

**Ingredients:**
*1 head cauliflower*
*1 onion, chopped*
*6 Tbs. butter*
*1 Tbs. flour*
*½ tsp baking powder*
*7 eggs*
**Spices:**
*1¼ Tbs. salt*
*¼ tsp pepper*
*½ tsp turmeric*

### DIRECTIONS FOR COOKING

**1.** Separate cauliflower flowerets; remove stems; boil in 5 cups of water with 1 Tbs. salt for 10 to 15 minutes or until tender; drain, mash, and set aside to cool.
**2.** Preheat oven to 350° F.
**3.** Sauté onions in 2 Tbs. butter. Set aside to cool.
**4.** Mix together all ingredients except for remaining butter and beat well.
**5.** Melt the remaining butter and use half of it to grease the bottom and sides of a flat-bottomed casserole dish. Pour in mixture and even out the surface. Then, pour the remaining butter evenly over the top. Bake for 30 minutes or until the top of the *kuku* is golden brown.

# Kuku Qandi
(sweetened potato "quiche")

*6 servings*

**Ingredients:**
*4 medium potatoes*
*4 eggs*
*2½ Tbs. powdered sugar*
*3 Tbs. butter*
**Spices:**
*½ tsp salt*
*¼ tsp saffron, dissolved in 2 Tbs. hot water*

## DIRECTIONS FOR COOKING

**1.** Wash and cook potatoes until soft.
**2.** Peel and mash potatoes; let cool.
**3.** Add eggs, sugar, and spices and mix well.
**4.** Melt 2 Tbs. of the butter in a non-stick skillet; pour in egg and potato mixture and shake skillet to make sure surface is even.  Cover and cook over medium-low heat for 10 minutes, or until set.
**5.** Remove cover and cook an additional 5 minutes.
**6.** Slice *kuku* into pie-shaped wedges in the skillet and turn over each piece to brown the underside for 10 minutes, distributing the remaining 1 Tbs. of butter under each piece.  Transfer to platter to serve.
NOTE:  This dish is traditionally served with *Zereshk Polo* or *Shirin Polo* at weddings.

Prepared by Fahimeh Z.

# Kuku Sabzi va Sibzamini

(layered green vegetable and potato "quiche,"
Tabriz style)

*6 to 8 servings*

**Ingredients:**
*3 potatoes*
*7 eggs*
*3 cups leeks, minced*
*¼ cup fresh chopped or 2 Tbs. dried fenugreek*
*1 cup parsley, minced*
*¼ cup fresh chopped or 2 Tbs. dried dill weed*
*½ cup fresh coriander, chopped*
*¼ cup butter, melted*
*¼ cup walnuts, chopped*
**Spices:**
*1 tsp salt*
*½ tsp turmeric*
*1 tsp Azerbaijan-style seasoning (see page 7)*

### DIRECTIONS FOR COOKING

**1.** Cook potatoes in 2 cups water until tender; peel, mash well, and allow to cool.
**2.** Mix together well mashed-potatoes, ½ tsp salt, and 3 eggs.
**3.** Preheat oven to 350° F.
**4.** Mix together all remaining ingredients, except butter and walnuts.
**5.** Use 3 Tbs. of the butter to grease a shallow, oblong casserole dish. Pour in the green herb and egg mixture, spread out evenly and bake for 5-10 minutes or until the mixture is set. Remove dish from the oven and spread potato mixture evenly on top. Sprinkle with walnuts.
**6.** Bake for an additional 15 minutes or until the top turns golden brown.

To serve: Cut in squares and serve with bread and yogurt or as an accompaniment to meat dishes.

# Kuku-ye Kadu

(zucchini patties)

*approximately 25 patties*

**Ingredients:**
*6 zucchinis, washed and grated*
*1 medium onion, finely grated*
*2 Tbs. flour*
*6 eggs*
*¼ cup olive oil*
**Spices:**
*½ tsp salt*
*¼ tsp black pepper*
*¼ tsp saffron dissolved in 2 Tbs. hot water*

### DIRECTIONS FOR COOKING

**1.** Mix together all ingredients except butter and beat well.
**2.** Heat half the olive oil in a skillet, then pour 1 Tbs. at a time of the mixture into the oil to form round patties the size of small pancakes. Brown over medium heat for 5 minutes, then turn and brown the other side.
**3.** Continue Step 2 until the mixture is used up. Add small amounts of oil to the skillet gradually.

## Kuku-ye Shevid va Baqala

(fava bean and dill weed "quiche")

*8 to 10 servings*

Ingredients:
*1 lb fresh shelled fava or lima beans*
*1 onion, chopped*
*6 Tbs. butter*
*6 eggs*
*½ cup chopped fresh or ¼ cup dried dill weed*
*2 Tbs. flour*
Spices:
*½ tsp salt*
*¼ tsp saffron dissolved in 2 Tbs. hot water*
*¼ tsp black pepper*

### DIRECTIONS FOR COOKING

1. If using fava beans, remove outer membrane. Simmer fava or lima beans in water for 10 minutes; drain.
2. Sauté onion in 2 Tbs. butter and set aside.
3. Mash beans; add eggs, sautéed onions, dill weed, flour, and spices and mix together well.
4. Melt 2 Tbs. of butter in a skillet, preferably a nonstick skillet; pour in mixture, cover and cook over low heat for 20 minutes or until it is set. Then, remove cover, increase heat to medium or medium-high for about 10 minutes or until the bottom of the *kuku* develops a thin, golden crust.
5. Place a large platter over the skillet; turn *kuku* out on the platter. Melt the remaining butter in the skillet and slide the *kuku* in crust-side up. Cook over medium or medium-high heat for about 10 minutes or until a crust is formed on the bottom. (If a nonstick skillet is not available, cut the *kuku* into 8-10 wedges and turn each wedge individually; or, this *kuku* may also be baked in a buttered casserole dish in a moderate, 350° F. oven for 30 minutes.)

To serve, place platter on top of pan and turn out *kuku* on platter; cut in wedges. Serve as an accompaniment to meat or rice dishes.

## Kuku-ye Mast

(yogurt "quiche" with scallions, carrots, and walnuts)

*6-8 servings*

Ingredients:
*2 cups plain yogurt*
*1 bunch scallions or green onions, chopped*
*4 carrots, grated*
*6 eggs*
*2 Tbs. flour*
*¼ cup walnuts, chopped*
*¼ cup butter*
Spices:
*¼ tsp saffron, dissolved in 2 Tbs. hot water*
*½ tsp salt*
*¼ tsp black pepper*

### DIRECTIONS FOR COOKING

1. Place yogurt in a cheesecloth and let the juice drain for several hours or overnight, until the yogurt thickens to the consistency of cream cheese.
2. Preheat oven to 350° F.
3. Mix together all ingredients except for half the walnuts and butter.
4. Melt butter and use half of it to grease a casserole dish. Pour in mixture and spread out evenly.
5. Distribute remaining walnuts over top. Pour remaining butter over top and bake for 30-40 minutes.

## Kuku-ye Lubiya Sabz

(green been "quiche" with almonds)

*6-8 servings*

**Ingredients:**
*1 lb fresh green beans*
*1 onion, sliced*
*6 Tbs. butter*
*1 Tbs. flour*
*5 eggs*
*½ tsp baking powder*
*¼ cup slivered almonds*

**Spices:**
*2½ tsp salt*
*1 tsp turmeric*
*½ tsp cinnamon*
*¼ tsp black pepper*

### DIRECTIONS FOR COOKING

**1.** Wash and snap off ends of beans; boil in 5 cups water with 2 tsp salt for about 20 minutes or just until tender. Drain; set aside to cool.
**2.** Preheat oven to 350° F.
**3.** Sauté onion in 2 Tbs. butter. Set aside to cool.
**4.** Mix together all ingredients except remaining butter.
**5.** Melt the butter and use half to grease a casserole dish. Pour in the mixture and spread evenly.
**6.** Pour remaining butter over top of mixture and bake for 30 minutes.

## Kuku-ye Kadu Tanbal

(pumpkin "quiche" with meat and yogurt)

*8 to 10 servings*

**Ingredients:**
*2 lbs fresh pumpkin*
*1 lb ground lamb or beef*
*¼ cup flour*
*½ cup plain yogurt*
*1 Tbs. brown sugar*
*8 eggs*
*¼ cup butter*

**Spices:**
*1 tsp salt*
*1 tsp nutmeg*

### DIRECTIONS FOR COOKING

**1.** Remove skin from pumpkin and cut pulp into small pieces; simmer in 3 cups water for 1 hour or until tender.
**2.** Sprinkle meat with seasonings and brown. Set aside to cool.
**3.** Mix together all ingredients except butter and beat well.
**4.** Melt butter and pour into a flat casserole dish; pour in mixture, evening out surface, and bake in preheated oven at 350° F. for 30-40 minutes.

(This *kuku* may also be fried, preferably in a non-stick skillet, in which case, cover and cook over medium heat for 20 minutes, or until firmly set. Cut into wedges; turn one at a time; cook until a crust is formed on the other side.)

# Morghaneh-ye Mast

(yogurt omelet, Mazandaran style)

*3-4 servings*

**Ingredients:**
*2 cups plain yogurt*
*1 medium onion, chopped*
*3 eggs*
*2 Tbs. butter*
**Spices:**
*½ tsp turmeric*
*¼ tsp salt*
*¼ tsp black pepper*

### DIRECTIONS FOR COOKING

**1.** Place yogurt in a cheesecloth and let the liquid drain for several hours or overnight, until the yogurt thickens to the consistency of cream cheese.
**2.** Sauté onion in half of the butter; stir in turmeric. Set aside to cool.
**3.** Fry eggs in remaining butter until yolk is solid. Set aside to cool.
**4.** Chop fried eggs, mix with onion and yogurt, and sprinkle with salt and pepper.

Serve with flat bread.

# Choghortmeh

(chicken "quiche," Rasht style)

*10-12 servings*

**Ingredients:**
*1½ lb skinless, boneless chicken thighs*
*1 onion, quartered*
*1 medium onion, chopped*
*4 eggs, beaten*
*¼ cup butter*
*2 Tbs. lemon juice*
*1 Tbs. flour*
**Spices:**
*1½ tsp salt*
*¼ tsp black pepper*
*¼ tsp saffron, dissolved in 2 Tbs. hot water*

### DIRECTIONS FOR COOKING

**1.** Place chicken, quartered onion, ½ tsp of the salt and 2 cups water in large pot, bring to a boil, reduce heat and simmer 45 minutes. Drain and set aside to cool.
**2.** Preheat oven to 350° F.
**3.** Mince chicken. This may also be done with a meat grinder or in a food processor.
**4.** Sauté chopped onion in 1 Tbs. butter; set aside to cool.
**5.** Mix together all ingredients except remaining butter and beat well.
**6.** Melt remaining butter and pour into a flat casserole dish; pour in mixture and bake for 30 minutes.

# Kuku-ye Mahi I

(fish cakes, Caspian Sea Coast style)

*4 to 6 servings*

**Ingredients:**
*1 lb whitefish*
*7 Tbs. butter*
*2 Tbs. lemon juice*
*1 onion, grated*
*4 eggs, beaten*
*3 Tbs. flour*
*½ tsp baking powder*
*½ bunch parsley, chopped*
**Spices:**
*1 tsp salt*
*¼ tsp black pepper*
*½ tsp turmeric*
*½ tsp powdered cumin*

## DIRECTIONS FOR COOKING

**1.** Preheat oven to 350° F.
**2.** Rub fish with ½ tsp salt. With 1 Tbs. of the butter, grease the bottom of a flat casserole dish; arrange fish in the casserole dish and dot with 1 Tbs. butter; sprinkle with lemon juice. Bake for 25-30 minutes. Cool, remove bones (if any), and finely chop.
**3.** Sauté onion in 1 Tbs. butter.
**4.** Mix together eggs, flour, baking powder, parsley, and spices and beat well; mix in fish.
**5.** Grease a flat-bottomed baking dish with half the remaining butter. Pour in the fish mixture and spread out evenly. Melt and pour remaining butter evenly over top of batter. Bake for 30 minutes or until well set. (This *kuku* can also be cooked on top of the stove in a non-stick frying pan, in which case, pour half the butter into the pan, top with batter, spread out evenly. Cover and cook over medium heat for 20 minutes. Then, turn *kuku* out on a platter; add remaining butter to frying pan; slide *kuku* into frying pan top side down and brown, uncovered, on second side.

# Kuku-ye Mahi II

(fish cakes)

*6 to 8 servings*

**Ingredients:**
*1 lb filet of trout or perch*
*6 Tbs. butter*
*2 Tbs. lemon juice*
*1 medium onion, grated*
*1 bunch parsley, chopped*
*4 Tbs. fresh chopped or 2 Tbs. dried dill weed*
*2 potatoes, finely grated*
*5 eggs, beaten*
**Spices:**
*½ tsp salt*
*¼ tsp black pepper*
*1 tsp curry powder*

## DIRECTIONS FOR COOKING

**1.** Using 2 Tbs. of the butter, grease the bottom of a casserole dish. Arrange fish on the bottom, sprinkle with lemon juice; cover and bake at 350° F. for 20 minutes. Set aside to cool.
**2.** Break fish into small pieces or dice; mix together with all remaining ingredients, except remaining butter.
**3.** Melt and pour half the butter in a skillet (preferably non-stick) and pour in the fish batter. Cover and cook over medium heat for 15 minutes. Then, reduce heat to low and cook an additional 15 minutes.
**4.** Place a platter over the skillet and turn out *kuku* on the platter. Then pour the remaining butter into the skillet and slide the *kuku* in on the side that is not browned. Brown, uncovered, on the second side over medium heat for 15-20 minutes.

# Mirza Qasemi
## (eggplant "quiche")

*3 to 4 servings*

**Ingredients:**
*1 medium eggplant*
*1 large onion, chopped*
*3 cloves garlic, minced*
*3 Tbs. olive oil*
*1 large tomato, peeled and chopped*
*2 eggs, slightly beaten*
**Spices:**
*½ tsp turmeric*
*½ tsp salt*
*¼ tsp black pepper*

### DIRECTIONS FOR COOKING

**1.** Roast whole eggplant over charcoal or bake in hot, 400°, oven until tender (about 15 - 20 minutes in the oven).
**2.** Allow eggplant to cool, then peel and mash.
**3.** Sauté onion and garlic in olive oil; stir in turmeric.
**4.** Add eggplant and sauté for a few more minutes.
**5.** Add tomato and cook 5 minutes more.
**6.** Stir remaining spices and eggs into the eggplant mixture and continue cooking for a few minutes more, until eggs are cooked. Serve with bread and yogurt or different types of *Torshi*.

Prepared by Janet N.

# Torsh Tareh
## (tart green vegetables with eggs, Northern Provinces style)

*5 to 6 servings*

**Ingredients:**
*1 medium onion, sliced*
*6 Tbs. butter*
*1 cup fresh black-eyed peas*
*1 cup lentils*
*1 bunch parsley*
*6 Tbs. fresh chopped dill weed*
*6 Tbs. fresh chopped coriander*
*1 cup leeks, chopped*
*2 cloves garlic, minced*
*½ cup rice flour*
*5 eggs, beaten*
*¼ cup lemon juice\**
**Spices:**
*1 tsp salt*

### DIRECTIONS FOR COOKING

**1.** Sauté onion in 2 Tbs. of the butter; transfer to a medium-size saucepan.
**2.** Add peas, lentils, salt, and 3 cups water and simmer over medium heat for 30-40 minutes or until peas and lentils are tender.
**3.** Melt remaining butter in skillet; add parsley, dill, coriander, leeks and garlic and stir over medium heat for 5 minutes. Add to pea-lentil-onion mixture.
**4.** Dissolve rice flour in ½ cup cold water and add gradually to vegetable mixture, stirring until well mixed.
**5.** Stir in beaten eggs for 2 minutes.
**6.** Stir in lemon juice. Serve with bread.

*Traditionally bitter orange juice is used in this recipe, which is rarely found, and thus lemon juice is substituted.

# Nargesi-ye Lubiya Sabz
## (green beans with eggs)

*6 servings*

**Ingredients:**
*1 lb fresh green beans*
*1 large onion, sliced*
*¼ cup butter*
*¼ cup slivered almonds*
*6 eggs*
**Spices:**
*1½ tsp salt*
*¼ tsp black pepper*
*¼ tsp paprika*

**DIRECTIONS FOR COOKING**

**1.** Snap off ends of green beans and slice into strips lengthwise. Cook in 2 cups water and 1 tsp. of the salt for 15 minutes or until tender; drain and set aside.
**2.** Sauté onions in butter in skillet.
**3.** Add almonds and stir for 2 minutes. Stir in beans. Spread mixture out evenly in bottom of skillet.
**4.** Break eggs evenly spaced over bean mixture; sprinkle with remaining salt, pepper, and paprika, adjust to taste; cover and cook over low heat for 5-10 minutes or until eggs are set.

# Nargesi-ye Kadu
## (zucchini with eggs)

*8 servings*

**Ingredients:**
*8 medium zucchinis*
*3 Tbs. olive oil*
*1 large onion, sliced*
*2 Tbs. butter*
*8 eggs*
**Spices:**
*½ tsp salt*
*¼ tsp black pepper*

**DIRECTIONS FOR COOKING**

**1.** Peel and cut zucchinis into ½" slices. Brown on both sides in olive oil; spread out zucchini evenly over the bottom of the skillet and set aside.
**2.** Sauté onions in butter and spread evenly over top of zucchini.
**3.** Break eggs evenly over top of zucchini and onion mixture; sprinkle with salt and pepper.
**4.** Cover and cook over medium heat 5-10 minutes or until eggs have set.

Prepared by Diane W.

## Nargesi-ye Esfenaj
(spinach with eggs)

6 servings

Ingredients:
*1 lb fresh spinach*
*2 medium onions, sliced*
*3 Tbs. butter*
*6 eggs*
Spices:
*1½ tsp salt*
*½ tsp black pepper*
*½ tsp paprika*

### DIRECTIONS FOR COOKING

1. Cook spinach in 1 cup water and 1 tsp. of the salt over low heat for 10 minutes.
2. Drain spinach in a colander, placing a plate or bowl on the spinach to help press out any extra water.
3. Sauté onion in butter in a skillet.
4. Stir spinach into the onions and spread out evenly in the bottom of the skillet.
5. Break eggs over spinach and onion mixture, sprinkle with salt, pepper, and paprika, and cook over low heat for 5-10 minutes or until eggs have set.

## Sheshandaz-e Beh
(baked eggs on a bed of quince)

*6 servings*

Ingredients:
*2 quinces*
*¼ cup butter*
*3 Tbs. lemon juice*
*3 Tbs. sugar*
*6 eggs*
Spices:
*¼ tsp salt*

### DIRECTIONS FOR COOKING

**1.** Quarter quinces and remove seeds and inner membranes; grate.
**2.** Sauté quince in butter; cover and cook over low heat for 35-40 minutes, stirring occasionally.
**3.** Add sugar and lemon juice and stir over low heat for an additional 2-3 minutes.
**4.** Transfer quince mixture to a flat bottom baking dish and spread out evenly. Break eggs on top distributed evenly and without breaking yolks; sprinkle with salt; cover and bake at 350° F. for 10-15 minutes or until eggs have set. Serve with bread.

---

## Gorzavij
(scrambled eggs with carrots, Gilan style)

*3 to 4 servings*

Ingredients:
*1 small onion, finely chopped*
*6 carrots, grated*
*3 Tbs. butter*
*6 eggs, beaten*
Spices:
*½ tsp salt*

### DIRECTIONS FOR COOKING

**1.** Sauté onion in butter.
**2.** Add carrots and brown for 3 to 4 minutes.
**3.** Add eggs and salt and stir over medium heat until the eggs are set.

# Sheshandaz-e Havij
(eggs on a bed of carrots and onions)

*6 servings*

**Ingredients:**
*1 medium onion, sliced*
*¼ cup butter*
*6 medium carrots, grated*
*2 Tbs. lemon juice*
*1 Tbs. sugar*
*6 eggs*
**Spices:**
*½ tsp salt*
*½ tsp cinnamon*

### DIRECTIONS FOR COOKING

**1.** Sauté onion in butter over medium heat in a non-stick skillet.
**2.** Add carrots and stir for 4-5 minutes.
**3.** Add lemon juice, sugar, and salt; reduce heat, cover and cook over low heat for 15 minutes, stirring occasionally.
**4.** Smooth out the surface of the carrot mixture. Break eggs on top of carrot mixture, being careful not to break the yolks; cover and cook over medium heat an additional 5 minutes or until eggs have set. Serve with bread.

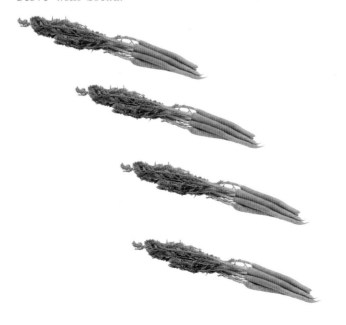

# Sheshandaz-e Sib
(baked eggs on a bed of apples)

*6 servings*

**Ingredients:**
*4 cooking apples, cored and sliced*
*¼ cup butter*
*3 Tbs. lemon juice*
*2 Tbs. sugar*
*6 eggs*
**Spices:**
*¼ tsp salt*

### DIRECTIONS FOR COOKING

**1.** Sauté apples in butter; cover and cook over low heat for 10 minutes, stirring occasionally.
**2.** Add sugar and lemon juice and stir over low heat for an additional 2 minutes; spread out evenly on bottom of skillet.
**3.** Break eggs on top distributed evenly and without breaking yolks; sprinkle with salt; cover and cook over low heat for 5 minutes or until eggs have set. Serve with bread.

# Baqala Qateq

(fava beans with dill weed and eggs, Northern
Provinces style)

*5 to 6 servings*

**Ingredients:**
*1½ lb fresh fava beans ( see tips below)*
*1 large onion, sliced*
*1 Tbs. butter*
*1 cup fresh chopped dill weed*
*2 cloves garlic, minced*
*4 eggs, beaten*
**Spices:**
*½ tsp salt*
*¼ tsp black pepper*

### DIRECTIONS FOR COOKING

**1.** Remove fava beans from pod and simmer over low
heat in 2 cups water for 10 minutes, or until tender.
**2.** Sauté onion in butter.
**3.** Drain beans and add to onions along with dill and
stir for 2 minutes.  Transfer to a large saucepan.
**4.** Mix in garlic, spices and 1 cup water to bean-on-
ion-dill mixture; cover and simmer for 20 minutes.
**5.** Slowly add beaten eggs. Cover and cook for 5 additional minutes.
Serve over rice.

**Tips and things**
When fresh fava beans are not available, substitute dried
fava beans; in which case, soak in a generous amount of
water for several hours and drain before cooking.  Lima
beans are the closest substitute for fava beans.

# Shirin Tareh

(scrambled eggs with leeks and garlic, Gilan style)

*5 to 6 servings*

**Ingredients:**
*3 Tbs. butter*
*2 cups chopped leeks*
*2 cups chopped spinach*
*2 cloves garlic, minced*
*5 eggs, beaten*
**Spices:**
*½ tsp salt*
*¼ tsp black pepper*

### DIRECTIONS FOR COOKING

**1.** Melt 2 Tbs. of the butter in a skillet. Add leeks and
spinach and brown for 2 to 3 minutes.
**2.** Melt remaining butter in another skillet. Add garlic and brown for two minutes, stirring occasionally.
**3.** Stir in eggs over the garlic and cook a few minutes
until set.
**4.** Add leeks and spinach along with salt and pepper
and mix together.
Serve with bread.

# Fish and Other Seafood
## *(Mahi, Meygu and Khaviyar)*

P rior to the past few decades, that is, before refrigerated transportation became available in Iran, *mahi,* or fish, was not a common part of the diet for most inland Iranians. Even for the traditional dish of the Persian New Year, *Noruz,* smoked fish was commonly used. However, fish has always been a substantial part of the diet of Iranians living on the costs of the Caspian Sea and the Persian Gulf. For this reason, most of the fish recipes in this section are regional dishes. However, because of the increased availability of fish inland, a number of modern fish dishes have appeared and are included here.

# Mahi Kabab I
### (fish kabob, Persian Gulf Coast style)

*5 to 6 servings*

**Ingredients:**
*1½ lb firm filet of fish*
*1 large onion, finely*
 *grated*
*¼ cup lemon juice*
*½ cup olive oil*

**Spices:**
*½ tsp salt*
*¼ tsp black pepper*
*¼ tsp paprika*
*¼ tsp saffron, dissolved*
 *in 2 Tbs. hot water*

## DIRECTIONS FOR COOKING

**1.** Cut fish into chunks (about 1" x 2").
**2.** Mix together all ingredients in a glass bowl and marinate for 1 hour.

**3.** Place 3 to 4 pieces of fish lengthwise on skewers and broil over hot charcoal, turning frequently. Baste with marinade sauce while cooking.

# Mahi Kabab II
### (fish kabob)

*5 to 6 servings*

**Ingredients:**
*1½ lb firm filet of fish*
*3 green peppers, cut in*
 *2" squares*
*1 medium onion, quartered*
 *and separated*
*¼ cup melted butter*

**Spices:**
*½ tsp salt*
*¼ tsp black pepper*
*¼ tsp garlic powder*
*¼ tsp turmeric*

## DIRECTIONS FOR COOKING

**1.** Cut fish into 1" cubes and sprinkle with salt, pepper, and garlic.
**2.** Place alternating pieces of fish, green pepper, and onion on skewers.
**3.** Mix together melted butter and turmeric, and brush fish and vegetables with this mixture.
**4.** Grill slowly over hot charcoal, keeping skewers about 6" from coals, turning frequently; continue to baste with the butter-turmeric mixture.
**Serve with fresh wedges of lemon or rice.**

# Mahi-ye Tupor
(stuffed fish, Mazandaran style I)

*6 servings*

**Ingredients:**
*1 bunch parsley, chopped*
*1 bunch coriander, chopped*
*¼ cup fresh mint, chopped*
*2 Tbs. dried tarragon*
*6 Tbs. butter*
*1 cup walnuts, finely chopped*
*¼ cup raisins*
*¼ cup zereshk\**
*1 3-lb fish*
*¼ cup lemon juice*
*1 cup tomato sauce*
*lemon slices*
*sprigs of parsley*
**Spices:**
*1 tsp salt*
*¼ tsp black pepper*

### DIRECTIONS FOR COOKING

**1.** Sauté parsley, coriander, mint, and tarragon in 4 Tbs. of the butter for 2 minutes.
**2.** Stir in walnuts, raisins, *zereshk*, salt and pepper. Set aside.
**3.** Split the fish open. Stuff with vegetable and nut mixture.
**4.** Grease the bottom of a flat baking dish with 1 Tbs. of the butter; place fish in the baking dish. Dot fish with remaining butter; pour lemon juice and tomato sauce over fish. Bake at 350° F. for 30 minutes.

To Serve: Use two large spatulas and carefully transfer fish to a platter. Pour the sauce from baking the fish over the fish. Garnish with lemon wedges and parsley.
*\*Zereshk* is a tart wild berry that is now available in dried form in virtually all Iranian grocery stores. To clean, generously cover with water and soak for several minutes. Remove from water carefully, making sure that any grains of sand contained in the dried *zereshk* have settled on the bottom of the container.

# Del-Kabab Mahi
(stuffed fish, Mazandaran style II)

*6 servings*

**Ingredients:**
*2 medium onions, finely chopped*
*½ cup olive oil*
*6 cloves garlic, minced*
*1 bunch parsley, chopped*
*2 bunches coriander, chopped*
*¼ cup fresh mint, chopped*
*1 bunch leeks or 2 bunches green onions, chopped*
*2 Tbs. chopped fresh or 1 Tbs. dried fenugreek*
*1 cup walnuts, finely chopped*
*2 cups pomegranate juice*
*1 Tbs. butter, melted*
*1 3-lb trout or salmon*
**Spices:**
*1 tsp salt*
*¼ tsp black pepper*
*2 tsp turmeric*
*1 tsp saffron, dissolved in ¼ cup hot water*

### DIRECTIONS FOR COOKING

**1.** Sauté onion in olive oil, add garlic, parsley, coriander, mint, leeks, and fenugreek and stir over medium heat for 2 minutes.
**2.** Stir in walnuts, spices, and 1 cup of the pomegranate juice. Set aside.
**3.** Split the fish open. Stuff with half the vegetable and nut mixture.
**4.** Grease the bottom of a flat baking dish with the butter; place fish in the baking dish. Cover fish with remaining vegetable and nut mixture and pour remaining pomegranate juice around the fish. Bake at 350° F. for 30 minutes.

To serve: Use two large spatulas and carefully transfer fish to a platter. Pour the sauce from baking the fish over the fish. Serve with plain rice.

## Khorak-e Mahi-ye Jonubi
(fish with almonds and parsley, Southern Iran style)

*4 to 5 servings*

**Ingredients:**
*2 lb fish*
*¼ cup olive oil*
*1 cup slivered almonds*
*¼ cup butter*
*1 bunch parsley, chopped*
*2 Tbs. lime juice*
**Spices:**
*½ tsp salt*
*¼ tsp black pepper*

### DIRECTIONS FOR COOKING

**1.** Cut off head and tail of fish and scale. Then, soak fish in very cold water for 15 minutes (to remove fishy taste and smell). Drain and pat dry with paper towels.
**2.** Sprinkle fish with spices and brown on both sides in olive oil.
**3.** Lightly brown almonds in butter. Add parsley and lime juice and stir for a few minutes.
**4.** Place fish on a serving platter and cover with almond and parsley sauce.

## Sorkhmahi-ye Jonubi ba Tamr-e Hendi
(fish with tamarind, southern-Iran style)

*4 to 6 servings*

**Ingredients:**
*¼ lb tamarind*
*2 lbs sea robin or red snapper*
*1 cup flour*
*½ cup olive oil*
*2 medium onions, chopped*
*2 cloves garlic, crushed*
*1 bunch parsley, chopped*
*1 bunch coriander, chopped*
*2 Tbs. tomato paste*
**Spices:**
*1 tsp turmeric*
*½ tsp salt*
*¼ tsp black pepper*

### DIRECTIONS FOR COOKING

**1.** Soak tamarind in 1 cup warm water for 1 hour. Discard seeds, if any, and cut into small pieces.
**2.** Clean fish and cut into 2" x 2" squares; then, dip into flour and fry on both sides in olive oil.
**3.** Sauté onions in butter; add garlic, parsley, coriander, seasonings and stir over medium heat for 2-3 minutes.
**4.** Add tomato paste and tamarind with water and mix well. Simmer over medium heat for 2 minutes.
**5.** Arrange pieces of fish in sauce in a skillet so that all pieces of fish are covered with the sauce. Simmer for 20 minutes.

## Mahi-ye Sefid ba Badam
(whitefish baked with slivered almonds)

*4 to 5 servings*

Ingredients:
*2 lb whitefish*
*¼ cup butter*
*¼ cup slivered almonds*
*2 Tbs. lemon juice*
*3 Tbs. chopped parsley*
Spices:
*½ tsp salt*
*¼ tsp black pepper*
*¼ tsp paprika*

### DIRECTIONS FOR COOKING

**1.** Cut off head and tail of fish and remove scales.
**2.** Grease a flat baking dish with butter and rub remaining butter over fish thoroughly.
**3.** Sprinkle fish with spices, almonds, and lemon juice. Cover and bake at 350° F. for 30-35 minutes.

TO SERVE: Cut off the outer edges of the fish with a knife and discard. Cut the top of the fish lengthwise gently just to the bone. Slide two pieces on top to the side and remove bones by holding the bone from where the head has been severed and lifting gently. Replace the two top pieces and garnish with parsley.

## Mahi-ye Sorkh Kardeh
(fried fish)

*4 to 5 servings*

Ingredients:                   Spices:
*2 lb filet of whitefish*      *½ tsp salt*
*¼ cup lemon juice*            *¼ tsp pepper*
*5 eggs, beaten*               *¼ tsp saffron, dissolved*
*½ cup flour*                  *in 2 Tbs. hot water*
*½ cup olive oil*

### DIRECTIONS FOR COOKING

**1.** Cut fish into 2" x 3" pieces. Pat dry with paper towel and sprinkle with lemon juice on all sides.
**2.** Make a batter mixing together eggs, spices, and flour.
**3.** Dip pieces of fish in batter and fry on both sides in oil over medium heat.

Prepared by Jaleh P.

## Mahi Dudi
(smoked fish)

*4 to 5 servings*
Ingredients:                   Spices:
*1 2-lb smoked fish*           *½ tsp pepper*
*3 fresh lemons*
*¼ cup butter*
*sprigs of parsley*

### DIRECTIONS FOR COOKING
**1.** Cut off head and tail of fish and then divide into 3 to 4 sections. If using dried smoked fish, soak in 8 cups water overnight. Change water several times.
**2.** Remove skin and debone. Pat dry with paper towel. Squeeze the juice of 2 lemons over fish.
**3.** Fry fish in butter over medium-low heat on both sides. Sprinkle with pepper and garnish with parsley and slices of lemon.

## Mahi-ye Sobur-e Tanuri
### (baked stuffed catfish, Khuzestan style)

*3 to 4 servings*

Ingredients:

*1 onion, chopped*
*2 Tbs. olive oil*
*2 cloves garlic, minced*
*2 Tbs. chopped chili pepper*
*2 cups chopped parsley*
*2 Tbs. tamarind paste*
*1 large catfish (approximately 3 lbs)*
*2 Tbs. butter, melted*

Spices:
*½ tsp salt*
*½ tsp black pepper*
*1 tsp turmeric*
*2 tsp powdered cumin*
*1 Tbs. coriander seeds*
*1 tsp fenugreek*

### DIRECTIONS FOR COOKING

**1.** Sauté onions in olive oil.  Stir in garlic and chili pepper and remove from heat.
**2.** Stir in parsley, tamarind paste, and spices.
**3.** Clean the fish, and stuff with the mixture.  Secure the open side of the fish with toothpicks.
**4.** Place fish in a baking dish, pour melted butter over the top and bake in 350° oven for 25 to 30 minutes.

Serve with bread or plain rice.

## Kotlet-e Mahi
### (fish patties)

*10 to 15 pieces*

Ingredients:
*1 lb filet of whitefish*
*2 Tbs. butter*
*½ cup celery, minced*
*1 medium onion, minced*
*3 eggs, beaten*
*1 cup dried bread crumbs*
*1 tsp baking soda*
*½ cup olive oil*
*1 cup flour*
*1 fresh lemon, sliced into rings*
*parsley*

Spices:
*½ tsp salt*
*½ tsp black pepper*

### DIRECTIONS FOR COOKING

**1.** Grease a baking dish with butter and place fish in dish; bake in 350° oven for 15 minutes.
**2.** Chop fish into small pieces and mix together well with all remaining ingredients except flour and oil.
**3.** Preheat half the oil in a skillet over low heat.  Make oval shaped patties (about 4" long).  Dip both sides in flour and fry over low heat; turn and brown second side, adding more oil if needed.  To serve, place on a platter and decorate with lemon rings and fresh parsley.

## Mahi-ye Qobad ba Hashu
(stuffed kingfish with rice, Khuzestan style)

*5 to 6 servings*

**Ingredients:**
*2 to 3 lbs kingfish, mackerel,
    whiting, or other such fish
1 onion, chopped
2 Tbs. olive oil
2 cloves of garlic, minced
2 Tbs. chopped chili pepper
2 cups chopped parsley
2 Tbs. tamarind paste
2 cups rice
½ cup butter, melted*

**Spices:**
*1¼ Tbs. salt
½ tsp black pepper
1 tsp turmeric
2 tsp powdered cumin
1 Tbs. coriander seeds
1 tsp fenugreek*

### DIRECTIONS FOR COOKING

**1.** Place fish in a baking dish and bake in 350° oven for 5 minutes.
**2.** Meanwhile, sauté onions in olive oil; stir in garlic and chili pepper and remove from heat. Add and mix in parsley, tamarind paste, ½ tsp of the salt, and other spices.
**3.** Clean the fish, and stuff with the mixture.
**4.** In a large pot, bring 4 cups of water and remaining salt to a boil. Add rice and boil for 10 minutes. Drain in a colander.
**5.** Grease the bottom of a non-stick pot with some of the butter. Cover the bottom of the pot with ¼ of the cooked rice. Then place the fish in the pot and top with remaining rice. Pour remaining melted butter on top. Cover and steam over low heat for 50 minutes to 1 hour.
To serve, dish out the rice on top around the rim of an oval platter. Gently transfer the fish to the middle of platter and cover with remaining rice and crust (*tahdig*).

## Tahandaz-e Mahi Zobeydi
(filet of flounder with rice, Khuzestan style)

*7 to 8 Servings*

**Ingredients:**
*1 onion, chopped
¼ cup olive oil
2 cloves of garlic, minced
2 Tbs. chopped chili pepper
2 cups chopped parsley
2 Tbs. tamarind paste
2 to 3 lbs filet of flounder
3 cups rice
½ cup butter, melted*

**Spices:**
*1½ Tbs. salt
½ tsp black pepper
1 tsp turmeric
2 tsp powdered cumin
1 Tbs. coriander seeds
1 tsp fenugreek*

### DIRECTIONS FOR COOKING

**1.** Sauté onions in 2 Tbs. of the olive oil. Stir in garlic and chili pepper and remove from heat.
**2.** Add parsley, tamarind paste, ½ tsp of the salt and remaining spices.
**3.** Lightly brown both sides of all pieces in remaining olive oil.
**4.** In a large pot, bring 6 cups of water and remaining salt to a boil. Add rice and boil for 10 minutes. Drain in a colander.
**5.** Grease the bottom of a non-stick pot with some of the butter. Cover the bottom of the pot with 1/3 of the cooked rice. Then place half of the pieces of fish over the rice, top with half of the onion and parsley mixture. Repeat this step. Top with remaining rice. Pour remaining melted butter on top. Cover and simmer for 50 minutes to 1 hour.
TO SERVE: Dish out the top layer of rice and place around the rim of an oval platter; gently transfer the pieces of flounder to the middle of the platter; repeat this process with next layer of rice and fish; cover last layer of fish with remaining rice and crust.

# Mahi-ye Komo

(baked stuffed sole, Khuzestan style)

*5 to 6 servings*

Ingredients:

*1 onion, chopped*
*2 Tbs. olive oil*
*2 cloves of garlic, minced*
*2 Tbs. chopped chili pepper*
*2 cups chopped parsley*
*2 Tbs. Tamarind paste*
*1 cup chopped walnuts*
*1 cup raisins*
*½ cup* zereshk
*3 lbs sole (whole)*
*2 Tbs. butter, melted*

Spices:

*½ tsp salt*
*½ tsp black pepper*
*1 tsp turmeric*
*2 tsp powdered cumin*
*1 Tbs. coriander seeds*
*1 tsp fenugreek*

## DIRECTIONS FOR COOKING

**1.** Sauté onion in olive oil.  Stir in garlic and chili pepper and remove from heat.
**2.**  Mix in parsley, tamarind paste, walnuts, raisins, *zereshk*, and spices.
**3.**  Clean the fish, and stuff with the mixture.  Secure the open side of the fish with toothpicks.
**4.**  Place fish in a baking dish, pour melted butter over the top and bake in 350° oven for about 30 minutes.
Serve with plain rice.

*\*Zereshk* is a tart wild berry that is now available in dried form in virtually all Iranian grocery stores.  To clean, generously cover with water and soak for several minutes.  Remove from water carefully, making sure that any grains of sand contained in the dried *zereshk* have settled on the bottom of the container.

# Qeliyeh-ye Mahi I

(kingfish stew)

*7 to 8 Servings*

Ingredients:

*¼ lb tamarind*
*½ cup olive oil*
*2 lbs fillet of kingfish*
*1 Tbs. flour*
*1 onion, chopped*
*4 cloves of garlic, minced*
*1 cup chopped parsley*
*3 Tbs. dried fenugreek leaves*

Spices:

*2 tsp salt*
*½ tsp black pepper*
*1 Tbs. curry powder*

## DIRECTIONS FOR COOKING

**1.** Soak tamarind in warm water for 2 hours.  Remove the skin and seeds and set aside.
**2.** Brown the fish in ¼ cup of the olive oil.
**3.** Lightly brown flour in a skillet.
**4.** Sauté onions in remaining olive oil.  Stir in garlic, parsley, and fenugreek.
**5.** Place the onion, garlic, and herb mixture on the fish.  Stir in spices in tamarind and pour over the top.  Simmer over medium heat for 15 minutes.

This dish can be served with bread or over plain rice.

## Qeliyeh-ye Mahi II
(fish stew, Khuzestan style)

*3 to 4 servings*

Ingredients:

*2 onions, chopped*
*2 Tbs. olive oil*
*2 cloves garlic, minced*
*2 Tbs. chopped chili pepper*
*3 cups chopped parsley*
*2 Tbs. tamarind paste*
*2 lbs filet of red snapper*
Spices:
*1 tsp salt*
*½ tsp black pepper*
*1 tsp turmeric*
*2 tsp powdered cumin*
*1 Tbs. coriander seeds*
*1 tsp fenugreek*

### DIRECTIONS FOR COOKING

**1.** Sauté onions in olive oil. Stir in garlic and chili pepper. Transfer to a medium-size pot.
**2.** Add remaining ingredients along with 4 cups of water and bring to a boil.
**3.** Cut fish into 1 inch pieces, add to the pot, and simmer for 40 to 50 minutes.

Serve with flat bread.

## Lavangi-ye Mahi
(stuffed fish, Astara style)

*5 to 6 servings*

Ingredients:
*2 cups chopped walnuts*
*½ cup olive oil*
*1 large onion, grated*
*¼ cup pomegranate concentrate*
*¼ cup lemon juice*
*1 Tbs chopped fresh mint*
*¼ cup chopped parsley*
*1 3-lb fish*
*¼ cup melted butter*
Spices:
*1 tsp salt*
*¼ tsp black pepper*
*1 tsp turmeric*

### DIRECTIONS FOR COOKING

**1.** Lightly brown walnuts in olive oil over medium heat.
**2.** Add onion and sauté lightly. Add pomegranate concentrate, lemon juice, mint, parsley, and spices and simmer for 3 to 5 minutes. Remove from heat.
**3.** Stuff fish with the prepared ingredients, secure with toothpicks.
**4.** Brush a baking dish with some of the melted butter. Place fish in the baking dish and brush with the remaining butter. Bake in a 350° preheated oven for 30 minutes.
Serve with bread or plain rice.

# Meygu Kabab
## (shrimp kabob)

*5 to 6 servings*

**Ingredients:**
*1½ lb large (jumbo) shrimps*
*1 large onion, finely grated (with juice)*
*¼ cup lemon juice*
*½ cup olive oil*
**Spices:**
*½ tsp salt*
*¼ tsp black pepper*
*¼ tsp paprika*
*¼ tsp saffron, dissolved in 2 Tbs. hot water*

### DIRECTIONS FOR COOKING

**1.** Mix together all ingredients in a glass bowl and marinate for 1 hour.
**2.** Place 8 to 10 pieces of shrimp on skewers and broil over hot charcoal, turning frequently.  Baste with marinade sauce while cooking. Garnish with broiled tomatoes and basil. For added flavor, squeeze lemon or lime over shrimp when eating.

# Iranian Caviar

Caviar and champagne, or rather champagne and caviar, are thought by many people around the world to be the inseparable twins that are associated with luxury living. The best-quality caviar, connoisseurs unanimously agree, comes from the Caspian Sea in northern Iran, where 90% of world production of caviar originates from the three species of sturgeon—Beluga, Osentra, and Sevurga. Like champagne, the production of caviar is an art, and again like champagne experts, caviar critics are meticulous in ranking the quality of various types of this delicacy. The appreciation of caviar is an acquired taste for most people, and this is true particularly for the average Iranian, who calls it *khaviyar*. Even for Iranians who like caviar, the cost is often prohibitive. For this reason, a large portion of all caviar from the Iranian side of the Caspian Sea is exported to other parts of the world.

Although some caviar lovers prefer to use it to season various dishes, such as eggs and vegetable dishes, and even to add flavor to salmon or white fish, the real caviar enthusiasts simply serve it on dried toast or crackers. This is in fact the way it is most often served in Iran. However, it is also served on buttered toast or crackers, sometimes as a seasoning for scrambled eggs, and most recently atop cream cheese or feta cheese. What cannot be excluded for many Iranian lovers of caviar, or the delicacy sometimes referred to as "the Caspian Pearl," however, is champagne, dry white wine, and of course, frozen vodka sprinkled with black pepper.

Photographs and serving suggestions courtesy of
Mark Bolourchi.
Pacific Plaza Imports.

## Hashu va Khaviar
(caviar, Khuzestan style)

### Types of World-famous Iranian Caviar

Beluga

Sevruga

Royal Ostera

*3 to 4 servings*

Ingredients:

*1 onion, finely chopped*
*½ cup butter*
*2 cloves of garlic, minced*
*2 Tbs. chopped finely chili pepper*
*2 cups chopped finely parsley*
*1 Tbs. tamarind paste*
*4 oz. caviar or any fish eggs*

**Spices:**
*½ tsp salt*
*½ tsp black pepper*
*½ tsp turmeric*
*2 tsp powdered cumin*
*1 Tbs. coriander seeds*
*1 tsp fenugreek*

### DIRECTIONS FOR COOKING

**1.** Sauté onions in butter. Stir in garlic, chili pepper, and spices.
**2.** Mix in all remaining ingredients, and cook over low heat for 5 to 10 minutes.
To serve: Cut into wedges and serve as a side dish with meals. Unlike most caviar dishes, this dish is served warm.

### Serving Suggestions

Stir caviar into softened butter and serve on top of grilled or poached fish.

Sprinkle caviar onto the top of deviled eggs or fold it into an egg salad.

Top broiled lobsters, oysters or clams with caviar before serving.

Wholesale Fish Market near Caspian Sea.
Photo by Rasoul M. Oskouy.

# Pottage, Porridge, and Soup
## *(Ash, Halim and Abgusht)*

*Ash* is a thick pottage that is generally served in winter. Its major ingredients include rice, grains, vegetables, legumes, meat, dried or fresh fruit, and nuts. Some *ash* dishes are served on special occasions, some are served to persons in ill health and are believed to have medicinal as well as nutritional qualities (not unlike 'Grandma's chicken soup'!). Most *ash* dishes are easy to prepare and make an ideal luncheon for a large group of people. Many of the following *ash* dishes include rice. Unlike the rice that is generally preferred in the chapter on "Rice and Rice Dishes," the rice that is preferred for use in *ash* should be softer, small-grained, lower-grade rice, which provides the necessary consistency for these dishes.

In contrast to *ash*, *halim* dishes are more creamy, almost paste-like in texture, a porridge in which the ingredients are finely mashed together so as to be almost indistinguishable.

*Abgusht* is a category of Iranian meat-based soups that are relatively inexpensive to prepare; these dishes have, therefore, played an important part of the diet of the 'common' man. Nevertheless, *abgusht* remains a favorite of rich and poor alike. It is usually served with Persian flat bread, fresh vegetables and herbs, such as green onions, radishes, and fresh mint, basil, and tarragon, and various types of *torshi* or pickled vegetables and relishes.

*Eshkeneh* is a meatless soup usually prepared on the spur of the moment. In Isfahan, it is referred to as *abgusht-e rowghani,* or oil-based *ash*. It is light and tasty and makes an excellent appetizer or light lunch or supper.

Most of the dishes in this section may be served as complete meals. This is especially true of *ash*.

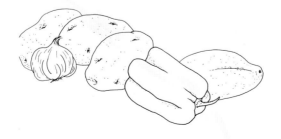

# Ash-e Torsh
(sweet-and-sour dried fruit pottage)

*5 to 6 servings*

**Ingredients:**
½ lb lean ground beef
    or lamb
1 small onion, grated
½ cup rice
¼ cup dried chickpeas
1 small onion, chopped
2 Tbs. butter
1 cup dried prunes
1 cup dried apricots
¼ cup chopped walnuts
1 cup chopped parsley
½ cup vinegar
1/3 cup sugar
1 Tbs. dried mint

**Spices:**
½ tsp cinnamon
½ tsp black pepper
3½ tsp salt

## DIRECTIONS FOR COOKING

**1.** In a bowl, mix the meat, grated onion, ¼ tsp of the cinnamon, ¼ tsp of the pepper, and ½ tsp of the salts. Make small meatballs the size of walnuts. Set aside.

**2.** Put 8 cups water in a 3-quart pot. Add remaining salt and chickpeas and boil for 20 minutes. Add rice and boil for an additional 15 minutes.

**3.** Meanwhile, sauté chopped onions in butter and set them aside.

**4.** Add prunes to the pot with rice and chickpeas and let cook for another 15 minutes.

**5.** Add meatballs, apricots, walnuts, parsley and sautéed onions and let cook about 20 minutes more over medium heat.

**6.** Add vinegar and sugar and let cook 15 minutes more.

GARNISH: Rub dried mint in the palm of your hand to make it powdery. Add remaining cinnamon and pepper to the mint. Add this to the *ash* just before removing it from the fire. If more seasoning is necessary, add to taste.

# Ash-e Mast
(yogurt pottage)

*6 to 8 servings*

**Ingredients:**
½ cup dried chickpeas
½ cup rice
¼ cup lentils
½ lb ground beef or lamb
1 medium onion, minced
1 bunch parsley, chopped
1 Tbs. dill weed
1 medium onion, thinly sliced
2 Tbs. butter
3 cups plain yogurt

**Spices:**
2 tsp salt
½ tsp black pepper

## DIRECTIONS FOR COOKING

**1.** Put chickpeas in a pot, cover with 5 cups water and boil for 20 minutes or until almost tender.

**2.** Add rice, lentils, and spices and cook 15 minutes more.

**3.** Mix together meat and minced onion; make into walnut-size meatballs and drop into boiling soup mixture. Stir occasionally to avoid sticking.

**4.** Sauté sliced onion in butter and set aside.

**5.** Add parsley and dill weed and cook an additional 5 minutes.

**6.** Stir in yogurt and transfer to serving bowl. Decorate top with sautéed onions.

# Ash-e Lapeh

(yellow split pea and rice pottage)

*8 to 10 servings*

**Ingredients:**
*2 cups rice*
*1 cup yellow split peas*
*1 bunch coriander, chopped*
*½ lb ground beef or lamb*
*1 medium onion, thinly sliced*
*2 Tbs. butter*
*4 Tbs. fresh chopped mint*
*¼ cup lemon juice*
**Spices:**
*1 Tbs. salt*
*2 tsp turmeric*
*1 tsp black pepper*

### DIRECTIONS FOR COOKING

**1.** Bring rice, 8 cups water, herbs, peas, and coriander to a boil in a large pot; boil about 20 minutes or until rice and peas are very soft.
**2.** Make small meatballs about the size of hazelnuts with the ground meat; drop in boiling rice mixture. Reduce heat and simmer 10 minutes more.
**3.** Sauté onion; stir in mint and set aside.
**4.** Stir in lemon juice. Place *ash* in serving bowl. Decorate top of pottage with onion-mint mixture.

# Ash-e Jow

(barley pottage)

*8 to 10 servings*

**Ingredients:**
*½ cup chickpeas*
*1½ lb stew beef or lamb, cut in small chunks*
*1 cup barley*
*½ cup lentils*
*1 bunch parsley, chopped*
*¾ cup green onions or chives, chopped*
*2 Tbs. butter*
*2 medium onions, thinly sliced*
*2 Tbs. chopped fresh mint*
*3 Tbs. lemon juice*
**Spices:**
*3 tsp salt*
*½ tsp black pepper*
*1 tsp turmeric*

### DIRECTIONS FOR COOKING

**1.** Place chickpeas, meat, 6 cups water, and seasonings in a large pot; bring to a boil, reduce heat and simmer until meat is tender (about 1 hour
**2.** Add barley, lentils, parsley, and green onions or chives and let simmer for 40 to 50 minutes longer. Stir occasionally to prevent sticking. Add additional water if necessary.
**3.** Meanwhile, sauté sliced onions, remove from heat, stir in mint, set aside.
**4.** To serve, place *ash* in a large bowl, stir half of the sautéed onion-mint mixture along with the lemon juice into the *ash*; use the remainder of the onion-mint mixture to garnish the top.

NOTE: *Ash-e Jow,* like other types of *ash,* is generally a winter dish and can be a complete meal, served with bread if desired.

# Ash-e Reshteh
(legume and noodle pottage)

*10 to 12 servings*

**Ingredients:**
*½ cup chickpeas*
*½ cup kidney beans*
*½ cup navy beans*
*½ cup lentils*
*1 bunch fresh parsley, chopped*
*3 bunches leeks or scallions, chopped*
*½ lb fresh spinach, chopped*
*½ lb linguini noodles or Persian noodles*
*3 Tbs. butter*
*2 large onions, sliced*
*1 Tbs. dried mint*
*1 cup plain yogurt or liquid whey*
**Spices:**
*2 tsp turmeric*
*1½ tsp salt*
*½ tsp black pepper*

Prepared by Amineh N.

**DIRECTIONS FOR COOKING**

**1.** If using dried legumes, cook each separately until tender and set aside.
**2.** Combine parsley, scallions, spices, and 6 cups water in a large pot. Boil 20 minutes, or until vegetables are tender.
**3.** Add spinach and cook 10 minutes more.
**4.** Break noodles into lengths of about 4"; add to *ash* mixture and boil until noodles are cooked.
**5.** Fry onions in butter until golden brown. Stir in mint.
**6.** Add cooked legumes to *ash*; let simmer 10-15 minutes.
**7.** Place *ash* in large serving bowl and decorate top with fried onions and mint mixture. A few tablespoons of beaten yogurt or liquid whey can also be used for decoration.
Serve *Ash-e Reshteh* with yogurt or whey at the side to be mixed with the *ash* to each individual's taste.
This dish is also sometimes served with *Qeymeh* (see recipe in "Khoresh and Khorak") at the side.

# Ash-e Sholeh Qalamkar
(bean and vegetable pottage)

*10 to 12 servings*

**Ingredients:**
*1 cup navy beans*
*1 cup kidney beans*
*1 lb stew beef or lamb, cut in thin strips*
*1 cup rice*
*½ cup lentils*
*½ cup mung beans*
*1 bunch parsley, chopped*
*2 bunches green onions, chopped*
*2 medium onions, thinly sliced*
*2 Tbs. butter*
**Spices:**
*2½ tsp salt*
*½ tsp black pepper*
*1 tsp turmeric*

Prepared by Kamron J.

**DIRECTIONS FOR COOKING**

**1.** Place all ingredients except onions, butter, and ¼ tsp of the pepper in a large pot with 5 cups water and bring to a boil; reduce heat and simmer for 1 hour or until all ingredients are very well cooked, almost falling apart, stirring occasionally.  Add more water if necessary.

**2.** Sauté onions in butter and set aside.

**3.** To serve, place *ash* in large bowl and decorate with sautéed onion; sprinkle with remaining pepper.  Serve accompanied with *torshi* (see recipes in section on *Torshi*) and flat bread (if desired).

NOTE: This delicious dish seems to have become less frequently served, particularly in large cities; however, the name, literally translated "Calico [originally a hand-stamped cloth] Pottage," is still prevalent in the common vocabulary, sometimes carrying the connotations of "hodgepodge" in English.

# Ash-e Bibi Seshanbeh
(bean and wheat pottage, Arak style)

*6 to 8 servings*

**Ingredients:**
*1 cup chickpeas*
*1 cup kidney beans*
*1 lb stew lamb or beef*
*4 Tbs. butter*
*½ cup lentils*
*2 onions, sliced*
**Spices:**
*2½ tsp cinnamon*
*2 tsp salt*
*1 tsp turmeric*
*½ tsp black pepper*

**DIRECTIONS FOR COOKING**

**1.** Simmer chickpeas and kidney beans in 7 cups water for 30 minutes, or until tender.
**2.** Sprinkle meat with 2 tsp of the cinnamon and brown in 2 Tbs. of the butter. Add to chickpea-kidney bean mixture along with mung beans, lentils, salt, turmeric, and pepper; simmer for another 35-40 minutes, stirring occasionally to prevent sticking.
**3.** Sauté onions in remaining butter.
**4.** Stir half the onions into *ash.* Transfer to a serving bowl or tureen and decorate with remaining onions. Sprinkle with remaining cinnamon.

# Ash-e Dugh I
(yogurt pottage with meat, Ardabil style)

*4 to 5 servings*

**Ingredients:**
*½ cup chickpeas*
*1½ cups plain yogurt*
*1 cup rice*
*1 cup chopped coriander*
*3 carrots, diced*
*¾ lb ground beef or lamb*
*4 Tbs. flour*
*1 small onion, grated*
*2 Tbs. butter*
*2 cloves garlic, minced*
*2 Tbs. dried mint*
**Spices:**
*1½ tsp salt*
*¼ tsp black pepper*

**DIRECTIONS FOR COOKING**

**1.** Simmer chickpeas in 2 cups water for 30 minutes, or until tender. Drain and set aside.
**2.** Beat yogurt; add 3 cups water and 1 tsp of the salt; mix well.
**3.** In a large pot, bring yogurt mixture and rice to a boil; reduce heat and simmer for 20 minutes, stirring frequently to prevent sticking.
**4.** Add coriander, carrots, and chickpeas to *ash* and let simmer for 10 minutes more.
**5.** Mix together meat, remaining salt, and pepper and form into small meatballs the size of hazelnuts. Drop into *ash* and simmer an additional 10 minutes.
**6.** Dissolve flour in ½ cup cold water and stir into *ash*.
**7.** Sauté onion in butter in a skillet; stir in garlic and mint and remove from heat.
**8.** To serve, pour into a tureen or serving bowl and decorate with onion-garlic-mint mixture.

## Ash-e Dugh II
(yogurt pottage, Ardabil style)

*6 to 8 servings*

Ingredients:
*½ cup dried chickpeas*
*½ cup rice*
*4 cups plain yogurt*
*2 eggs*
*½ lb ground beef or lamb*
*1 medium onion, minced*
*1 bunch parsley, chopped*
*1 stock leeks or 1 bunch green onions, chopped*
*4 cloves garlic, chopped*
*2 Tbs dried mint, crushed*
Spices:
*2½ tsp salt*
*½ tsp black pepper*

### DIRECTIONS FOR COOKING

**1.** Put chickpeas in a pot, cover with 5 cups water and boil for 20 minutes or until almost tender. Drain and set aside.
**2.** Cook rice in 2 cups water for 15 minutes. Set aside.
**3.** Beat yogurt well; add 4 cups water, mix and bring to a boil in a large pot.
**4.** Lightly beat eggs with flour and add to the pot. Stir for a few minutes to mix well in the yogurt broth.
**5.** Mix together meat, minced onion and ½ tsp salt; make into walnut-size meatballs and drop into boiling soup mixture.
**6.** Add parsley, leeks, and garlic and cook an additional 15 minutes.
**7.** Add spices and chickpeas and simmer for 15 minutes.
**8.** Transfer to a serving bowl and sprinkle with mint.

## Ash-e Kashkak
(vegetable pottage, Khosbijan style)

*3 to 4 servings*

| Ingredients: | Spices: |
| --- | --- |
| *½ cup chickpeas* | *1½ tsp salt* |
| *½ cup kidney beans* | *½ tsp black pepper* |
| *½ cup lentils* | |
| *1 cup bulgur* | |
| *1 large onion, chopped* | |
| *3 Tbs. butter* | |

### DIRECTIONS FOR COOKING

**1.** Simmer chickpeas and kidney beans in 5 cups water for 40 minutes or until tender.
**2.** Add lentils, bulgur, and spices, and simmer an additional 20 minutes.
**3.** Sauté onions in butter. Stir into pottage just before serving.

## Ash-e Qonabid
(kohlrabi pottage with legumes, Qom style)

*8 to 10 servings*

| Ingredients: | Spices: |
| --- | --- |
| *1 cup black-eyed peas* | *1½ tsp salt* |
| *1 cup mung beans* | *1 tsp turmeric* |
| *1 cup rice* | *1 tsp black pepper* |
| *1 large onion, sliced* | |
| *1½ lb kohlrabi, chopped* | |
| *1 cup lentils* | |
| *2 Tbs. lemon juice* | |
| *2 Tbs. dried mint* | |

### DIRECTIONS FOR COOKING

**1.** Bring black eyed peas, mung beans, rice, 8 cups water, and seasonings to a boil in a large pot; reduce heat and simmer for 40 minutes.
**2.** Sauté onions in butter. Stir in kohlrabi for 2-3 minutes. Add along with lentils to pottage and simmer for an additional 20 minutes. Stir in lemon juice and simmer an additional 10 minutes.
**3.** Transfer to a tureen and sprinkle with dried mint.

## Ash-e Kashk-e Tabrizi

(bulgur pottage with green vegetables and legumes, Tabriz style)

*8 to 10 servings*

**Ingredients:**
*1 cup chickpeas*
*1 cup kidney beans*
*1 cup lentils*
*1 cup rice*
*½ cup bulgur*
*1 cup parsley, chopped*
*1 cup coriander, chopped*
*1 cup leeks, chopped*
*¼ cup fresh tarragon, chopped*
*1½ lbs carrots, sliced*
*¾ lb cabbage, chopped*
*2 cups chicken broth*
*1½ cups liquid whey*
*1 large onion, sliced*
*3 Tbs. olive oil*
*¼ cup fresh mint, chopped*
**Spices:**
*2 tsp salt*
*1 tsp turmeric*

### DIRECTIONS FOR COOKING

**1.** Simmer chickpeas and kidney beans in 6 cups water for 40 minutes or until tender; drain and set aside.
**2.** Simmer lentils in 3 cups water for 20 minutes; drain and set aside.
**3.** Boil rice and bulgur in 4 cups water for 20 minutes. Add chickpeas, kidney beans, lentils, parsley, coriander, leeks, tarragon, carrots, cabbage, chicken broth and spices and simmer for 30-40 minutes, stirring occasionally to prevent sticking.
**4.** Sauté onion in olive oil; remove from heat and stir in mint.
**5.** When ready to serve, stir whey into pottage; transfer to tureen and decorate with onion-mint mixture.

## Tandir Ashi

(bulgur pottage with chickpeas and meat, Azerbaijan style)

*5 to 6 servings*

**Ingredients:**
*1 cup chickpeas*
*1 lb small-grained bulgur*
*4 onions, chopped*
*¼ lb stew beef or lamb*
*2 Tbs. butter*
**Spices:**
*1 tsp salt*
*2 tsp powdered, dried rose petals**

### DIRECTIONS FOR COOKING

**1.** Boil chickpeas in 5 cups water in a large pot for 20 minutes or until tender.
**2.** Add all remaining ingredients except for butter and rose petals; simmer for 1 hour, stirring occasionally.
**3.** Transfer the *ash* into a tureen; drop butter in the middle and sprinkle the top of the *ash* with rose petals.

* Powdered dried rose petals add a subtle flavor and aroma to a variety of Persian dishes. Aromatic, generally pink roses are the best choice for drying and using in food preparation.

## Ashma Jow

(barley pottage, Azerbaijan style)

*4 servings*

### Ingredients:
*½ lb barley*
*1½ cups chicken broth*
*1 medium potato, grated*
*1 carrot, grated*
*½ cup leeks, chopped*
*1 Tbs. butter*
*2 Tbs. wheat flour*
*½ cup milk*
*2 Tbs. parsley, chopped*
*¼ cup cream*

### Spices:
*1 tsp salt*
*¼ tsp paprika*

### DIRECTIONS FOR COOKING

**1.** Soak barley in 3 cups water overnight.

**2.** Bring barley-water to a boil in a medium pot; simmer for 30 minutes.

**3.** Add chicken broth, potato, carrot, leeks, and spices. Simmer for an additional 15 minutes.

**4.** Lightly brown wheat flour in butter; stir into the *ash* mixture.

**5.** Add milk and stir over medium heat for 1 or 2 minutes.

**6.** Transfer mixture into a tureen; sprinkle with parsley and top with cream.

## Ash-e Gowjeh Farangi

(tomato pottage with split peas, scallions, and ground meat, Northern Iran style)

*7 to 8 servings*

### Ingredients:
*¼ cup yellow split peas*
*1 cup rice*
*1 bunch parsley, chopped*
*2 bunches scallions or green onions, chopped*
*1 large onion, chopped*
*3 Tbs. olive oil*
*1 small onion, grated*
*1 lb ground beef or lamb*
*½ cup rice flour*
*2 large tomatoes, cut and mashed*
*2 Tbs. butter*
*¼ cup chopped fresh mint*

### Spices:
*2½ tsp salt*
*½ tsp black pepper*
*1 tsp cinnamon*

### DIRECTIONS FOR COOKING

**1.** Place split peas, rice, parsley, green onions, 5 cups water, 1½ tsp of the salt, and pepper in a large pot. Bring to a boil, reduce heat and simmer for 40 minutes.

**2.** Sauté chopped onion in olive oil and add to above mixture.

**3.** Mix together grated onion, remaining salt, cinnamon, ground meat, and rice flour. Shape into meatballs the size of walnuts and drop into *ash* mixture.

**4.** Add tomatoes and simmer an additional 30 minutes.

**5.** Melt butter over medium heat; add mint and stir for about 1 minute; remove from heat.

**6.** Transfer *ash* into a large tureen; decorate top with mint and butter mixture.

# Ash-e Rashti

(pottage with kidney beans, beets,
and meat, Rasht style)

*8 to 10 servings*

**Ingredients:**
*1 cup kidney beans*
*2 bunches parsley, finely chopped*
*2 bunches scallions or green onions, finely chopped*
*1 lb beets, diced*
*1 lb ground beef or lamb*
*½ cup rice flour*
*¼ cup sugar*
*¼ cup sour grape juice\**
*6 eggs*
**Spices:**
*¼ tsp powdered saffron, dissolved in 2 Tbs. hot water*
*3 tsp salt*
*½ tsp black pepper*
*2 tsp marjoram*

**DIRECTIONS FOR COOKING**

**1.** Place beans, parsley, green onions, and 4 cups water in a large pot; bring to a boil, reduce heat and simmer for 1 hour or until beans are tender.
**2.** Add beets and simmer for 30 minutes more.
**3.** Mix together meat, dissolved saffron, 1 tsp of the salt, and pepper; make into meat balls the size of walnuts and drop into the *ash*.
**4.** Dissolve rice flour in 1 cup water; stir in remaining salt and marjoram.
**5.** Stir in sugar and sour grape juice.
**6.** Break eggs gently into *ash*, one by one; do not stir, allow eggs to poach, 3 or 4 minutes, or until they are firm but not hard; then remove the poached eggs and set aside.
**7.** Transfer *ash* into a tureen and decorate with poached eggs.

*\*Lemon or lime juice can be substituted.*

# Ash-e Shalgham

(turnip pottage with meat, rice, and lentils,
Bakhtiari style)

*8 to 10 servings*

**Ingredients:**
*1 lb beef or lamb, minced*
*¼ tsp meat tenderizer*
*¼ cup butter*
*1 medium onion, chopped*
*1 cup rice*
*2 lbs small turnips*
*½ cup lentils*
*¼ cup vinegar*
**Spices:**
*1 tsp cinnamon*
*1 tsp turmeric*
*2 tsp salt*
*1 tsp black pepper*

**DIRECTIONS FOR COOKING**

**1.** Sprinkle meat with cinnamon and meat tenderizer. Brown in butter in a skillet for 10 minutes over medium heat. Stir in onions; brown for 5 more minutes.
**2.** Transfer meat mixture to a large pot and add 5 cups water; simmer the meat mixture for 30-40 minutes over medium heat.
**3.** Add rice, turnips (if turnips are large, cut in quarters), lentils, and remaining spices. Simmer for 1 hour, stirring occasionally to prevent sticking.
**4.** Stir in vinegar just before serving.

# Ash-e Kadu Tanbal

(pumpkin pottage with rice and lentils,
Tehran Province style)

*8 to 10 servings*

**Ingredients:**
*2 lbs fresh pumpkin*
*½ cup rice*
*1 cup lentils or yellow split peas*
*2 cups plain yogurt*
*2 Tbs. brown sugar*
**Spices:**
*1 tsp salt*
*1 tsp nutmeg*

**DIRECTIONS FOR COOKING**

**1.** Remove the skin and cut pumpkin pulp into 1-inch cubes.

**2.** Place pumpkin with rice, lentils or split peas, 6 cups water, and salt in a large pot; bring to a boil, then reduce heat and simmer for 1 ½ hours, stirring occasionally to prevent sticking, or until pumpkin becomes soft. If the *ash* becomes too thick, add more water.

**3.** Just before serving, stir in yogurt, nutmeg and brown sugar.

OPTIONAL: When serving, stir in some croutons or pieces of *Nan-e Khoshkeh* (Iranian cracker bread; see recipe in the "Breads" section.)

# Ash-e Alucheh Baraquni

(pottage with chicken, split peas,
and prunes, Isfahan style)

*10-12 servings*

**Ingredients:**
*1 lb boneless, skinless chicken thighs, cut in ½" cubes*
*2 Tbs. olive oil*
*1 medium onion, quartered*
*1 lb dried prunes*
*1 cup yellow split peas*
*1½ cup rice*
*1 bunch parsley, chopped*
*1 bunch coriander, chopped*
*2 Tbs. sugar*
*1 medium onion, sliced*
*2 Tbs. butter, melted*
*¼ cup fresh mint, chopped*
**Spices:**
*2 tsp salt*
*2 tsp cinnamon*

**DIRECTIONS FOR COOKING**

**1.** Brown chicken lightly in olive oil.

**2.** Place chicken, quartered onion, and 6 cups water in a large pot and simmer for 15 minutes.

**3.** Add prunes, peas, rice, parsley, coriander, salt, cinnamon. Bring to a boil; reduce heat and simmer for 1 hour, stirring occasionally. Add more water if necessary.

**4.** Add sugar and stir for a few minutes.

**5.** Sauté sliced onion in butter; add mint and remove from heat.

**6.** Place *ash* in a large tureen and decorate top with onion-mint mixture.

# Ash-e Sak
(pottage with ground meat, spinach, and beets, Mazandaran style)

*8 to 10 servings*

**Ingredients:**
*½ cup kidney beans*
*2 large onions, chopped*
*¼ cup butter*
*½ lb ground beef or lamb*
*½ cup lentils*
*1 lb fresh spinach, chopped*
*1 bunch parsley, chopped*
*2 bunches green onions, chopped*
*1 lb fresh beets, sliced*
*1 cup rice flour*
*½ cup sour grape juice\**
*3 eggs, beaten*
*½ cup walnuts, chopped*
**Spices:**
*2½ tsp salt*
*½ tsp black pepper*
*1 tsp turmeric*
*½ tsp cinnamon*

## DIRECTIONS FOR COOKING

**1.** Simmer kidney beans in 2-3 cups water over medium heat for 40 minutes, or until tender.

**2.** Sauté onions in butter and divide in half. Set aside one-half for garnish.

**3.** Place half of the sautéed onions, 6 cups water, 2 tsp of the salt, pepper, and turmeric in a large pot; bring to a boil and reduce heat.

**4.** Mix together meat with remaining salt and cinnamon, make small meat balls the size of hazelnuts and drop into *ash*.

**5.** Add lentils, spinach, parsley, green onions, and beets to *ash* and simmer over medium heat for 30-40 minutes.

**6.** Add kidney beans to *ash* along with the water they have cooked in.

**7.** Dissolve rice flour in ¾ cup water and add to *ash* along with sour grape juice\*. Stir well and simmer for 20-30 minutes more.

**8.** Just before serving, thoroughly stir in beaten eggs.

**9.** Place in a tureen and garnish with the remaining sautéed onions and walnuts.

\*If not available, 1/3 cup of lime juice can be substituted.

# Ash-e Ghureh

(sour grape pottage with split peas, greens,
and meat, Najafabad style)

*8 –10 servings*

Ingredients:
*1 large onion, chopped*
*¼ cup butter*
*1 bunch scallions, chopped*
*1 bunch parsley, chopped*
*1 bunch coriander, chopped*
*½ cup yellow split peas*
*1 cup rice*
*2 cups sour grapes*
*1 lb ground lamb or beef*
*1 small onion, grated*
*3 Tbs. wheat flour*
*¼ cup fresh mint, chopped*
Spices:
*1 tsp oregano*
*2½ tsp salt*
*½ tsp black pepper*

## DIRECTIONS FOR COOKING

**1.** Sauté onion in half of the butter.
**2.** Place sautéed onion, 5 cups water, scallions, parsley, coriander, peas, rice, 2 tsp of the salt, and remaining spices in a large pot; bring to a boil; reduce
heat and simmer for 30 minutes.
**3.** Add sour grapes and simmer another 30 minutes,
stirring occasionally to prevent sticking. Add more
water if necessary.
**4.** Mix meat, grated onion, flour and remaining salt
and form into meatballs the size of small walnuts.
Drop into *ash* and simmer over low heat until ready
to serve.
**5.** Place in a large tureen. Add mint to melted butter
and pour over top.

# Ash-e Jujeh

(chicken pottage)

*5 to 6 servings*

Ingredients:
*½ lb boneless skinless chicken breasts*
*1 cup lentils*
*1 cup rice*
*½ cup chopped parsley*
*½ cup chopped coriander*
*½ cup chopped leeks*
*1 cup chopped spinach*
*1 onion, chopped*
*3 Tbs. butter*
*2 Tbs. powdered dried mint*
Spices:
*1 tsp salt*
*½ tsp black pepper*
*½ tsp turmeric*

## DIRECTIONS FOR COOKING

**1.** Cut chicken breasts into half-inch cubes, place in a
pot with 4 cups water, lentils, rice, parsley, coriander, leeks, spinach, salt, and black pepper. Simmer
over low heat for 1 hour.
**2.** Sauté onion in butter. Stir in mint and turmeric
and remove from heat.
**3.** Transfer *Ash-e Jujeh* to a soup tureen and decorate
top with sautéed onion and mint.

Serve with lemon juice or plain yogurt.

# Ash-e Anar

(pomegranate pottage with beets and split peas)

*8 to 10 servings*

**Ingredients:**
*1 medium beet or 1 can of sliced cook beets*
*1 cup yellow split peas*
*¼ cup butter*
*1 large onion, sliced*
*¼ cup chopped fresh or 3 Tbs. dried mint*
*1 bunch scallions, chopped*
*2 cups rice*
*1 cup pomegranate sauce*
*1 Tbs. dried mint*
**Spices:**
*3 tsp salt*
*½ tsp black pepper*
*2 Tbs. turmeric*

### DIRECTIONS FOR COOKING

**1.** If using fresh beets, slice and cook in 4 cups of water along with split peas for 20 minutes or until half cooked. If using cooked beets leave aside to be added later.

**2.** Sauté onion in butter until golden brown.

**3.** Add half of sautéed onion, 2 cups water, rice, and seasoning to the beet and peas and cook for an additional 20 minutes, then reduce heat and simmer for 30 more minutes. Add additional water if necessary.

**4.** Add pomegranate and simmer for an additional 10 minutes. If using cooked beets, add 2 minutes before serving.

**5.** Place in a large tureen. Decorate with remaining sautéed onion and mint.

# Omaj

(legume and dumpling pottage)

*10 to 12 servings*

**Ingredients:**
*2 cups flour*
*½ cup kidney beans*
*½ cup navy beans*
*½ cup lentils*
*1 bunch fresh parsley, chopped*
*1 bunches leeks or scallions, chopped*
*½ lb fresh spinach, chopped*
*¼ cup butter*
*1 Tbs. dried mint*
*vinegar (optional)*
**Spices:**
*¼ tsp saffron* (optional)
*2 tsp turmeric*
*1½ tsp salt*
*½ tsp black pepper*

### DIRECTIONS FOR COOKING

**1.** Use 1½ cups flour and ½ cup water to make dough. Kneed well and set aside.

**2.** If using dried legumes, cook each type separately until tender and set aside.

**3.** Combine parsley, scallions, spices, and 4 cups water in a large pot. Boil 20 minutes, or until vegetables are tender.

**4.** Add spinach, butter, and spices and cook 10 minutes more.

**5.** Make walnut-size dumplings with the dough and drop in the pot. Cook for an additional 10 minutes.

**6.** Mix remaining flour in ¾ cup cold water and add to the pot. Stir for a minute or two.

**7.** Add legumes and cook for 10 minutes.

To serve, pour *Omaj* in a large serving bowl, sprinkle with dried mint, and serve with vinegar, if desired.

Prepared by Kamron J.

# Kolah Jush
(whey soup)

*5 to 6 servings*

**Ingredients:**
*2 medium onions, thinly sliced*
*¼ cup butter*
*¼ cup chopped walnuts*
*1 cup liquid whey*
*2 Tbs. wheat flour*
*2 Tbs. dried mint*
**Spices:**
*2 tsp salt (if whey is salty, omit)*
*½ tsp turmeric*
*¼ tsp black pepper*

### DIRECTIONS FOR COOKING

**1.** Sauté onions in butter.
**2.** Stir in walnuts and brown a few minutes.
**3.** Transfer onion-walnut mixture and butter into a pot. Mix together all remaining ingredients along with 1½ cups water. Bring to a boil; reduce heat and let simmer for 5 minutes.

NOTE: Serve with hot flat bread.

# Abdugh Khiyar
(cold yogurt and cucumber soup)

*4 to 5 servings*

**Ingredients:**
*2 cups plain yogurt*
*2 cucumbers, grated*
*1 small onion, grated*
*2 tsp. dried mint*
*¼ cup chopped walnuts*
*¼ cup raisins*
**Spices:**
*½ tsp salt*

### DIRECTIONS FOR COOKING

**1.** In mixing bowl, beat yogurt until it is smooth. Add 2 cups water and spices and stir well to completely dissolve yogurt and salt in the mixture.
**2.** Add and mix together all remaining ingredients.

NOTE: *Abdugh Khiyar* should be served with *nan-e khoshkeh* (see recipe in the "Breads" section) or other form of dry, firm cracker (such as melba toast), which is usually broken into bite-size pieces, dropped into the soup, and eaten with a spoon. This dish makes an excellent appetizer and is often served in Iran as a late-night summer snack.

# Shuli
(pottage of legumes, beets, and spinach, Yazd style)

*5 to 6 servings*

**Ingredients:**
*1 cup kidney beans*
*1 cup chickpeas*
*2 medium-sized beets, sliced*
*2 lb fresh spinach, chopped*
*½ cup fresh dill weed, chopped*
*1 large onion, sliced*
*¼ cup butter*
*½ cup vinegar*
**Spices:**
*2 tsp salt*
*½ tsp black pepper*

### DIRECTIONS FOR COOKING

**1.** Simmer kidney beans and chickpeas in 6 cups water for 1 hour, or until tender.
**2.** Add beets, lentils, spinach, dill, and spices; simmer for 30 minutes.
**3.** Dissolve flour in 1½ cups cold water and stir into the pottage for 10 minutes over medium-low heat, stirring occasionally to prevent sticking.
**4.** Sauté onion in butter; set aside.
**5.** Stir in vinegar. Transfer to a large serving bowl or soup tureen and decorate with sautéed onion.

NOTE: *Shuli* is generally served as a midmorning or afternoon snack, especially on family picnics.

# Sholeh Mash
(mung bean pottage)

*6 to 8 servings*

**Ingredients:**
*1 large onion, sliced*
*2 Tbs. butter*
*½ lb ground beef or lamb*
*¾ cup mung beans*
*½ cup rice*
*½ cup pinto beans*
**Spices:**
*2 tsp salt*
*½ tsp black pepper*
*½ tsp turmeric*

### DIRECTIONS FOR COOKING

**1.** Brown onion in butter.
**2.** Add meat and spices and stir over medium heat for about 5 minutes, or until meat is cooked.
**3.** Add remaining ingredients along with 5 cups water and cook over medium heat for 1 hour, or until beans are quite soft.
**4.** Remove from heat and mash slightly. Serve either hot or cold, with flat bread.

## Mash Piyazu
(bean and onion pottage)

*8 to 10 servings*

**Ingredients:**
*1 cup kidney beans*
*1 cup lentils*
*1 cup mung beans*
*¾ cup cracked wheat (make sure it is not pre-cooked)*
*¾ cup rice*
*12 medium onions*
*1 clove garlic, minced*
*½ cup butter*
**Spices:**
*3 tsp salt*
*2 tsp turmeric*
*1 tsp black pepper*

### DIRECTIONS FOR COOKING

**1.** Simmer kidney beans in 6 cups water over medium heat for 45 minutes.
**2.** Add lentils and mung beans and simmer another 30 minutes.
**3.** Add wheat and rice and simmer another 30 minutes, adding more water if necessary. Stir occasionally to prevent sticking.
**4.** Peel the onions. Add 5 whole onions to the pot; simmer for another 30 minutes.
**5.** Using a slotted spoon, remove onions from mixture and mash; then return onions to the pot and mix well.
**6.** Slice the remaining onions and sauté (add garlic, if desired) in butter. Stir in spices and add to the pot. Let simmer for another 10 minutes.
Serve with bread.

NOTE: This dish is a specialty of the city of Qazvin and is generally served in winter.

## Adasi
(lentil porridge)

*6 to 8 servings*

**Ingredients:**
*1 lb lentils*
*½ cup butter, melted*

**Spices:**
*1 tsp salt*
*1 tsp dried oregano*
*sugar (optional)*

### DIRECTIONS FOR COOKING

**1.** Boil lentils in 6 cups water about 30 minutes or until very soft. Mash well. Mix in salt and oregano. Place in serving bowl.
**2.** Pour butter over top, or put a pat of butter in individual serving bowls and add *adasi* on top.
**3.** Sprinkle with sugar and additional oregano, if desired.

NOTE: A traditional winter breakfast dish, *adasi* is scooped up with flat, pita-type bread. Also served side-by-side with *halim* (see recipe on next page).

# Halim
(meat and wheat porridge)

*8 to 10 servings*

**Ingredients:**                          **Spices:**
*1 lb stew beef or lamb*                  *1 tsp salt*
*2 cups Instant Cream of*                 *cinnamon*
  *Wheat*
*½ cup butter*
*sugar*

## DIRECTIONS FOR COOKING

**1.** Place meat in a pot with 4 cups water; boil for 1 hour, or until the meat falls apart.
**2.** Remove meat from broth, let cool for 10 minutes. Set broth aside.
**3.** Pulverize meat in a food processor, then add to the broth.
**4.** Stir in Cream of Wheat, 5 cups water, and salt to the pot. Simmer gently over low or medium-low heat for 30 minutes, frequently stirring and mashing with a potato masher to prevent a crust from forming on the bottom of the pot.
**5.** Transfer *halim* into a large serving bowl. Decorate top with melted butter, and sprinkle with sugar and cinnamon to taste.

NOTE: This is a traditional winter breakfast, usually bought in specialty shops, very often served side-by-side with *adasi* (see recipe on the previous page) and is scooped up with flat bread.

# Halim-e Shir
(wheat porridge with turkey)

*8 to 10 servings*

**Ingredients:**
*1¼ lb skinless, boneless white turkey meat, cooked*
*2 cups Instant Cream of Wheat*
*3 cups milk*
*½ cup butter*
*sugar*
**Spices:**
*1 tsp salt*
*cinnamon*

## DIRECTIONS FOR COOKING

**1.** Cut ¼ lb of the turkey into thin strips and set aside.
**2.** Cut the remainder of the turkey into small chunks and pulverize in a food processor.
**3.** Transfer pulverized turkey to a medium-size pot, add Cream of Wheat, milk, 2 cups water, and salt. Simmer gently over low or medium-low heat for 30 minutes, frequently stirring and mashing with a potato masher to prevent a crust from forming on the bottom of the pot.
**4.** Transfer *halim-e shir* into a large serving bowl. Decorate top with melted butter and strips of turkey; sprinkle with sugar and cinnamon to taste.

NOTE: Like the beef or lamb *halim*, this is a traditional winter breakfast very often served side-by-side with *adasi* (see recipe above in this chapter) and is scooped up with flat bread.

# Halim Badenjan
(eggplant paste)

*6 to 8 servings*

**Ingredients:**
*1 lb beef or lamb*
*2 eggplants*
*¼ cup olive oil*
*1 cup wheat flour*
*1½ cup liquid whey or plain yogurt*
*1 large onion, sliced*
*3 Tbs. butter*
*2 Tbs. dried mint*

**Spices:**
*2 tsp turmeric*
*2 tsp salt*
*½ tsp black pepper*
*¼ tsp paprika*

## DIRECTIONS FOR COOKING

**1.** Boil meat in 3 cups water until very tender.  Remove meat from broth and set broth aside.

**2.** Let meat cool for 10-15 minutes; cut meat into chunks, and place in a food processor and pulverize it until it becomes a soft paste.

**3.** Peel eggplants, cut lengthwise in 3 or 4 pieces; brown lightly in olive oil on both sides.

**4.** In a medium-size pot, combine broth, meat paste, eggplants, and spices; simmer over medium heat for 20 minutes.

**5.** Dissolve flour slowly in 1 ½ cups cold water; add to *halim* and mash well with potato masher.  Let simmer for 10 minutes more, stirring constantly to avoid sticking.

**6.** Stir in liquid whey or plain yogurt.  Should be the consistency of a thick paste.

**7.** Brown onions in butter, stir in mint.

**8.** Transfer *halim* to a serving bowl; top with onion-mint mixture and sprinkle with paprika.  Serve hot or cold with thin, flat bread.

NOTE: *Halim badenjan* makes an excellent dip. Cut recipe in half.  Makes 2½ to 3 cups of dip.

Prepared by Fahimeh Z.
Additional garnishing includes crushed walnuts

# Abgusht-e Nokhod (or Nokhodab) va Gusht-e Kubideh
(chickpea soup and meat paste)

*4 to 6 Servings*

**Ingredients:**
*1 lb stew beef or lamb*
*1 large onion, quartered*
*½ cup chickpeas*
*2 dried limes, or juice of 3 key limes*
*2 Tbs. rice*
*6 small potatoes, peeled*
*2 large tomatoes, quartered*
**Spices:**
*2 tsp salt*
*½ tsp black pepper*
*1 tsp turmeric*

## DIRECTIONS FOR COOKING

**1.** Put all ingredients, except for potatoes and tomatoes, along with 6 cups of water in a pot and bring to a boil; reduce heat to low and let simmer for 1 to 1½ hours, or until meat is tender. Add more water if additional cooking time is required to tenderize meat.

**2.** Add potatoes and tomatoes and simmer for an additional 30 minutes.

**3.** With a slotted spoon, remove meat, potatoes, and most of the chickpeas and rice from the soup. Set soup aside over low heat to keep warm (the tomatoes will be mostly dissolved at this time).

**4.** Separate meat from vegetables; pulverize meat in a food processor.

**5.** Combine potatoes and chickpeas with pulverized meat and mash into a smooth paste.

**6.** To serve, spread out smoothly on a platter, using a spatula or spoon with some of the soup to facilitate smoothing the paste. Sprinkle with additional black pepper to taste.

NOTE: The soup is served in bowls with torn pieces of flat Persian or pita-type bread soaking up the juices (much as some people crumble crackers in soup). The meat paste is eaten by scooping up with flat bread.

*Abgusht* in general, and this one in particular, is thought of by many as the "poor man's meal," since, by "adding water to the soup" (a Persian expression), one could feed a large family or unexpected guests. However, a good *abgusht* makes an excellent meal.

Although not a Persian tradition, the meat paste makes an ideal hors d'oeuvre.

# Abgusht-e Sabzi (Bozbash) va Gusht-e Kubideh

(green vegetable soup and meat paste)

*6 to 8 servings*

**Ingredients:**
*1½ lb stew beef or lamb*
*1 cup navy beans*
*1 large onion, quartered*
*2 cups chopped leeks or green onions*
*1 bunch parsley, chopped*
*3 dried limes, or ¼ cup lemon juice*
*6 small potatoes, peeled*
**Spices:**
*2 tsp salt*
*1 tsp black pepper*
*1 tsp turmeric*

## DIRECTIONS FOR COOKING

**1.** Place all ingredients, except for potatoes, in a large pot with 6 cups water. Bring to a boil, reduce heat and let simmer for 1½ hour.
**2.** Add potatoes and simmer for another 30 minutes.
**3.** With a slotted spoon, remove most of the meat, potatoes, beans, and vegetables; keep soup warm.
**4.** Separate the meat and pulverize in a food processor. Return pulverized meat to potatoes and beans and mash together well. Spread out on a platter and sprinkle with black pepper to taste.
**5.** Serve soup and mashed meat-vegetable paste separately with flat bread, accompanied by pickled vegetables (see *Torshi*).

NOTE: If the meat paste is not desired, this soup can be served after Step 2.

# Bozbash-e Araki

(apricot soup, Arak style)

*3 to 4 servings*

**Ingredients:**
*2 onions, sliced*
*3 Tbs. butter*
*1 lb stew beef or lamb*
*1 cup yellow split peas*
*¾ lb dried apricots*
*½ cup sugar*
*½ cup vinegar*
*¼ cup fresh mint, chopped*
**Spices:**
*1 tsp salt*
*1 tsp turmeric*
*½ tsp cinnamon*
*¼ tsp black pepper*

## DIRECTIONS FOR COOKING

**1.** Sauté onion in butter in a skillet; divide in half and set half aside.
**2.** Add meat to onions in skillet and brown.
**3.** Mix in yellow split peas to meat and onion mixture and stir for 1 minute.
**4.** Transfer meat mixture to a medium-size pot; add 3 cups water and spices and simmer for 1 hour, or until meat is tender.
**5.** Add dried apricots and simmer for an additional 10 minutes.
**6.** Add sugar and vinegar and stir for 2 to 3 minutes.
**7.** Stir in remaining sautéed onions and mint.
Serve with flat bread.

# Abgusht-e Dizi

(*dizi* style soup and meat paste)

6 servings

**Ingredients:**
1 cup pinto beans
1 cup chickpeas
3 medium onions, chopped
2½ lbs stew lamb, or three lamb shanks
2½ Tbs. tomato paste
6 small potatoes
4 dried limes
1 large tomato, cut in half

**Spices:**
1 tsp salt
½ tsp black pepper
1 tsp turmeric
a dash of saffron dissolved in warm water

## DIRECTIONS FOR COOKING

**1.** Cook beans and chickpeas in water for 1 hours or until tender. Drain and set aside.

**2.** Put lamb shanks and onion in a large pot with 4 cups of water. Cook over medium heat until the meat is cooked.

**3.** Add potatoes, beans, tomatoes, limes, tomato paste, and spices. Cook on low heat for 30 minutes.

To serve: Remove solid ingredients from soup. The soup may be served in small bowls with flat, pita-type bread or sangak bread. The solid ingredients can be served as is or mashed together with a mortar into a paste and spread out on a platter to be scooped up with pieces of flat bread. Traditionally, this dish is cooked in pots known as *dizi* and served individually. Different types of *Torshi*, *sabzi khordan*, and onion may also be served.

A *dizi*

Prepared by Kamron J.

# Abgusht-e Baghbani
(gardener's soup and meat paste)

*6 servings*

**Ingredients:**
*1 cup pinto beans*
*1 cup chickpeas*
*3 medium onions, chopped*
*3 Tbs. olive oil*
*2½ lbs stew beef or lamb, or three lamb shanks*
*2 cloves garlic, chopped*
*1½ Tbs. tomato paste*
*4 small potatoes, peeled*
*1 eggplant, peeled and cut into chunks*
*5 okra pods*
*1 small bell pepper, cut into chunks*
*1½ Tbs. sour grape juice or lemon juice*
**Spices:**
*1 tsp salt*
*½ tsp black pepper*
*1 tsp turmeric*
*¼ tsp cinnamon*

## DIRECTIONS FOR COOKING

**1.** Cook beans and chickpeas in 4 cups water for 1 hours or until tender.  Set aside.
**2.** Sauté onions in olive oil until golden brown.
**3.** Put onions, meat, garlic, and spices in a large pot with 5 cups water.  Simmer over medium heat for 1 hour, or until the meat is cooked.
**4.** Cut off ends of okra and add along with potatoes, eggplant, green pepper, and sour grape or lemon juice; simmer for 30 minutes, or until potatoes are tender.
**5.** Add cooked beans and chickpeas and simmer for 10 more minutes.

To serve: Remove solid ingredients from soup. The soup may be served in small bowls with flat, pita-type bread or sangak bread.  The solid ingredients can be served as is or mashed together into a paste and spread out on a platter to be scooped up with pieces of flat bread.

# Abgusht-e Ajil
(nut soup, Tehran style)

*8 to 10 servings*

**Ingredients:**
*1 lb stew beef or lamb*
*1 cup navy beans*
*1 onion, quartered*
*1 cup walnuts*
*1 cup pistachios*
*1 cup almonds*
*1 quince, cored and sliced*
*2 large potatoes, pealed and quartered*
*2 apples, cored and quartered*
*10 pitted prunes*
*10 dried apricots*
*½ cup red wine vinegar*
*½ cup sugar*
**Spices:**
*1 Tbs. whole caraway seeds*
*1 tsp salt*
*½ tsp black pepper*
*1 tsp. turmeric*
*½ tsp saffron*

## DIRECTIONS FOR COOKING

**1.** Place meat, navy beans, onion, and caraway seeds in a pot with 6 cups water; bring to a boil, and simmer for 1 hour.
**2.** Add walnuts, pistachios, almonds, quince, and potatoes and simmer for 15 minutes.
**3.** Add all other ingredients and simmer for an additional 15 minutes.
**4.** If desired, remove the ingredients from the soup and mash with a potato masher or in a food processor and serve on a platter sprinkled with additional saffron.

Serve with flat bread.

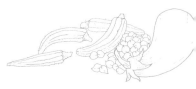

# Abgusht-e Qonabid
(kohlrabi soup, Qom style)

*5 to 6 servings*

Ingredients:
*1 lb stew beef or lamb*
*1 Tbs. butter*
*1 cup navy beans*
*1 lb kohlrabi, chopped*
*2 medium onions, quartered*
*1 Tbs. powdered dried lime or 2 Tbs. lemon juice*
Spices:
*2 tsp cinnamon*
*1 tsp salt*
*½ tsp black pepper*

**DIRECTIONS FOR COOKING**

**1.** Sprinkle meat with cinnamon and brown lightly in skillet in butter.
**2.** Place meat, remaining spices, and beans in 4 cups water in a large pot; bring to a boil, reduce heat, and simmer for 30 minutes, or until meat is tender.
**3.** Add kohlrabi and onions to soup and simmer an additional 30 minutes.
**4.** A few minutes before serving, stir in powdered limes or lemon juice.
Serve with flat bread and Persian pickles or relish (see recipes for *Torshi*).

# Abgusht-e Beh
(quince soup with meat and potatoes, Isfahan style)

*6 to 8 servings*

Ingredients:
*¼ cup butter*
*2 medium onions, sliced*
*1 lb stew beef or lamb*
*2 large quinces, cored and sliced in wedges*
*2 medium potatoes, peeled and quartered*
*1 Tbs. sugar*
*1 Tbs. lemon juice*
Spices:
*1 tsp cinnamon*
*1 tsp salt*
*¼ tsp black pepper*
*1 tsp turmeric*

**DIRECTIONS FOR COOKING**

**1.** Sauté onions in butter in a skillet.
**2.** Add meat and brown lightly.
**3.** Transfer meat and onion mixture to a large pot. Add spices and 5 cups water. Bring to a boil; reduce heat and simmer for 1 hour.
**4.** Add quince to soup mixture and simmer for 30 minutes.
**5.** Add potatoes, sugar, and lemon juice and simmer another 20 minutes.

To serve: Remove solid ingredients from soup; set soup aside. Mash solid ingredients into a paste and smooth out on a platter. Serve soup and paste separately accompanied with bread as a complete meal for lunch or dinner.

## Abgusht-e Badenjan
(eggplant soup with meat and potatoes)

*6-8 servings*

**Ingredients:**
*1 lb stew beef or lamb*
*2 medium onions, quartered*
*2 medium eggplants, peeled and sliced lengthwise*
*¼ cup butter*
*½ cup yellow split peas*
*2 potatoes, peeled and sliced*
*¼ cup sour grapes or 2 Tbs. lemon juice*
*2 Tbs. tomato paste*
**Spices:**
*3 tsp salt*
*½ tsp black pepper*
*1 tsp turmeric*

### DIRECTIONS FOR COOKING

**1.** Place meat, onions, 6 cups water, 2 tsp. of the salt, and remaining spices in a large pot; bring to a boil; reduce heat and simmer for 1 hour.
**2.** Meanwhile, sprinkle eggplants with remaining salt; set aside for ½ hour; then wipe salt off with paper towel and lightly brown eggplants in butter.
**3.** Add eggplants, split peas, potatoes, and sour grapes (if using instead of lemon juice) to soup and simmer for 30 minutes more.
**4.** If using lemon juice instead of sour grapes, add to soup along with tomato paste and simmer for 5 minutes more.

## Abgusht-e Jow
(barley soup)

*5 to 6 servings*

**Ingredients:**

*½ lb. stew meat*
*1 cup barley*
*5 carrots, grated*
*½ cup chopped parsley*
*2 Tbs. flour*
*1 cup cream*
**Spices:**
*2 tsp salt*
*1 tsp black pepper*

### DIRECTIONS FOR COOKING

**1.** Simmer meat with 4 cups of water for 30 minutes. Remove meat from broth with a slotted spoon and allow to cool.
**2.** Add barley to the broth with 2 additional cups of water and allow to simmer for 45 minutes. Remove meat from broth and set broth aside.
**3.** Pulverize meat in a food processor and add to barley broth.
**4.** Add carrots, parsley, and spices and simmer for 10 more minutes.
**5.** Dissolve flour in half a cup of cold water and then add to the broth. Stir a few minutes.
**6.** Before serving, stir in the cream.

## Abgusht-e Zaban
### (tongue soup)

*6 to 8 servings*

**Ingredients:**
*2 lamb tongues or 1 beef tongue*
*3 medium onions, sliced*
*¼ cup fresh parsley, chopped*
*2 Tbs. fresh mint, chopped*
*2 Tbs. lime juice or vinegar*
**Spices:**
*2½ tsp salt*
*½ tsp black pepper*
*½ tsp turmeric*

### DIRECTIONS FOR COOKING

**1.** Scrub tongues in warm water with a brush or the edge of a knife.
**2.** Place in a medium-size pot together with 6 cups water, onions, and spices. Cover pot and bring to a boil; reduce heat and let simmer 2 hours.
**3.** With a sharp knife, remove skin from tongue(s) and return tongue(s) to pot.
**4.** When the tongue is tender, add parsley, mint, and lemon juice or vinegar; let simmer an additional 20 minutes.

## Eshkeneh
### (egg drop soup)

*6 to 8 servings*

**Ingredients:**
*2 medium onions, thinly sliced*
*½ cup butter*
*¼ cup dried mint*
*4 eggs*
**Spices:**
*1 tsp salt*
*½ tsp black pepper*
*½ tsp turmeric*

### DIRECTIONS FOR COOKING

**1.** Sauté onions in butter.
**2.** In a medium pot, add onions and spices to 4 cups water; bring to a boil; reduce heat and simmer for 5 minutes.
**3.** Break the eggs one at a time and drop them into the soup mixture; let simmer 2 more minutes. Serve with hot bread and yogurt.

## Eshkeneh-ye Anar
### (pomegranate soup)

*3 to 4 servings*

**Ingredients:**
*1 medium onion, chopped*
*3 Tbs. butter*
*2 Tbs. sugar*
*2 Tbs. flour*
*3 eggs*
*½ cup pomegranate syrup*
**Spices:**
*½ tsp salt*
*½ tsp turmeric*

### DIRECTIONS FOR COOKING

**1.** Sauté onion in butter.
**2.** Transfer sautéed onion to medium-size pot; add 3 cups water, sugar, and spices, and bring to a boil.
**3.** Dissolve flour in ½ cup cold water and stir into boiling soup mixture.
**4.** Slowly add eggs to soup.
**5.** Stir in pomegranate syrup and simmer 5 minutes.

## Eshkeneh-ye Albalu
### (egg drop soup with tart cherries)

*4 to 6 servings*

**Ingredients:**
*2 onions, chopped*
*¼ cup butter*
*3 Tbs. flour*
*4 eggs*
*1 lb fresh tart cherries, pitted*
*1 Tbs. honey*
**Spices:**
*1 tsp turmeric*
*1 tsp salt*
*¼ tsp black pepper*
*1 tsp powdered fenugreek*

### DIRECTIONS FOR COOKING

**1.** Sauté onions in butter.
**2.** Transfer sautéed onions into a medium-sized pot. Add 4 cups water and spices and bring to a boil.
**3.** Mix flour in ½ cup cold water and beat into a smooth paste. Stir slowly into soup mixture.
**4.** Add eggs slowly.
**5.** Add cherries and honey to soup; simmer for 10 minutes.

## Mahi-ye Shurpazan
(smoked salt fish soup, Khuzestan style)

*6 to 8 Servings*

Ingredients:
*½ lb. smoked fish*
*1 onion, chopped*
*2 Tbs. olive oil*
*2 cloves garlic, minced*
*2 cups chopped parsley*
*2 Tbs. finely chopped chili pepper*
*2 Tbs. tamarind paste*
Spices:
*1 tsp black pepper*
*2 tsp turmeric*
*½ tsp powdered cumin*

### DIRECTIONS FOR COOKING

**1.** Soak the fish in a large amount of water for several hours or over night. Change the water two or three times in order to remove most of the salt.
**2.** Cut the fish into 1 inch square pieces and boil in 8 cups of water in a large pot. Taste the water to make sure that it is not too salty. If it is salty, drain and repeat this step.
**3.** Sauté onions in olive oil. Stir in garlic.
**4.** Add all ingredients to the boiling fish and simmer for 30 to 40 minutes; add additional water if necessary.

This dish is served as a very thin broth with some of the fish and other ingredients in each bowl. Serve with flat bread and pickled vegetables.

## Kalleh Pacheh
(sheep's head and feet)

*7 to 8 servings*

Ingredients:
*1 sheep's head*
*4 lamb's feet*
*2 onions, quartered*
*3 cloves garlic*
Spices:
*salt*
*black pepper*

### DIRECTIONS FOR COOKING

**1.** Singe the hair on the sheep's head on an open fire or with a torch.
**2.** Place sheep's feet in boiling water and remove hair with a sharp paring knife. This requires some patience, as you need to allow the feet to cool enough to be able to touch them. Repeat placing them in boiling water and cleaning them until all hair is removed. Split the hoof to remove the hair clump in each foot.
**3.** Cut off the nose, and cut the head in half. Clean and wash thoroughly in cool water. Remove the tongue in one peace.
**4.** Place the sheep's head, tongue, and feet in a large pot with 2 gallons of boiling water. Then reduce heat to low and simmer for 6 to 8 hours.
**5.** Remove head, tongue, and feet from the broth. Separate meat and brains from the bones; cut them into smaller pieces. Peel the tongue and cut into 7 to 8 pieces.
**6.** Add meat, brains, and tongue to the broth. Salt and pepper to taste in individual servings.

Serve with flat bread and green herbs, such as basil, tarragon, mint, and green onions.

# Meatballs and Stuffed Dishes
## (Dolmeh, Kufteh and Pirashki)

*olmeh* is basically a stuffed vegetable or bread dish. The recipes that follow are among the most traditional and most common in Iran. However, in recent years, other stuffed vegetables, such as tomatoes and bell peppers, also have found their way into Persian kitchens. They can be served as main dishes or as accompaniments to other foods. *Dolmeh* is popular not only in Iran but in Middle Eastern and other countries. However, Iranian *dolmeh* is distinctive in flavor from those found in other places.

*Pirashki* dishes are stuffed dough or bread generally fried or baked. Different kinds of *pirashki* are sometimes sold by street vendors.

*Kufteh* dishes are meatballs, of varying sizes, generally made of ground meat, rice, and various vegetables and herbs. The term *kufteh* literally means 'pounded' and describes a variety of meat and rice balls that are prepared by pounding the meat and other ingredients in stone mortars with wooden pestles. Some of these dishes are even stuffed. In fact, they vary almost as much as individual imaginations. The dishes in this section include the most widespread and generally recognized, as well as unique modern and regional varieties. Like *dolmeh, kufteh* can be either featured as a main dish or served as a side dish.

# Dolmeh-ye Sib
(stuffed apples)

*8 servings*

## Ingredients:
*2 medium onions, finely chopped*
*¼ cup butter*
*1 lb ground beef or lamb*
*¼ cup yellow split peas*
*8 large cooking apples*
*2 Tbs. brown sugar*
*¼ cup lemon juice*

## Spices:
*1 tsp salt*
*¼ tsp pepper*
*½ tsp powdered cardamom*

### DIRECTIONS FOR COOKING

**1.** Sauté onions in butter.

**2.** Sprinkle meat with salt and pepper and add to onions. Brown thoroughly.

**3.** Add split peas and 1 cup water to meat-onion mixture; simmer until meat is cooked.

**4.** Core each apple leaving a thickness of ¾" to ½".

**5.** Stuff each apple with the meat mixture.

**6.** Arrange apples in a wide pan or deep baking dish.

**7.** Dissolve brown sugar in 1 cup hot water, add lemon juice, pour around the apples; sprinkle the tops of each apple with cardamom; bake in 350° oven for 45 minutes. Add additional water if necessary.

**8.** Transfer each *dolmeh* with a spatula carefully onto a platter and pour some of the liquid from the pot or baking dish evenly over the apples.

# Dolmeh-ye Barg-e Mo
## (stuffed grape leaves)

*6 to 8 servings; more as an hors d'oeuvre*

**Ingredients:**
¼ cup yellow split peas
½ cup rice
1 medium onion, chopped
¼ cup olive oil
3 Tbs. dried mint
1 bunch scallions, chopped
1 egg, slightly beaten
½ cup zereshk
1 jar grape leaves
¼ cup lemon juice or vinegar
2 Tbs. sugar

**Spices:**
1½ tsp salt
¼ tsp black pepper
½ tsp turmeric
½ tsp cinnamon

## DIRECTIONS FOR COOKING

**1.** Cook split peas in 2 cups water until tender. Drain and set aside to cool.
**2.** Boil rice in 2 cups water for 10 minutes. Drain and set aside to cool.
**3.** Sauté onion in butter. Stir in scallions and cook a few minutes more. Set aside to cool.
**4.** Mix together rice, spit peas, onion, scallions, egg, *zereshk*, and spices in a large bowl.
**5.** Drain and rinse the grape leaves and spread out flat. Put about 1 Tbs. (alter according to size of leaf) of stuffing mixture on each leaf. Fold edges over and roll up.
**6.** Line bottom of pot with unused leaves. Arrange stuffed grape leaves, seam side down, in pot.
**7.** Mix together lemon juice or vinegar, sugar, and 1 cup water and pour over leaves. Cover and simmer over low heat until tender, about 30 minutes. (Can also be baked in 350° oven for 30 minutes.)
May be served hot or cold with plain yogurt.

Prepared by Maryam J.

# Dolmeh-ye Barg-e Mo ba Gousht

(stuffed grape leaves with meat)

*8 to 10 servings*

## Ingredients:

*¾ lb ground beef or lamb*
*1 Tbs. lemon juice*
*½ cup partially cooked rice*
*½ cup cooked split peas*
*¾ cup fresh parsley, chopped*
*¾ cup fresh coriander, chopped*
*2 Tbs. dried tarragon*
*¾ cup scallions, chopped*
*2 cloves garlic, crushed*
*2 Tbs. tomato paste*
*½ cup yogurt*
*1 jar grape leaves*

## Spices:

*1 tsp turmeric*
*1 tsp salt*

**DIRECTIONS FOR COOKING**

**1.** Mix together all ingredients except for grape leaves.
**2.** Rinse salt off grape leaves.
**3.** Lay out flat or put in the palm of your hand one leaf at a time and place 1 - 1½ Tbs. of the mixture on top. To wrap the stuffing in the leaf, first, fold the bottom edge tightly over the stuffing, then the sides, and then roll up.
**4.** Line the bottom of a deep pot with torn and un-used leaves and place stuffed leaves, seam side down, in the pot.
**5.** Add 1½ cups water and cook over low heat for 30 to 40 minutes, or until the water is completely absorbed.

Serve with plain yogurt.

Prepared by Fereshteh K.

# Dolmeh-ye Beh
(stuffed quinces)

*6 servings*

**Ingredients:**
*2 medium onions, chopped*
*¼ cup butter*
*1 lb ground beef or lamb*
*¼ cup rice*
*½ cup sugar*
*6 medium quinces*
*¼ cup vinegar*
**Spices:**
*1 tsp salt*
*¼ tsp pepper*

**DIRECTIONS FOR COOKING**

**1.** Sauté onions in butter.
**2.** Sprinkle meat with spices and add to onions. Brown thoroughly.
**3.** Dissolve ¼ cup of the sugar in 1 cup hot water and add to meat along with rice; let simmer over low heat for 10 minutes, stirring occasionally to prevent sticking.
**4.** Clean the quinces well, rubbing off the fuzz if necessary, and rinse in water. Slice off about ¼ inch of the tops of each quince and set aside. With an apple corer or a spoon, scoop out the seeds and some of the pulp, leaving a thickness of ¾" to ½".
**5.** Stuff each quince with the meat mixture along with its liquid.
**6.** Place tops of each quince back and secure with a few toothpicks.
**7.** Arrange quinces in a wide pan or deep baking dish with tops up.
**8.** Mix 1 cup water, remaining sugar, and vinegar, pour over the quinces and simmer over moderate heat or in 350° oven for 1½ - 2 hours. Cooking time may vary with the ripeness and size of the quinces. Add additional water if necessary. The *dolmeh* is ready when the quinces are cooked to the consistency of a baked potato.
**9.** To serve, transfer each *dolmeh* carefully to a platter and pour some of the liquid from the pot or baking dish evenly over the quinces.

# Garni Yarikh
(stuffed eggplants, Azerbaijan style)

*6 to 8 servings*

**Ingredients:**
*½ lb ground beef or lamb*
*¼ lb green beans, chopped*
*½ cup parsley, chopped*
*2 cloves garlic, crushed*
*2 green hot peppers*
*2 Tbs. butter*
*3 cups tomato juice*
*4 to 6  small gourmet eggplants*
*¼ cup olive oil*
*¼ cup slivered almonds*
*3 tomatoes, halved*

**Spices:**
*2 tsp salt*
*½ tsp saffron, dissolved in 4 Tbs. hot water*

**DIRECTIONS FOR COOKING**

**1.** Brown meat in its own fat in a skillet; set aside.
**2.** Lightly sauté green beans, parsley, garlic, and peppers in butter.  Add 1 cup of the tomato juice; cover and simmer over low heat for 15 minutes.  Stir into meat.
**3.** Peel eggplants.  Make a lengthwise incision in each eggplant, being careful not to break them in half.  Brown eggplants on all sides in oil.  Arrange in a flat casserole dish slit side up.
**4.** Fill each eggplant with meat and vegetable mixture.
**5.** Stir almonds thoroughly in saffron solution and top eggplant fillings with this mixture.
**6.** Arrange tomatoes on top of eggplants; pour remaining tomato juice over them; cover and bake at 350° F. for 30-40 minutes.

Prepared by Fahimeh Z.

# Dolmeh Badenjan
(stuffed eggplant)

*4 servings*

Ingredients:
*4 medium eggplants*
*1 large onion, finely chopped*
*½ cup olive oil*
*1 lb ground beef or lamb*
*1 bunch scallions or green onions, chopped*
*1 cup parsley, chopped*
*1 tsp. dried tarragon*
*2 hard-boiled eggs, chopped*
*2 cups tomato juice*
*1 cup yogurt*
Spices:
*1 tsp salt*
*¼ tsp black pepper*
*1 tsp turmeric*

**DIRECTIONS FOR COOKING**

**1.** Peel eggplants. Cut off tops just below the stem; save tops. Scoop out pulp with spoon or apple corer. Set aside.
**2.** Sauté onion in ¼ cup of the olive oil.
**3.** Add the meat and brown.
**4.** Stir in scallions and parsley and keep stirring for a few minutes more.
**5.** Mix in tarragon, eggs, and spices and remove from heat.
**6.** Stuff each eggplant loosely with meat mixture. Replace tops and secure with toothpicks.
**7.** Brown eggplants on all sides in skillet in remaining olive oil. Add more oil while browning if necessary. Handle gently to prevent breakage.
**8.** Arrange eggplants in a baking dish.
**9.** Pour the tomato juice over the eggplants. Cover and bake in 350° oven for 30 minutes.
To serve, transfer eggplants to serving dish with a wide spatula. Add yogurt to tomato juice in pan. Mix well and pour over eggplants.

# Dolmeh Kalam
(stuffed cabbage leaves)

*4 to 5 servings*

Ingredients:
*¼ cup yellow split peas*
*¾ cup rice*
*1 medium onion, finely chopped*
*2 Tbs. butter*
*1 lb ground beef or lamb*
*½ cup parsley, chopped*
*1 head cabbage*
*¼ cup sugar*
*1/3 cup vinegar*
Spices:
*1 tsp salt*
*¼ tsp pepper*
*½ tsp cinnamon*

**DIRECTIONS FOR COOKING**

**1.** Cook split peas in 2 cups boiling water until tender, about 25 minutes. Drain and set aside.
**2.** Cook rice in lightly salted boiling water about 15 minutes. Drain and set aside.
**3.** Sauté onion in butter. Remove onions from butter and set skillet aside.
**4.** In a large bowl, mix meat, split peas, rice, onion, parsley, and spices. Mix well.
**5.** Separate cabbage leaves from stem. Boil them gently in a large pot of lightly salted water for about 3 minutes. Drain gently, taking care not to break the leaves. Spread out flat.
**6.** Take 1 leaf at a time in hand; put about 1½ Tbs. stuffing mixture on it. Fold over the edges of each leaf and roll up starting from stem end.
**7.** Line bottom of baking dish with unused leaves. Arrange stuffed leaves, seam side down, in dish.
**8.** Mix 1 cup water, sugar, and vinegar in buttered skillet (used to sauté onions). Pour over leaves. Bake, covered, in 350° oven for 30 minutes. (Can also be cooked over low heat on the stove for 30 minutes.)

# Ermani Bademjan

(tomatoes stuffed with meat, Jolfa style)

*6 servings*

**Ingredients:**
*1 lb ground beef or lamb*
*1 onion, grated*
*1 bunch parsley, chopped*
*6 large tomatoes*
**Spices:**
*1 tsp salt*
*½ tsp black pepper*
*1 tsp Azerbaijan-style seasoning (see explanation in "Miscellaneous" section)*

### DIRECTIONS FOR COOKING

**1.** Mix together meat and onions and lightly brown in a skillet. Add salt, pepper, and ½ cup water and simmer over medium heat for 5 minutes.
**2.** Stir in parsley and Azerbaijan-style seasoning; cover and set aside.
**3.** Wash tomatoes and cut off tops. Remove the seeds and soft membranes, taking care not to break through the skins.
**4.** Stuff each tomato with meat mixture. Arrange in a large, flat-bottomed covered saucepan.
**5.** Pour in 1 cup water; cover and simmer over low heat for 20 minutes. Remove tomatoes from sauce carefully with a spatula or large spoon and arrange on a platter to serve. Serve with rice.

# Dolmeh-ye Havij

(carrots stuffed with meat and onions, Azerbaijan style)

*8 servings*

**Ingredients:**
*8 large, plump carrots*
*2 Tbs. butter*
*½ lb ground beef or lamb*
*1 medium onion, grated*
*2 Tbs. sugar*
*¼ cup lemon juice*
**Spices:**
*½ tsp salt*
*cinnamon*

### DIRECTIONS FOR COOKING

**1.** Peel carrots. With a sharp knife, hollow out part of each carrot lengthwise, taking care not to break them. Sauté lightly in butter.
**2.** Mix together meat, onion, and salt; stuff carrots with this mixture.
**3.** Arrange stuffed carrots in a flat casserole dish; add 1 cup water; cover and bake at 350º F. for 30 minutes.
**4.** Dissolve sugar in ¼ cup hot water; add lemon juice, and pour about 1 Tbs. evenly over each stuffed carrot. Cover and bake for an additional 5 minutes.
**5.** Sprinkle with cinnamon before serving.

## Dolmeh-ye Felfel-e Sabz
(bell peppers stuffed with meat and rice)

*8 servings*

### Ingredients:
*½ lb ground beef or lamb*
*1 bunch scallions, chopped*
*1 bunch parsley, chopped*
*½ cup rice*
*½ cup lentils*
*2 Tbs. fresh coriander, chopped*
*2 Tbs. tomato paste*
*8 bell peppers*
*1½ cup tomato juice*
### Spices:
*1 tsp salt*
*½ tsp turmeric*
*½ tsp cinnamon*
*¼ tsp black pepper*

### DIRECTIONS FOR COOKING

**1.** Preheat oven to 350° F.
**2.** Brown meat in its own fat. Mix in scallions and parsley and brown for 5 minutes; set aside.
**3.** Boil rice and lentils in 3 cups water for 20 minutes. Drain and add to meat mixture.
**4.** Mix in ½ tsp of the salt, along with the cinnamon, pepper, coriander, and tomato paste.
**5.** Rinse bell peppers and cut off tops (save); remove seeds and pulp and fill each with the meat mixture. Replace tops of bell peppers and secure with toothpicks.
**6.** Arrange peppers in a deep casserole dish. Mix remaining salt and pepper and tomato juice and pour over peppers in casserole dish. Cover and bake for 45 minutes.

## Dolmeh-ye Gowjeh Farangi
(tomato stuffed with ground meat and yellow split peas)

*8 servings*

### Ingredients:
*1 lb ground beef or lamb*
*½ cup yellow split peas*
*8 large tomatoes*
*¼ cup butter*
### Spices:
*½ tsp cinnamon*
*1 tsp salt*
*½ tsp black pepper*

### DIRECTIONS FOR COOKING

**1.** Preheat oven to 350° F.
**2.** Sprinkle meat with spices and brown in a skillet in its own fat.
**3.** Simmer split peas in 2 cups water for 30 minutes. Drain.
**4.** Mix split peas in with meat and set aside.
**5.** Rinse tomatoes and pat dry; cut off tops; hollow out seeds and soft pulp, taking care not to perforate the skins.
**6.** Add tomato pulp to the meat mixture, cover and simmer over low heat for 5 minutes. Then, remove from heat and mash.
**7.** Fill each tomato with meat mixture.
**8.** Melt butter in a saucepan and pour into a casserole dish. Arrange tomatoes in the dish, cover and bake for 30 minutes.

From left, clockwise: Green and yellow bell peppers ; stuffed tomato.
Prepared by Janet N.

## Lavangi-ye Badenjan
### (stuffed eggplants, Astara style)

*5 to 6 servings*

Ingredients:
*3 eggplants*
*2 cups chopped walnuts*
*½ cup olive oil*
*1 large onion, grated*
*¼ cup pomegranate concentrate*
*¼ cup lime juice*
*1 Tbs chopped fresh mint*
*¼ cup chopped coriander*
*2 Tbs chopped fresh or dried tarragon*
*¼ cup melted butter*
**Spices:**
*3 tsp salt*
*¼ tsp black pepper*
*1 tsp turmeric*

### DIRECTIONS FOR COOKING

**1.** Wash eggplants, make a slit lengthwise in each, and boil in a large pot with 6 cups of water and 2 tsp salt for ten minutes. Drain in a calendar, and using a plate, squeeze out the excess water. Set aside to cool.
**2.** Lightly brown walnuts in olive oil over medium heat.
**3.** Add onion and sauté lightly. Add pomegranate concentrate, lime juice, mint, coriander, tarragon, and spices and simmer for three to five minutes. Remove from heat.
**4.** Stuff eggplants with the prepared ingredients and brown in melted butter.
**5.** Brush a baking dish with melted butter (use additional butter, if necessary) and bake in a 350° oven for 45 minutes.

Serve with bread or plain rice.

## Dolmeh-ye Sibzamini
### (potatoes stuffed with meat and parsley)

*6 servings*

Ingredients:
*¼ lb ground beef or lamb*
*1 large onion, chopped*
*1 Tbs. butter*
*3 Tbs. tomato paste*
*½ bunch parsley, chopped*
*2 hard-boiled eggs, chopped*
*6 large potatoes*
**Spices:**
*1 tsp salt*
*¼ tsp pepper*

### DIRECTIONS FOR COOKING

**1.** Mix together meat, onion, and ½ tsp of the salt, and the pepper and brown in butter.
**2.** Dissolve tomato paste in ¼ cup water, add to meat mixture; simmer 10 minutes.
**3.** Add parsley and eggs; mix well and set aside.
**4.** Wash potatoes, then cut a slice off the top and hollow out with a spoon or apple corer without breaking the skins, leaving a little less than ½" thickness.
**5.** Fill each potato with meat mixture; arrange in a casserole dish.
**6.** Mix together remaining salt and 1 cup water and pour along the sides of the potatoes in the casserole dish. Cover and bake in a moderate, 350° F., oven for 1 hour. Occasionally check to see if water has evaporated; add additional water if necessary.

# Dolmeh Kadu
## (stuffed zucchini)

*8 servings*

### Ingredients:
*½ lb ground beef or lamb*
*1 small onion, grated*
*4 medium zucchinis*
*¼ cup plain yogurt*
*1 Tbs. butter*
### Spices:
*1 tsp salt*
*¼ tsp black pepper*
*1 tsp turmeric*

### DIRECTIONS FOR COOKING

**1.** Preheat oven to 350° F.
**2.** Mix together meat, onion, ½ tsp of the salt and all remaining spices and brown in meat's own fat for 10 minutes over medium heat.
**3.** Wash and halve zucchini lengthwise; scoop out some of the pulp leaving ¼" of zucchini and skin.
**4.** Fill each zucchini with meat mixture and arrange in a casserole dish.
**5.** Spread 1 Tbs. of the yogurt on each filled zucchini.
**6.** Melt butter in saucepan; add ¼ cup water and remaining salt. Pour around *dolmeh;* cover and bake for 30 minutes.

# Lavash Dolmasi
## (stuffed flat bread, Azerbaijan style)

*10-12 pieces*

### Ingredients:
*1 lb ground beef or lamb*
*1 large onion, grated*
*1 bunch parsley, chopped*
*2 loaves* lavash* *bread, or 10-12 flour tortillas*
*½ cup olive oil*
*sprigs of fresh mint*
### Spices:
*2 tsp Azerbaijan-style seasoning (see recipe in "Miscellaneous" section)*
*1 tsp salt*
*1 tsp turmeric*
*½ tsp saffron, dissolved in 2 Tbs. hot water*

### DIRECTIONS FOR COOKING

**1.** Mix together meat, onion, spices, and parsley and brown in a skillet. Divide into 10 to 12 portions; set aside.
**2.** Cut *lavash* bread in 10-inch squares or trim tortillas to form squares.
**3.** Sprinkle both sides of each piece of bread with warm water; place 1 portion of meat mixture on each piece and fold the four corners of the bread neatly over the mixture, making sure to cover all the stuffing.
**4.** Brown stuffed bread in olive oil, seam side down first; turn over and brown on the second side.
**5.** Arrange stuffed bread on a platter; decorate with mint. Serve along with any of the variety of Azerbaijan-style pickles or relishes (see *Torshi*), or with yogurt.

*See bread section.

# Pirashki I

(fried pie stuffed with meat, coriander, and *zereshk*, Azerbaijan style)

*10 to 12 servings*

**Ingredients:**
*½ tsp. baking powder*
*2 cups flour*
*½ cup milk*
*¾ cup olive oil*
*½ lb ground beef or lamb*
*1 cup chopped coriander*
*4 Tbs. fresh mint, chopped*
*¼ cup zereshk*
*a few sprigs parsley*

**Spices:**
*1 tsp salt*
*½ tsp black pepper*
*½ tsp turmeric*

### DIRECTIONS FOR COOKING

**1.** Mix together baking powder, flour, milk, ½ tsp of the salt, and 1 Tbs. of the olive oil; knead for a few minutes; cover and set aside in a warm spot to rise for about 1 hour.

**2.** Place meat, coriander, *zereshk*, and remaining salt and spices in a skillet and brown without oil. Set aside.

**3.** Take a piece of dough the size of a small orange and spread out very thin with your hand or a rolling pin. Use additional flour as needed to facilitate flattening the dough.

**4.** Place 2 Tbs. of the meat mixture in the center of the flattened dough; wrap and secure edges of dough. Repeat Steps 3 and 4 until all the dough and meat mixtures are used up.

**5.** Heat remaining olive oil in a skillet over medium-low heat and brown both sides of each *pirashki*.

**6.** Arrange the *pirashki* pies on a platter and garnish with parsley. Serve with yogurt or plain.

Prepared by Maryam J.

# Pirashki II
### (fried meat pies, Azerbaijan style)

*10 to 15 servings*

## Ingredients:
*1 tsp baking powder*
*¾ cup plain yogurt*
*1 egg*
*1 Tbs. powdered sugar*
*3 cups flour*
*4 cups olive oil*
*1 medium onion, chopped*
*2 Tbs. butter*
*½ lb ground beef or lamb*
*1 Tbs. tomato paste*
*¼ cup parsley, chopped*
## Spices:
*1½ tsp salt*
*½ tsp black pepper*

## DIRECTIONS FOR COOKING

**1.** Mix together ½ tsp of the salt, baking powder, yogurt, egg, and sugar in a mixing bowl.

**2.** Mix in flour and 2 Tbs. of the olive oil to this mixture; knead and let rise in a warm place for 2 hours.

**3.** Sauté onions in butter.

**4.** Add ground meat, spices, and tomato paste, stir and cook for 10 minutes over medium heat.

**5.** Remove from heat; add parsley and mix well.

**6.** Take pieces of dough as large as a small apple and flatten into round patties the size of the palm of your hand and about 1/8" thick. Use extra flour if necessary to help shape the patties.

**7.** Put 2 Tbs. of the meat mixture on the dough patties; fold over the edges to form a semi-circle and press together the edges to keep the mixture from pouring out when frying.

**8.** Continue Steps 6 and 7 until all the dough and meat mixtures are used up.

**9.** Heat remaining olive oil in a skillet and fry *pirashki,* half covered in oil, until golden brown. Remove from oil and drain on paper towels.

**10.** Place on a platter and decorate with parsley.

# Dolmeh-ye Nan-e Lavash
(flat bread stuffed with ground meat)

*16 pieces*

**Ingredients:**
*1 lb ground beef or lamb*
*1 onion, finely chopped*
*3 Tbs. flour*
*¼ cup tomato paste*
*16 pieces of lavash flat bread\* (for explanation, see previous recipe), 10" x 10"*
*½ cup butter*

**Spices:**
*1 tsp salt*
*½ tsp black pepper*
*½ tsp saffron, dissolved in 2 Tbs. hot water*

**DIRECTIONS FOR COOKING**

**1.** Sprinkle meat with salt and pepper and brown along with onion.

**2.** Dissolve flour in ¼ cup cold water and mix well along with tomato paste into meat and onion mixture. Simmer over medium heat for 5 to 10 minutes or until most of the water has evaporated.

**3.** Stir saffron solution into meat mixture and remove from heat.

**4.** Take one piece of bread at a time and place about 2 Tbs. of meat mixture on it; wrap the bread securely around the meat mixture and fry in butter with the seam side down. Turn carefully and fry the other side and transfer to a serving dish.

\*Wheat or flour tortillas can be substituted.

# Kukeh-ye Qarch
(mushroom pie with green vegetables, Khuzestan style)

*3 to 4 servings*

**Ingredients:**
*1 tsp active dry yeast*
*3 cups flour*
*1 lb mushrooms, sliced*
*½ cup butter*
*½ cup leeks, chopped*
*1 bunch parsley, chopped*
*1 bunch coriander, chopped*
*½ lb spinach, chopped*
*1 Tbs. dried fenugreek leaves*

**Spices:**
*1½ tsp salt*
*½ tsp black pepper*

**DIRECTIONS FOR COOKING**

**1.** Dissolve yeast in 1 cup warm water. Thoroughly stir in ½ tsp of the salt and 2½ cups of the flour. Kneed dough for about 10 minutes.

**2.** Sauté mushrooms in half of the butter over medium heat.

**3.** Add leeks, parsley, coriander, spinach, and fenugreek and stir for 2 to 3 minutes.

**4.** Add remaining salt and pepper along with ½ cup water; cover and simmer for 30 minutes or until water is almost completely absorbed.

**5.** Divide dough into 8 to 10 parts and roll out each piece on a flat surface (sprinkled with flour to prevent sticking) into a round loaf approximately 1/8" thick.

**6.** Place 2 to 3 Tbs. of mushroom and vegetable mixture in the middle of the dough. Fold over dough, press edges together to secure in a semicircle.

**7.** Brush a flat-bottomed baking dish with some of the remaining butter; arrange the pies on this dish; brush all pieces thoroughly with remaining butter and bake in 350° F. oven for 15 to 20 minutes or until dough turns golden brown.

## Kufteh Naneh
("Nanny's" meatballs)

*10 to 12 servings*

Ingredients:
6 slices white bread
¼ cup milk
2 lb ground beef or veal
3 eggs
2 medium onions, grated
2 clove garlic, crushed
1 cup flour
1 cup olive oil
4 onions, minced
1 Tbs. tomato paste
1 dried lime
8 small potatoes
1½ cups cream
¼ cup chopped parsley

Spices:
1 Tbs. salt
2 tsp turmeric
½ tsp saffron
½ tsp black pepper

### DIRECTIONS FOR COOKING

**1.** Soak bread in milk for 1 hour, then mash well.
**2.** Mix mashed bread, meat, eggs, grated onions, garlic, 2 tsp of the salt, and turmeric; and divide into 12 parts, then roll into meatballs.
**3.** Roll meatballs in flour and brown on all sides in ¾ cup of the olive oil; remove from oil and set aside.
**4.** Sauté onions in the remaining oil.
**5.** In a large pot, bring to a boil the onions, tomato paste, dried lime, 3 cups water, and remaining spices.
**6.** Reduce heat to medium-low and add meatballs to the soup; simmer for 30 to 40 minutes, stirring occasionally to prevent meatballs from sticking to the pot.
**7.** Boil the whole potatoes in a separate pot in 3 cups water for 30 to 40 minutes or until tender. Remove from water and peel.
**8.** Remove meatballs from sauce and arrange on a serving platter; place potatoes around them.
**9.** Pour the sauce over the meatballs and potatoes, top with cream, and garnish with chopped parsley.

## Kabab Moshti
(carrot meatball "stew")

*5 to 6 servings*

Ingredients:
1 lb meat, finely ground
6 carrots, finely grated
½ cup roasted chickpea flour
¼ cup butter or olive oil
½ cup granulated or brown sugar
Spices:
2 tsp salt
2 tsp turmeric

### DIRECTIONS FOR COOKING

**1.** In a mixing bowl, combine meat, carrots, chickpea flour, and 1 tsp salt and turmeric each. Shape into oblong, oval-shaped meatballs the size of an egg.
**2.** Melt butter or pour olive oil in a frying pan and brown meatballs on both sides.
**3.** Put 2 cups water in a pot along with sugar and remaining spices and bring to a boil.
**4.** Add meatballs; reduce heat and simmer over low heat for 20 minutes

Serve as a main dish with flat bread or over plain rice.

# Kufteh Tabrizi I
(meatballs, Tabriz style)

*6 servings*

**Ingredients:**
*½ cup rice*
*1 cup yellow split peas*
*1 lb ground beef or lamb*
*1 medium onion, grated*
*1 egg, slightly beaten*
*2 Tbs. dried mint*
*6 prunes*
*2 hardboiled eggs, peeled*
*¼ cup raisins*
*¼ cup walnuts*
**Spices:**
*1 tsp cinnamon*
*1 tsp salt*
*½ tsp black pepper*

## DIRECTIONS FOR COOKING

**1.** Cover rice with warm, slightly salted water and soak for 20 minutes.

**2.** Cook yellow split peas in boiling, slightly salted water for 20 to 30 minutes. Drain and set aside.

**3.** Put meat in a large bowl. Drain rice and add to meat along with onion, beaten egg, mint, and spices. Mix well and divide into two equal portions.*

**4.** Form two large meatballs, placing 3 prunes,1 hardboiled egg, half the raisins and half the walnuts in the center of each.

**5.** Place meatballs in a large, covered, oven-proof pot; add 1 cup water; bake in a moderate, 350° oven for 1 hour.

*Alternatively, meatballs can be made smaller, individual servings the size of a large apple, for instance, in which case, cut the hard-boiled eggs in thirds, and place a piece of egg, one prune, a portion of raisins and walnuts in the center of each meatball.

Prepared by Maryam J.

# Kufteh Tabrizi II
(meatball wrapped around a stuffed chicken, Tabriz style)

*6 to 8 servings*

**Ingredients:**
*1 cup yellow split peas*
*1 lb ground beef or lamb*
*1 large onion, grated*
*1 Tbs. tomato paste*
*1 Tbs. rice*
*1/3 cup leeks, finely chopped*
*2 Tb. dried sweet fennel*
*1 egg, beaten*
*2 medium onions, sliced*
*½ cup olive oil*
*10 pitted prunes*
*5 pitted dates*
*¼ cup walnuts, chopped*
*¼ cup* zereshk
*1 Cornish hen*
*1 hardboiled egg*
*1 cup tomato sauce*
*2 tomatoes, quartered*

**Spices:**
*½ tsp turmeric*
*1 tsp Azerbaijan-style seasoning (see recipe in "Miscellaneous" section)*
*2 tsp salt*
*½ tsp saffron*

## DIRECTIONS FOR COOKING

**1.** Simmer split peas in 1 cup water for 25 minutes or until tender; mash well.
**2.** Knead meat, onion, tomato paste, 2 Tbs. water, and split peas well in a mixing bowl for 5 minutes.
**3.** Boil rice in ½ cup water and turmeric for 10 minutes; drain.
**4.** Add rice, leeks, fennel, beaten egg, and remaining spices to meat and mix well; set aside.
**5.** Sauté sliced onions in half of the olive oil; remove from heat.
**6.** Mix in prunes, dates, walnuts, and *zereshk* to onions; divide in half.
**7.** Simmer Cornish hen in 2 cups water and saffron in a pot for 1 hour, until well cooked, but not falling apart.
**8.** Remove Cornish hen from broth (set broth aside) and stuff cavity with boiled egg and half of onion-fruit-nut mixture.
**9.** Brush sides of a large mixing bowl with some of the olive oil; press half the meat mixture evenly around the bottom and sides of the bowl about 1 inch thick. Place whole Cornish hen in this mixture and evenly spread onion-fruit-nut mixture around it. Spread remaining meat mixture evenly around top and sides of Cornish hen, connecting it with the meat mixture in the bowl to form a large round meatball.
**10.** Gently turn meatball over into a skilled greased with the remaining olive oil; brown top of meatball lightly in oil.
**11.** Add tomato sauce to broth. Transfer meatball gently to a deep saucepan or Dutch oven. Pour broth mixture over top. Place tomatoes on top. Place lid on pot, slightly open and simmer meatball for 40 minutes.

To serve: Transfer meatball gently to a platter, using large spatulas. Pour sauce from pot over the top.

# Kufteh Kari
(curried meatballs)

*10-12 servings*

## Ingredients:
*1 cup rice*
*1 lb ground beef or lamb*
*¼ cup chopped parsley*
*¼ cup leeks, chopped*
*2 Tbs. dried dill weed*
*1 small onion, grated*
*¼ cup roasted chickpea flour*
*2 eggs*
*1 large onion, sliced*
*2 Tbs. butter*
*2 Tbs. lemon juice*

## Spices:
*2 tsp salt*
*½ tsp black pepper*
*3 tsp curry powder*

## DIRECTIONS FOR COOKING

**1.** Bring rice, ½ tsp. of the salt, and 2 cups water to a boil in a medium-size pot; reduce heat and simmer over low heat for 5 to 10 minutes or until all water is absorbed by rice, stirring occasionally to prevent sticking; set aside..
**2.** Mix together in a large mixing bowl meat, parsley, leeks, dill weed, ½ tsp of the salt, pepper, 2 tsp of the curry powder, chickpea flour, and eggs.
**3.** Add rice to this mixture and stir together well. Form into 10 to 12 meatballs.
**4.** Sauté onions in butter.
**5.** Transfer sautéed onions to a large saucepan; add remaining spices, 2 cups water, and lemon juice.
**6.** Arrange meatballs in the sauce; cover and simmer over low heat for 45 minutes.

Prepared by Nahid N.

## Kufteh-ye Shevid-o Baqala

(dill weed and lima or fava bean meatballs)

*4 to 6 servings*

Ingredients:
*¾ cup rice*
*1 lb fresh or frozen fava beans (or lima beans)*
*1 lb ground beef or lamb*
*1 medium onion, grated*
*½ cup dried dill weed*
*2 eggs, slightly beaten*
*1 Tbs. lemon juice*
**Spices:**
*1½ tsp salt*
*½ tsp black pepper*
*1 tsp turmeric*

### DIRECTIONS FOR COOKING

**1.** Soak the rice in slightly salted water for 1 hour; drain and set aside.

**2.** Cook the beans in boiling salted water until tender, about 10 minutes, or cook frozen beans according to package instructions. Drain and set aside.

**3.** Put the meat in a large bowl. Add two-thirds of the rice along with the beans, 7 Tbs. of the dill weed, the eggs, 1 tsp of the salt, the pepper, and ½ tsp of the turmeric; mix well. Divide this mixture to form meatballs the size of large apples.

**4.** Mix together a sauce of the remaining rice, dill weed, turmeric, and salt along with the lemon juice and 3 cups water.

**5.** Place meatballs in a pot along with the sauce mixture and simmer over low heat for 1 hour.

## Kufteh Somaq

(sumac and rice meatballs)

*8 servings*

Ingredients:
*1 cup yellow split peas*
*½ cup rice*
*1 onion, chopped*
*1 Tbs. butter*
*1½ lb lean ground lamb or beef*
*1 cup chopped leeks*
*1 cup chopped parsley*
*1 cup chopped coriander*
*½ cup chopped tarragon*
*2 eggs*
**Spices:**
*1½ tsp salt*
*¼ cup sumac*
*½ tsp black pepper*
*1 tsp powdered fennel seeds*
*1 tsp turmeric*
*1 tsp marjoram*

### DIRCTIONS FOR COOKING

**1.** Cook yellow split peas and rice in 3 cups water with ½ tsp of the salt for 10 minutes. Drain and set aside.

**2.** Sauté onion in butter. Divide in half and set aside.

**3.** Mix half of the onion and half the sumac (2 Tbs.) with all the ingredients, knead well. Divide into 8 parts and form each into a ball.

**4.** In a large saucepan bring 4 cups water and remaining sumac and remaining onion to a boil. Then gently place the meatballs in the boiling sauce and simmer for 45 minutes.

# Kufteh Berenji
(meatballs with rice, split peas, and herbs)

*5 to 6 servings*

## Ingredients:
*1 large onion, chopped*
*2 Tbs. butter*
*½ cup rice*
*½ cup yellow split peas*
*1 lb ground beef or lamb*
*½ cup chopped leeks*
*½ cup chopped parsley*
*½ cup chopped coriander*
*1 egg*
*½ cup raisins*

## Spices:
*1 tsp salt*
*1 tsp turmeric*
*1 tsp fenugreek*
*½ tsp black pepper*

### DIRECTIONS FOR COOKING

**1.** Sauté onion in butter.
**2.** Place rice and split peas with 1 cup water in a small pot, bring to a boil, remove from heat, and set aside, covered, for 10 minutes.

**3.** In a large saucepan, place half of the sautéed onion and 3 cups water. Bring to a boil, turn heat to medium-low, and keep on stove.
**4.** Mix together meat, remaining onion, rice-split pea mixture, leeks, parsley, coriander, egg, and spices. Knead for a few minutes, then divide the mixture into five or six portions.
**5.** Make meatballs of each portion with a few raisins in the middle, and drop into the boiling water with onions.
**6.** Turn the heat down to low and simmer for 20 to 30 minutes. The meatballs can also be placed on a baking dish with the water-onion mixture and baked in a 350° oven for the same amount of time.
Serve with yogurt or *torshi*, Persian pickled vegetables.

Prepared by Fahimeh Z.

# Dastpich
(meat roll stuffed with eggs, parsley, walnuts, and *zereshk*)

*4 to 5 servings*

### Ingredients:
*1 medium onion, grated*
*1 lb ground beef or lamb*
*3 hard-boiled eggs, chopped*
*¼ cup chopped walnuts*
*1 Tbs. parsley, chopped*
*1 Tbs.* zereshk
*3 Tbs. olive oil*
*1 small onion, sliced*
*1 Tbs. butter*
*1½ cups tomato sauce*
*several sprigs parsley*
### Spices:
*1½  tsp salt*
*¾ tsp black pepper*

Prepared by Afsaneh. O.

### DIRECTIONS FOR COOKING

**1.** Mix together grated onion, meat, ½ tsp of the salt, and ¼ tsp of the pepper.

**2.** Place a sheet of wax paper on a flat surface and spread the meat mixture out on the paper into an oblong shape, about 8 inches long and 1/3 inch thick.

**3.** Mix together eggs, walnuts, parsley, *zereshk*, ½ tsp of the salt and ¼ tsp of the pepper, and spread out evenly on top of the meat.  Carefully roll the meat around the mixture.

**4.** Heat oil in a non-stick skillet and brown rolled meat on all sides, seam side down first; turn gently taking care not to break the *dastpich*.

**5.** Sauté sliced onion in butter.

**6.** Mix together sautéed onion, tomato sauce, and remaining ½ tsp salt and ¼ tsp pepper; pour over the rolled meat mixture in the skillet, cover, and simmer for 30 minutes.

**7.** To serve, gently transfer *dastpich* from the skillet to a platter; slice about 1 inch thick and decorate with parsley and cooked vegetables, such as carrots, potatoes, and/or green beans.

Note: In Azerbaijan, *dastpich* is made in individual-size servings instead of a large dish that is sliced.  However, using this recipe, sliced pieces of *dastpich* can be used in sandwiches or served with plain rice and vegetables.

# Qeymerizeh
(chickpea meatballs)

*5 to 6 servings*

**Ingredients:**
*1 lb ground beef or lamb*
*½ cup roasted chickpea flour*
*2 onions, finely chopped*
*2 large tomatoes, quartered*
*2 dried limes*
**Spices:**
*1½ tsp salt*
*½ tsp black pepper*
*1 tsp turmeric*

### DIRECTIONS FOR COOKING

**1.** Mix together thoroughly meat, chickpea flour, 1 tsp of the salt, pepper, ½ tsp of the turmeric, and onions; set aside.
**2.** Bring 5 cups water to a boil. Add remaining ingredients.
**3.** Make walnut-size meatballs out of the meat mixture and drop into boiling soup.
**4.** Reduce heat; let simmer for 20-30 minutes.

Serve with flat bread and *sabzikhordan* (see recipe in the salad section).

# Sargonjeshki
(meatball soup)

*5 to 6 servings*

**Ingredients:**
*1 dried lime*
*1 medium onion, quartered*
*1 lb ground beef or lamb*
*2 medium potatoes, peeled and sliced*
*2 tomatoes, quartered*
*2 Tbs. tomato paste*
**Spices:**
*1 ½ tsp salt*
*½ tsp black pepper*
*1 tsp turmeric*

### DIRECTIONS FOR COOKING

**1.** Bring 3 cups water to a boil and add dried lime, spices, and onion.
**2.** Make balls the size of hazel nuts out of the meat and drop into the boiling water. Reduce heat to medium.
**3.** Add potatoes and tomatoes and simmer for 15 minutes more.
**4.** Stir in tomato paste and simmer for another 15 minutes.

Serve with flat bread and *sabzikhordan* (see recipe in the salad section).

# Salads and Accompaniments
## *(Burani, Morabba and Torshi)*

**D**espite the fact that in more recent years, tossed salads of various kinds have become common in Iran, especially in the larger cities, salads in the American sense are not among the traditional Iranian foods. However, a number of the salads presented here are traditional and can be served with most meals.

Among the modern salads adopted from or inspired by Western cuisines, perhaps none has become as popular, especially in large cities, as *Salad Oliviyeh,* a combination of potato salad, chicken salad, and sometimes egg salad. Most versions of this salad are basically similar; however, two versions are described in this section.

*Burani* refers to a category of foods that include yogurt and are served either hot or cold. Some *burani* dishes are best served as salads.

*Torshi* refers to traditional Iranian pickles and relishes, many of which are found in this chapter. This chapter also includes a number of regional pickles and relishes, some prepared with vinegar and some with salt water. *Khiyar shur,* or saltwater pickles, is particularly popular in Iran and is used most often in sandwiches. Most *torshi* pickles and relishes are best when they have been stored for about six months.

Many varieties of *morabba* (preserves) are found throughout Iran, and differ according to the types of fruits available in particular regions. Some of the most common are found in this chapter.

Vegetable Bazaar, Shemiran, Iran.
Photo by Susan Sprachman.

# Mast
(yogurt)

Yogurt is used in many Persian dishes and is often served as a side dish for lunch and/or dinner. Yogurt can be made very easily and economically at home.

*about 9 cups*

**Ingredients:**
*½ gallon whole milk*
*1 cup plain yogurt*

### DIRECTIONS FOR PREPARATION

**1.** Bring milk just to a boil and remove immediately from heat; let cool until lukewarm.
**2.** Mix yogurt with one cup of the milk in a separate bowl; add to remaining milk and mix well.
**3.** Pour into clean, covered glass or ceramic containers. (Large pickle jars make ideal containers.)
**4.** Cover and place in a Styrofoam or other ice chest (without ice!) or cooler and cover to keep an even temperature for about 8 hours. (If you prefer a more tart yogurt, increase this time up to 24 hours.) Refrigerate for several hours before serving.

NOTE: Keep a cup of this yogurt to make your next batch. Yogurt can be re-used this way several times before a fresh yogurt starter is needed. To obtain a very thick, creamy, tasty yogurt, experiment with various combinations of brands of milk and yogurt.

# Mast-e Kiseh'i
(condensed yogurt)

*about 1 cup*

**Ingredients:**
*2 cups yogurt*
**Spices:**
*¼ tsp salt (optional)*

### DIRECTIONS FOR PREPARATION

**1.** Mix salt with yogurt (if salt is desired).
**2.** Pour yogurt into a bag made of thin white cotton fabric. Tie the open end with a string and suspend over a bowl where it can drip for several hours. (Save the liquid in the bowl for *qaraqarut*, which follows this recipe.)

NOTE: The end result will be a thick, creamy paste (the thickness depends on how long the yogurt is left to drip), which can be used as a spread by itself or mixed with mint and a touch of salt and pepper.

Traditionally, thickened yogurt was especially important for travelers since it would take up less space. Today it is considered a special treat.

*Mast-e kiseh'i* makes an excellent substitute for whey (*kashk*), sour cream, or even cream cheese, depending on the thickness.

## Mast-o Khiyar
### (yogurt and cucumbers)

*4 servings*

**Ingredients:**
*2 cups plain yogurt*
*2 cucumbers, chopped or sliced*
*¼ cup chopped walnuts*
*¼ cup raisins*
*1 Tbs. dried mint*
*1 Tbs. grated onion (optional)*
**Spices:**
*1 tsp salt*
*¼ tsp black pepper*

#### DIRECTIONS FOR PREPARATION

**1.** Place yogurt in a bowl; beat with a spoon until smooth.
**2.** Add remaining ingredients and fold together. Serve cold.

NOTE: A favorite with most Iranians, this accompaniment goes well with almost any other dish. It is generally considered a seasonal salad, as cucumbers were not, in the past, available year round; but, since cucumbers are now available here virtually in all seasons, it can be enjoyed all year.

Prepared by Shiva J., age 12.

## Mast-o Labu
### (yogurt and beets)

*4 servings*

**Ingredients:**
*2 cups cooked beets, sliced*
*2 cups plain yogurt*

#### DIRECTIONS FOR PREPARATION

In a serving bowl, gently fold beets into yogurt.

NOTE: This accompaniment is generally considered a winter dish, as beets are most often available then. They are sold hot by street vendors in Iran. This dish is also known as *burani-ye choghondar*.

## Mast-o Musir
### (yogurt and shallots)

*4 servings*

**Ingredients:**
*5 shallots*
*2 cups plain yogurt*
**Spices:**
*½ tsp salt*
*¼ tsp black pepper*

#### DIRECTIONS FOR PREPARATION

**1.** Peel shallots. Cut off stems and thinly slice.
**2.** Soak in 2 cups cool water for a day or two, changing the water several times.
**3.** Drain. Add spices to yogurt and fold in shallots. Refrigerate one day before serving.

## Mast-o Tut Farangi
### (yogurt with strawberries)

*3 to 4 servings*

Ingredients:
*1 lb fresh ripe strawberries*
*2 Tbs. powdered sugar*
*1½ cup plain yogurt*

#### DIRECTIONS FOR PREPARATION

**1.** Wash strawberries and remove stems. Pat dry and place in a serving bowl. (If strawberries are very large, they can be cut in half.) Sprinkle with powdered sugar.
**2.** Stir yogurt vigorously with a spoon; pour over strawberries. Refrigerate for 30 minutes before serving.

## Salad-e Karafs-o Gerdu
### (salad with celery and walnuts)

*4 to 5 servings*

Ingredients:
*2 cups celery hearts, finely chopped*
*½ cup white wine vinegar*
*¼ cup olive oil*
*1 cup chopped walnuts*
*1 Tbs. dried dill weed*
Spices:
*½ tsp salt*
*¼ tsp black pepper*

#### DIRECTIONS FOR PREPARATION

**1.** Soak celery in vinegar and seasonings for several hours at room temperature in a glass or china bowl.
**2.** Mix in remaining ingredients and refrigerate for 1 hour.

## Salad-e Shirazi
### (cucumber and tomato salad)

*5 to 6 servings*

Ingredients:
*3 large tomatoes, chopped*
*3 medium cucumbers, chopped*
*1 medium red onion, chopped*
*¾ cup white wine vinegar or lemon juice*
Spices:
*1 tsp salt*
*½ tsp black pepper*

#### DIRECTIONS FOR PREPARATION

Mix together all ingredients in a glass or ceramic bowl; refrigerate for several hours before serving.

NOTE: This salad is a good accompaniment to most Persian dishes; in fact, to many Iranians the term "salad" refers to this dish alone.

Prepared by Parsa J., age 14.

# Salad Oliviyeh I

(potato salad with chicken, eggs, and olives)

*8 to 10 servings*

**Ingredients:**
*1 large onion, peeled and quartered*
*1½ lb boneless, skinless chicken breasts*
*8 large potatoes*
*1½ cups fresh or frozen green peas*
*3 pickled cucumbers, chopped*
*3 hardboiled eggs, chopped*
*½ cup sliced green olives*
*1 small onion, grated*
*1¾ cups mayonnaise*
*¼ cup lemon juice*
*½ cup whole green pitted olives*
*1 small pickled cucumber, sliced*
**Spices:**
*1 Tbs. salt*
*1 tsp black pepper*
*paprika*

## DIRECTIONS FOR PREPARATION

**1.** Place quartered onion, 1 tsp of the salt, and chicken in 2 cups of water in a pot; simmer for approximately 40 to 50 minutes or until very tender; remove chicken from broth and let cool. Dice the chicken and set aside.

**2.** Cook potatoes in 4 cups water for 30 minutes or until thoroughly cooked (cooking time will vary depending on type and size of potatoes; set aside to cool. Peel and dice.

**3.** Cook fresh or frozen green peas directions for 5 to 10 minutes or until tender.

**4.** Mix together lemon juice and 1½ cups of the mayonnaise, remaining salt and pepper in a large glass or ceramic bowl.

**5.** Add chicken, potatoes, peas, chopped pickles, chopped eggs, sliced olives, and grated onions to mayonnaise mixture in bowl and mix together well.

**6.** Form *salad oliviyeh* into a mound on a large serving platter and smooth the top out evenly.

**7.** With a spatula, spread remaining mayonnaise evenly over top.

**8.** Decorate with whole olives and sliced pickles and sprinkle top with paprika. Serve chilled.

Prepared by Fahimeh Z.

# Salad Oliviyeh II
(chicken and potato salad with peas, pickles, and olives)

*8 to 10 servings*

**Ingredients:**
*1½ lb boneless, skinless chicken breasts*
*1 large onion, chopped*
*8 large potatoes*
*1½ cups fresh or frozen green peas*
*3 carrots, diced*
*3 cucumber pickles, chopped*
*¼ cup chopped parsley*
*½ cup green olives, sliced*
*¾ cup mayonnaise*
*½ cup cream*
*2 Tbs. hot mustard*
*¼ cup white wine vinegar*
*½ cup whole, pitted green olives*
*¼ cup whole, pitted ripe olives*
**Spices:**
*1 Tbs. salt*
*½ tsp black pepper*
*paprika*

**DIRECTIONS FOR PREPARATION**

**1.** Cook chicken in 2 cups water with onion and 1 tsp. of the salt for 40 to 50 minutes, or until chicken is tender. Remove chicken from broth, allow to cool. Finely chop and set aside.
**2.** Wash and cut potatoes in half and cook in 4 cups water for 30 to 40 minutes or until tender. Cool, peel, and dice.
**3.** Cook peas and carrots in 1 cup water for 10 to 15 minutes or until tender. If using frozen peas, follow package directions. Set aside to cool.
**4.** Mix together chopped chicken, potatoes, peas and carrots, pickles, and chopped olives.
**5.** Mix ½ cup of the mayonnaise with cream, mustard, vinegar, remaining salt, and pepper and pour over chicken and potato salad; mix well.
**6.** Transfer *salad oliviyeh* to a large platter; shape into a smooth mound and spread remaining mayonnaise evenly over top and sides. Decorate with olives and sprinkle with paprika. Chill for at least 2 hours before serving.

Prepared by Mitra N.

## Salad-e Gowjeh Farangi ba Morgh
(salad of tomato stuffed with
cold chicken and rice)

*8 servings*

**Ingredients:**
*1 lb boneless, skinless chicken breasts*
*1 medium onion, grated*
*½ cup rice*
*2 Tbs. chopped fresh mint*
*¼ cup chopped walnuts*
*¼ mayonnaise*
*2 Tbs. lemon juice*
*8 large tomatoes*
*2 Tbs. chopped fresh parsley*
**Spices:**
*4 tsp salt*
*¼ tsp black pepper*

**DIRECTIONS FOR PREPARATION**

**1.** Simmer chicken with onion in 2 cups water and 1 tsp of the salt for 45-50 minutes, or until tender. Remove chicken from broth and allow to cool, then chop.
**2.** Rinse rice in hot tap water; drain. Bring 2 cups water and remaining salt to a boil; add rice and boil rapidly for 15-20 minutes or until kernels are tender but still separate, not mushy, stirring occasionally to prevent sticking. Drain and set aside to cool.
**3.** Rinse tomatoes; cut off tops, and hollow out.
**4.** Mix together all ingredients except tomatoes and parsley and stuff tomatoes. Arrange on a serving platter and sprinkle with parsley. Refrigerate for at least 30 minutes before serving.

## Salad-e Karafs-o Gerdu
(salad with celery and walnuts)

*4 to 5 servings*

**Ingredients:**
*2 cups celery hearts, finely chopped*
*½ cup white wine vinegar*
*¼ cup olive oil*
*1 cup chopped walnuts*
*1Tbs. dried dill weed*
**Spices:**
*½ tsp salt*
*¼ tsp black pepper*

DIRECTIONS FOR PREPARATION

**1.** Soak celery in vinegar and seasonings for several hours at room temperature in a glass or china bowl.
**2.** Mix in remaining ingredients and refrigerate for 1 hour.

# Panir-e Khanegi
(homemade feta-style cheese)

*about 1½ to 2 lbs*

**Ingredients:**
*1 gallon whole milk*
*1½ cups vinegar*
*3 Tbs. bleu cheese*
**Spices:**
*1 Tbs. salt*

### DIRECTIONS FOR PREPARATION

**1.** Bring milk to a boil. Add vinegar and allow to boil for a few minutes, until the milk curdles.
**2.** Place a piece of think white cotton cloth over a colander in the sink. (The cloth should be larger than the colander.)
**3.** Pour the curdled milk into the cloth and allow the liquid to drain off.
**4.** While the curdles are still hot, stir in bleu cheese and salt and mix together well.
**5.** Fold over edges of the cloth to cover the mixture. To further drain the liquid, place a plate and some kind of weight, like a large glass of water, on top of the folded cloth. Allow mixture to cool for about 1 hour with the weight on top.
**6.** Remove the weight and place the colander on a bowl or plate and refrigerate for 2 to 3 hours.
**7.** Remove from refrigerator; remove cloth from cheese; cut cheese into several pieces and store in refrigerator in a tight container.

# Sabzikhordan
(fresh herb and vegetable accompaniment)

*8 to 10 servings*

**Ingredients:**
*1 bunch radishes*
*1 bunch green onions*
*1 large bunch fresh spearmint*
*1 large bunch fresh basil*
*1 large bunch fresh tarragon*
*1 large bunch of savory (marzeh)*
*1 bunch Persian watercress* (shahi)

### DIRECTIONS FOR PREPARATION

**1.** Wash radishes and cut off ends, or slice, if desired.
**2.** Wash green onions; cut off ends and cut into 3" to 4" pieces, including the green parts.
**3.** Remove leaves from stems of spearmint, basil, tarragon, and savory discarding stems. Cut off ends of watercress and combine with other greens.
**4.** Wash and let drain in a colander.
**5.** Mix together all vegetables and serve as an accompaniment to most Persian dishes.
NOTE: This accompaniment is often served with flat bread and feta cheese or plain yogurt. The greens are eaten rolled up with a piece of cheese in a bite-size piece of bread or rolled up in the bread and dipped in yogurt. Be more creative: add walnuts and cucumber.

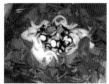

## Burani-ye Gusht-o Adas
(meat paste with lentils and yogurt)

*3 to 4 servings*

**Ingredients:**
*1 lb lean beef or lamb*
*1 small onion, quartered*
*1 eggplant*
*1 cup lentils*
*2 cups plain yogurt*
**Spices:**
*1 tsp salt*
*¼ tsp black pepper*

### DIRECTIONS FOR PREPARATION

**1.** Cook meat with onion, salt and 3 cups water for 1 hour, or until tender. Remove meat from broth; set broth aside; let meat cool. Pulverize meat in a food processor.
**2.** Peel and cut eggplants into small pieces and add to broth along with lentils and pulverized meat. Simmer for 20-30 minutes. Mash together well.
**3.** Remove from heat, fold in yogurt, transfer to a serving dish and sprinkle with pepper. Serve with flat bread.

## Gabakh Buranisi
(cooked pumpkin with cinnamon and nuts, Azerbaijan style)

*4 to 5 servings*

**Ingredients:**
*2 lb fresh pumpkin*
*¼ cup butter*
*½ cup sugar*
*¼ cup sour grape juice (or lemon juice)*
*¼ cup chopped walnuts*
**Spices:**
*2 tsp cinnamon*

### DIRECTIONS FOR PREPARATION

**1.** Cut pumpkin open; remove all seeds and membranes. Cut into small chunks; remove and discard the thick outer shell.
**2.** In a skillet, lightly brown pumpkin in butter. Transfer to a large pot.
**3.** Add sugar, grape or lemon juice, and 1 cup water. Cover and simmer over low heat for 30 minutes, or until juice has almost completely evaporated.
**4.** Transfer to a platter; sprinkle with cinnamon and walnuts. Use as a side dish.

## Burani-ye Kangar

(cardoon salad with yogurt and mint)

*3 to 4 servings*

**Ingredients:**
*2 stalks cardoons*
*¼ cup butter*
*3 cups plain yogurt*
*1 Tbs. chopped fresh mint*
**Spices:**
*2½ tsp salt*
*¼ tsp black pepper*
*¼ tsp paprika*

### DIRECTIONS FOR PREPARATION

**1.** Cut off and discard the prickly parts of the cardoons; boil in 5 cups water and 2 tsp of the salt for 15-20 minutes. Drain well and pat dry with a paper towel.
**2.** Chop cooked cardoons and sauté in butter.
**3.** Arrange cardoons in a serving dish. Mix remaining salt and pepper into yogurt and spread evenly over cardoons.
**4.** Sprinkle mint and paprika over top.

NOTE: If cardoons are not available, substitute 4 fresh artichoke hearts.

## Burani-ye Esfenaj

(yogurt and spinach)

*4 to 5 servings*

**Ingredients:**
*1 lb fresh spinach*
*2 medium onions, thinly sliced*
*2 Tbs. butter*
*1 cup plain yogurt*
*2 hardboiled eggs, sliced (optional)*
**Spices:**
*½ tsp salt*
*½ tsp black pepper*
*paprika*

### DIRECTIONS FOR PREPARATION

**1.** Cook spinach in 2 cups water for 10 minutes; drain well; chop and set aside.
**2.** Sauté onions in butter.
**3.** Add spinach and stir in with onions for 5 minutes. Mix in salt and pepper.
**4.** Serve hot or cold with yogurt. (Yogurt may be mixed with the spinach or served as an accompaniment.)
**5.** Decorate with sliced eggs, if desired. Sprinkle with paprika.

NOTE: For variety, add ½ cup finely chopped parsley to spinach in Step 1.

# Burani-ye Badenjan I
(chilled eggplant with yogurt)

*5 to 6 servings*

**Ingredients:**
*3 medium eggplants*
*½ cup olive oil*
*2½ cups yogurt*
*1 clove garlic, minced*
*1 Tbs. fresh dill weed, chopped*
*1 Tbs. fresh mint, chopped*
**Spices:**
*1 tsp salt*
*½ tsp black pepper*

**DIRECTIONS FOR PREPARATION**

**1.** Peel and slice eggplants lengthwise in ½"-thick pieces.
**2.** Brown eggplants on both sides in some of the oil in a skillet, adding small amounts of the olive oil gradually to prevent the eggplants from absorbing too much of it. Set aside to cool.
**3.** In a bowl, mix together yogurt, garlic, pepper and herbs. Spread 2 to 3 tablespoons of the yogurt mixture on the bottom of a serving dish. Arrange a layer of eggplants on top to completely cover the yogurt mixture. Then, cover eggplants with another layer of yogurt. This layering can be done two or three times, ending in yogurt.

Serve hot or cold with flat bread.

# Burani-ye Badenjan II
(chilled eggplant with yogurt, Mazandaran style)

*5 to 6 servings*

**Ingredients:**
*2 large eggplants*
*2½ cups yogurt*
*2 cloves garlic, minced*
*1 bunch parsley, chopped*
*2 Tbs. fresh mint, chopped*
**Spices:**
*1 tsp salt*
*½ tsp black pepper*

**DIRECTIONS FOR PREPARATION**

**1.** Rinse eggplants and bake in a preheated 350° oven for 30 minutes. Eggplants can also be placed on a grill until cooked.
**2.** Remove from oven or grill and rinse for several minutes in cold water. Set aside to cool.
**3.** Peel and mash eggplants in a bowl (use a food processor if necessary) and mix together with the remaining ingredients.

Serve with flat bread.

# Nazkhatun

(eggplants with pomegranate juice,
Northern Provinces style)

*6 to 8 servings*

**Ingredients:**
*4 medium eggplants*
*4 medium tomatoes*
*3 Tbs. sour grape juice or lemon juice*
*1 cup pomegranate juice*
*1 small onion, grated*
**Spices:**
*1 tsp salt*
*¼ tsp black pepper*
*2 tsp marjoram*

#### DIRECTIONS FOR PREPARATION

**1.** Preheat oven to 350° F. Wash eggplants, and bake for 40 minutes. Remove from oven and allow to cool; then peel and finely chop.
**2.** Bring 2 cups water and ½ tsp of the salt to a boil. Put whole tomatoes in boiling water for 5 minutes; drain and rinse with cold water. (This step will facilitate peeling the tomatoes.) Peel and cut into small pieces.
**3.** Mix together eggplants, sour grape or lemon juice, and pomegranate juice in a saucepan; cover and bring to a boil, then reduce heat and simmer over low heat for 40 minutes, or until the juice has evaporated.
**4.** Add tomatoes, onions, and remaining spices and stir for 2 minutes, then remove from heat. Serve with flat bread as a snack or light lunch or supper.

# Dopiyazeh

(mashed potatoes, Isfahan style)

*5 to 6 servings*

**Ingredients:**
*6 potatoes*
*2 medium onions, finely chopped*
*¼ cup butter*
**Spices:**
*2 tsp cinnamon*
*1 tsp salt*
*¼ tsp black pepper*

#### DIRECTIONS FOR COOKING

**1.** Wash, then boil potatoes in 2 cups water for 30 minutes, or until well cooked. Peel and mash.
**2.** Sauté onions in half of the butter.
**3.** Mix potatoes, onions, and spices well. Grease a casserole dish with some of the remaining butter and spread potato-onion mixture into it evenly. Melt remaining butter and pour over top. Bake in preheated oven at 350° F. for 10 minutes.

NOTE: *Dopiyazeh* is a popular accompaniment to grilled sausages or hot dogs.

# Torshi Badenjan I
(whole pickled eggplants)

**Ingredients:**
*2 long, thin gourmet eggplants*
*7½ cups white wine vinegar*
**Spices:**
*3½ tsp salt*
*½ tsp black pepper*
*½ tsp turmeric*
*1 tsp celery seed*
*½ tsp marjoram*
*½ tsp savory*

## DIRECTIONS FOR PREPARATION

**1.** Rinse eggplants in warm water; cut off tops. Make a lengthwise incision along the side of each eggplant, making sure not to cut so deep or long that eggplants separate in half.
**2.** Bring eggplants to a boil in 5 cups of the vinegar and 2 Tbs. of the salt in a large pot; boil 10 minutes; remove from pot and drain in a colander, placing a heavy pot or some other weight over them, and leave them to drain for an hour, to remove all excess vinegar.
**3.** Sprinkle the insides of the eggplants with 1 tsp of the salt and remaining spices. Place in a large pickling glass jar.
**4.** Mix together remaining vinegar and remaining salt and pour over eggplants in the jar, making sure they are covered with the vinegar; add more vinegar if needed to cover eggplants. Store in refrigerator or a very cool place for at least one month before serving.

NOTE: An important ingredient used in pickled eggplant in Iran, *siyah daneh* (nigella seeds), is not readily available in American stores; however, with the increasing number of Iranian specialty grocery stores, this seed may be found. If so, it adds an unusually pleasing flavor: add 1 Tbs.

# Torshi Badenjan II
(Azerbaijan-style pickled eggplant)

**Ingredients:**
*4 gourmet eggplants*
*4 cups white wine vinegar*
*3 cloves garlic, minced*
*¼ cup dried mint*
**Spices:**
*2 tsp salt*

## DIRECTIONS FOR PREPARATION

**1.** Make a lengthwise incision in each eggplant (do not remove the stem). Simmer eggplants in 2 cups of the vinegar for 15 minutes; drain in a colander by placing a heavy platter on top.
**2.** Sprinkle incision of each eggplant with garlic, mint and salt.
**3.** Place eggplants in a large glass jar. Fill with remaining vinegar; seal and store in a cool place for at least one month before serving.

Prepared by Fahimeh Z.

# Torshi Liteh
(eggplant and carrot relish)

Ingredients:
*1 eggplant, peeled and finely chopped*
*2 carrots, peeled and chopped*
*½ cup chopped fresh parsley*
*½ cup chopped fresh mint*
*1½ cups white wine vinegar*
Spices:
*1 tsp salt*
*½ tsp turmeric*
*¼ tsp black pepper*
*½ tsp dried marjoram*
*1 tsp nigella seeds (if available)*

## DIRECTIONS FOR PREPARATION

**1.** Put all ingredients in a medium-size pot and cook over medium heat for 20 minutes.
**2.** Allow to cool. Refrigerate for at least one month before serving.

NOTE: This relish can accompany most Persian dishes and is most often served along with *abgusht*.

Prepared by Farideh M.

# Torshi Khiyar
(pickled cucumbers)

Ingredients:
*10 pickling cucumbers*
*3 cups white wine vinegar*
Spices:
*1 Tbs. salt*
*1 tsp dill seed*
*1 tsp coriander seed*
*6 peppercorns*

## DIRECTIONS FOR PREPARATION

**1.** Wash cucumbers in cool water and pat dry with paper towel.
**2.** Pack tightly in large pickling jar(s).
**3.** Add remaining ingredients, making sure all cucumbers are covered with vinegar. Seal and store in a cool place for at least one month before serving.

# Torshi Karafs
(pickled celery)

Ingredients:
*1 stalk celery*
*1 medium onion, peeled and quartered*
*2 cloves garlic, peeled*
*2-3 cups white wine vinegar*
Spices:
*1 tsp salt*

## DIRECTIONS FOR PREPARATION

**1.** Wash and cut celery into ½" pieces. Allow to air dry.
**2.** Place celery along with onions, garlic, and salt in a large jar and cover completely with vinegar. Store in a cool place for at least one month before serving.

# Torshi Piyaz
## (pickled onions)

Ingredients:
*10 small whole onions (about the size of walnuts in the shell) or 3 large onions, quartered*
*2 cups white wine vinegar*
*2 Tbs. fresh (or 1 Tbs. dried) tarragon leaves*
Spices:
*1 tsp salt*
*6 peppercorns*
*1 tsp celery seed*

### DIRECTIONS FOR PREPARATION

**1.** Peel and cut the roots off the onions.
**2.** Dissolve salt in vinegar.
**3.** Place onions in a glass jar and add vinegar and remaining spices.  Seal and store in a cool place for at least one month before serving.
NOTE: Red wine vinegar or balsamic vinegar may be substituted for white vinegar.

Prepared by Kamron J. using balsamic vinegar.

# Sir Torshi
## (pickled garlic)

Ingredients:
*20 cloves of garlic*
*3 cups white wine vinegar*
*2 Tbs. fresh (or 1 Tbs. dried) tarragon leaves*

### DIRECTIONS FOR PREPARATION

1. Cut the roots off the garlic. Do not remove the outer skin
2. Place garlic in a glass jar and add vinegar and tarragon.  Seal and store in a cool place for at least six months before serving.

This pickle improves in taste with aging.  Seven-year old Sir Torshi, which is relatively sweet, was traditionally prescribed for Rheumatic arthritis.
NOTE: Red wine vinegar or balsamic vinegar may be substituted for white vinegar.

Prepared by Kamron J. using red wine vinegar.

## Torshi Gol Kalam
(pickled cauliflower)

**Ingredients:**
*1 medium head of cauliflower*
*2 cups white wine vinegar*
*a few celery leaves*
**Spices:**
*1 tsp salt*
*5 peppercorns*

### DIRECTIONS FOR PREPARATION

**1.** Break cauliflower into flowerettes.
**2.** Rinse and air dry.
**3.** Place in a large jar with remaining ingredients. Store in a cool place for 3 to 4 weeks before serving.

## Torshi-ye Bamiyeh
(pickled okra)

**Ingredients:**
*20 whole okras*
*2 cups white wine vinegar*
**Spices:**
*1tsp salt*
*6 peppercorns*
*1 tsp coriander seed*

### DIRECTIONS FOR PREPARATION

1. Rinse okra in cool water and pat dry with paper towel.
2. Dissolve salt in vinegar.
3. Place okra in a glass jar and add vinegar and remaining spices. Seal and store in a cool place for at least one month before serving.

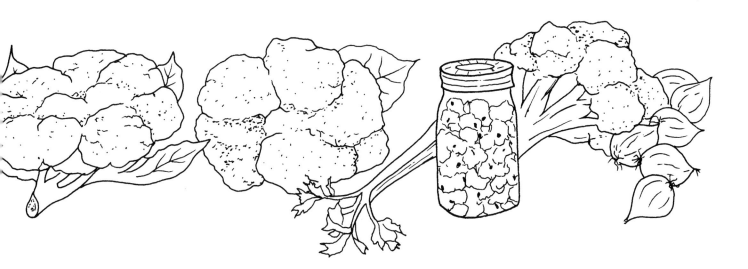

# Torshi-ye Nazkhatun
(eggplants with sour grape juice relish,
Mazandaran style)

*6 to 8 servings*

**Ingredients:**
*2 large eggplants*
*1 bunch parsley, chopped*
*1 bunch fresh basil, chopped*
*3 cloves garlic, minced*
*1 cup sour grape juice or lemon juice*
**Spices:**
*1 tsp salt*
*¼ tsp black pepper*

### DIRECTIONS FOR PREPARATION

**1.** Preheat oven to 350° F. Wash eggplants, and bake in oven on oven racks for 40 minutes. Remove from oven and allow to cool; then peel and mash (use a food processor, if desired).
**2.** Mix together eggplants, parsley, basil, garlic, and sour grape or lemon juice in a bowl. Add salt and pepper.
**3.** Refrigerate for an hour. Serve as a relish.

# Ghureh Ghureh
(pickled sour grapes)

**Ingredients:**
*1 lb sour grapes*
*1½ cups sour grape juice (or white wine*
*    vinegar, if not available)*
**Spices:**
*2 tsp salt*

### DIRECTIONS FOR PREPARATION

**1.** Separate grapes from stems. Rinse in cold water and allow to dry.
**2.** Place in large glass jar and add vinegar and salt. Seal and store in a cool place for at least one month before serving.

NOTE: *Ghureh ghureh* is used (removed from the sour grape juice or vinegar) in many *khoresh* dishes in place of lemon juice, dried lime, or sour plums.

## Torshi-ye Haft Bijar

(pickle of mixed vegetables and herbs)

### Ingredients:

*4 gourmet eggplants*
*3 cups white wine vinegar*
*6 pearl onions, peeled and halved*
*1 cup coarsely chopped celery leaves*
*1 cup cauliflower, broken into small pieces*
*1 cup coarsely chopped cabbage*
*3 carrots, sliced*
*2 cloves garlic*
*1 cup chopped parsley*
*1 cup chopped coriander*
*½ cup chopped fresh tarragon*
*½ cup chopped fresh mint*
*2 green chili peppers*

### Spices:

*2 tsp salt*
*2 tsp black pepper*
*2 tsp turmeric*
*2 tsp fennel seeds*

### DIRECTIONS FOR PREPARATION

**1.** Wash eggplants and pat dry with a paper towel; cut off the stem; make a lengthwise slit in each eggplant.
**2.** Simmer eggplants in 1 cup of vinegar for 30 minutes. Then drain in colander; place a plate and a heavy object on them to squeeze out excess vinegar and liquid. Allow to cool.
**3.** Place eggplants in a large jar with all other their ingredients and remaining vinegar. Top with additional vinegar if necessary to cover all ingredients. Keep in a cool place for at least one month before serving.

Prepared by Afsaneh O.

# Hal Badenjan

(Azerbaijan-style eggplant relish)

Ingredients:
2 cloves shallots
2 gourmet eggplants
2 cups white wine vinegar
½ lb fresh plums
2 carrots, grated
1 pickling cucumber, washed and chopped
   (do not peel)
1 small onion, grated
1 cup chopped cauliflower
1 cup chopped cabbage
3 green chili peppers

Spices:
1½ tsp salt
½ tsp turmeric
1 Tbs. Azerbaijan-style seasoning (see "Spices"
   section)

**DIRECTIONS FOR PREPARATION**

**1.** Soak shallots in 2 cups water for 24 hours, changing water occasionally.
**2.** Peel eggplants, chop, and simmer in mixture of 1 cup of the vinegar, ½ tsp of the salt, and turmeric for 15 minutes. Allow to cool.
**3.** Boil plums in 2 cups water for 5 minutes. Then, drain and run cool water over them; peel, remove pits. Add plums to the eggplants.
**4.** Add carrots and cucumber to mixture.
**5.** Drain shallots; chop.
**6.** Add shallots to eggplant mixture along with remaining ingredients; mix well. Place mixture in a glass jar; tightly seal; store in a cool place for at least one month before serving.

# Makhlut-e Shur

(mixed fruit and vegetable relish pickled in salt water, Azerbaijan style)

Ingredients:
4 pickling cucumbers
2 medium carrots, peeled and chopped
1 stalk celery, washed and chopped
1 green (unripe) tomato, chopped
1 green chili peppers
2 cloves garlic, peeled
½ lb wild plums (or 4 cored and chopped
   crabapples)
several sprigs fresh sweet fennel
several sprigs fresh spearmint
several sprigs fresh dill weed
several sprigs fresh parsley
several sprigs fresh coriander

Spices:
3 Tbs. salt

**DIRECTIONS FOR PREPARATION**

**1.** Wash cucumbers, cut off ends, and chop without removing skins.
**2.** Mix together and place in a mason jar: cucumbers, carrots, celery, tomato, pepper, garlic, and wild plums or crabapples.
**3.** Mix together all herbs and add to ingredients in jar.
**4.** Boil 2 cups water with salt and pour over mixture gradually. Cover jar immediately and leave in direct sunlight for 3 to 4 days.
**5.** Set aside to age for 3 to 4 weeks. Refrigerate after opening.

## Khiyar Shur-e Tabrizi
(cucumbers pickled in salt water, Tabriz style)

**Ingredients:**
*6 pickling cucumbers*
*2 small green chili peppers*
*1/8 cup fresh (or 1 Tbs. dried) tarragon leaves*
*3 cloves garlic, peeled*
**Spices:**
*1 Tbs. sweet fennel seeds*
*4 Tbs. salt*

### DIRECTIONS FOR PREPARATION

**1.** Make a lengthwise incision at the side of each cucumber, making sure not to cut cucumbers so deep that they separate in half.
**2.** Arrange cucumbers tightly in a large mason jar. Add peppers, tarragon, garlic, and sweet fennel seeds.
**3.** Bring 2 cups water and salt to a boil in a stainless steel pot, making sure salt dissolves completely.
**4.** Pour boiling salt water gradually over pickles in jar, making sure to cover all ingredients and that water reaches almost to the rim of the jar.
**5.** Cover and place the jar in direct sunlight for 3 days, then in a cool place for 10 to 15 days. Refrigerate after opening.

NOTE: This type of pickle is perhaps the most common in Iran, found in modern sandwich shops as well as homes.

## Kalam Shur
(cabbage and cauliflower pickled in salt water, Azerbaijan style)

**Ingredients:**
*1 medium head cabbage*
*1 small head cauliflower*
*1 pickling cucumber*
*3 cloves garlic, peeled*
*2 green chili peppers*
*1 cup tomato juice*
*1 Tbs. white wine vinegar*
*several sprigs fresh dill weed*
*several sprigs fresh sweet fennel*
*several sprigs fresh tarragon*
*several sprigs fresh spearmint*
**Spices:**
*2 tsp salt*

### DIRECTIONS FOR PREPARATION

**1.** Cut cabbage into chunks. Also, break cauliflower into flowerettes and mix together with cabbage.
**2.** Wash cucumber, cut off ends, and chop without removing peel; mix in with cabbage and cauliflower; add garlic and peppers and place in a large glass jar.
**3.** Bring to a boil 1 cup water, salt, and tomato juice; add vinegar. Remove from heat and pour into jar over vegetables.
**4.** Add herbs; close lid and refrigerate or store in a cool place for at least three weeks.

NOTE: This pickle is generally made in autumn to be eaten in winter.

## Morabba-ye Gerdu
### (walnut preserves)

**Ingredients:**
*2 cups walnuts*
*3 cups sugar*
*2 Tbs. lemon juice*

### DIRECTIONS FOR PREPARATION

**1.** Boil walnuts in 4 cups of water until the membrane is loose and separating from the nuts. Remove membrane from walnut.
**2.** Bring sugar and 1½ cups water to a boil, making sure sugar is completely dissolved. Stir in lemon juice; add walnuts and simmer for 45 minutes. Cool. Store in a mason jar in a cool, dry place. Refrigerate after opening.

## Morabba-ye Pust-e Hendavaneh
### (watermelon rind preserves)

**Ingredients:**
*Rind of half a watermelon*
*6 cups quicklime solution (optional)*
*¼ cup lime juice*
*5 cups sugar*

### DIRECTIONS FOR PREPARATION

**1.** Peel the thin green skin of watermelon rind and cut one-inch squares. Make sure that no watermelon pulp remains on the rind.
**2.** Soak in quicklime solution overnight. This will make the rind crispy. Rise well and soak in cool water for five to six hours. Drain and set aside
**3.** Bring sugar and 2 cups water to a boil, making sure sugar is completely dissolved. Stir in lemon juice; add watermelon rind and simmer for 30 minutes. Cool. Store in a mason jar in a cool, dry place. Refrigerate after opening.

## Morabba-ye Sib
### (apple preserves)

**Ingredients:**
*6-8 medium cooking apples*
*3 cups sugar*
*¼ cup lemon juice*

### DIRECTIONS FOR PREPARATION

**1.** Peel, core, and slice apples in ½" pieces.
**2.** Bring 1 cup water to a boil over high heat.
**3.** Add sugar and stir until completely dissolved.
**4.** Add lemon juice and stir. Reduce heat to medium.
**5.** Add sliced apples. Let mixture simmer over very low heat for about 30 minutes. Occasionally, gently push apples down into syrup with spatula. When cooked, mixture should have a slight reddish tint, if not, cook longer. Let cool and store in tightly sealed jars.

Prepared by Kamron J.

## (quince preserves)

### Ingredients:
*2 medium quinces*
*4 cups sugar*
*¼ cup lemon juice*

### DIRECTIONS FOR PREPARATION

**1.** Wash quinces; cut in quarters; cut off the core and cut into thin, ¼", slices.

**2.** Bring to a boil 1½ cups water, sugar and lemon juice in a medium-size pot.

**3.** Add quince; reduce heat to low and let simmer for 1 hour, stirring occasionally. The preserves are ready when the quinces have absorbed some of the syrup have turned a deep reddish-purple color.

**4.** Let cool and store in a cool place in a sealed jar.

## Morabba-ye Kadu Tanbal
(pumpkin preserves)

**Ingredients:**
*3 cups sugar*
*¼ cup lemon juice*
*3 cups fresh pumpkin, cut in 1"or smaller cubes*

### DIRECTIONS FOR PREPARATION

**1.** Bring 1 cup water to a boil over high heat; add sugar, stirring constantly until it completely dissolves.
**2.** Stir in lemon juice.
**3.** Add pumpkin; reduce heat to low and simmer, stirring occasionally, for about 1 hour, or until pumpkin is tender and saturated with the sugar syrup. Allow to cool before serving. Store in tightly sealed jars.

## Morabba-ye Balang
(*Balang* preserves, Isfahan, Shiraz, Tabriz style)

**Ingredients:**
*4 dried* balang* *halves*
*3 cups sugar*
*¼ cup lemon juice*

### DIRECTIONS FOR PREPARATION

**1.** Soak *balang* for several days in generous amounts of cool water, changing the water every 3 or 4 hours.
**2.** When the *balang* is soft, squeeze out the extra water absorbed, peeling, and cut into 1" pieces.
**3.** Place *balang*, sugar and 1½ cups water in a pot, bring to a boil, reduce heat and let simmer for 30 minutes, stirring occasionally.
**4.** Add lemon juice and simmer for another 30 minutes, stirring occasionally.
**5.** Let cool and store in well-sealed glass jars.
*Balang* [citron] is a type of citrus fruit, usually sold dried; available in some Iranian and Middle Eastern specialty stores.

## Morabba-ye Albalu
(tart cherry preserves)

**Ingredients:**
*1 lb tart cherries, pitted*
*2 Tbs. lemon juice*
*3 cups sugar*
*1 tsp. vanilla extract*

### DIRECTIONS FOR PREPARATION

**1.** Bring tart cherries, 1 cup water, and lemon juice to a boil in a saucepan.
**2.** Add sugar, reduce heat to low, and simmer for 30 minutes, stirring occasionally.
**3.** Stir in vanilla; remove from heat. Allow to cool. Store in tightly sealed jars.

Prepared by Fahimeh Z.

# Morabba-ye Anjir

(fig jam)

### Ingredients:
*3 cups sugar*
*2 Tbs. lemon juice*
*10 fresh figs*

#### DIRECTIONS FOR PREPARATION

**1.** Bring sugar and 1 cup water to a boil, making sure sugar is completely dissolved.
**2.** Stir in lemon juice, add figs, and simmer for 30 minutes. Cool. Store in a mason jar in a cool, dry place. Refrigerate after opening.

# Morabba-ye Havij

(carrot preserves)

### Ingredients:
*6 carrots*
*3 cups sugar*
*¼ cup lemon juice*
### Spices:
*¼ tsp cardamom*

#### DIRECTIONS FOR PREPARATION

**1.** Peel carrots and cut into thin strips, about 1" long and 1/8 " thin. This step can be done easily in a few seconds with the large-holed grater on a food processor.
**2.** Bring 1 cup water to a boil over high heat.
**3.** Add sugar and stir until all sugar is dissolved.
**4.** Add lemon juice and stir. Reduce heat to low.
**5.** Add carrots and simmer over very low heat for 20 to 25 minutes.
**6.** Sir in cardamom. Allow to cool. Store in a tightly sealed jar.

# Morabba-ye Zereshk

(*zereshk* preserves)

### Ingredients:
*2 cups* zereshk
*3 cups sugar*
*2 Tbs. lemon juice*

#### DIRECTIONS FOR PREPARATION

**1.** Soak *zereshk* in warm water for 20 minutes. Remove *zereshk* from water with a spatula in order to make sure no sand is left in it.
**2.** Bring sugar and 1 cup water to a boil, making sure sugar is completely dissolved. Stir in lemon juice; add *zereshk* and simmer for 30 minutes. Cool. Store in a mason jar in a cool, dry place. Refrigerate after opening.

# Morabba-ye Khiyar

(cucumber preserves, Hamadan style)

### Ingredients:
*5 small pickling cucumbers*
*¼ cup lime juice*
*3 cups sugar*
*2 Tbs. lemon juice*

#### DIRECTIONS FOR PREPARATION

**1.** Peel and cut cucumbers lengthwise in quarters. Cut off and discard the middle portion with seeds, if any.
**2.** Mix together lime juice and 6 cups water and soak cucumbers in this solution overnight.
**3.** Drain cucumbers.
**4.** Bring sugar and 1½ cups water to a boil, making sure sugar is completely dissolved. Stir in lemon juice; add cucumbers and simmer for 30 minutes. Cool. Store in a mason jar in a cool, dry place. Refrigerate after opening.

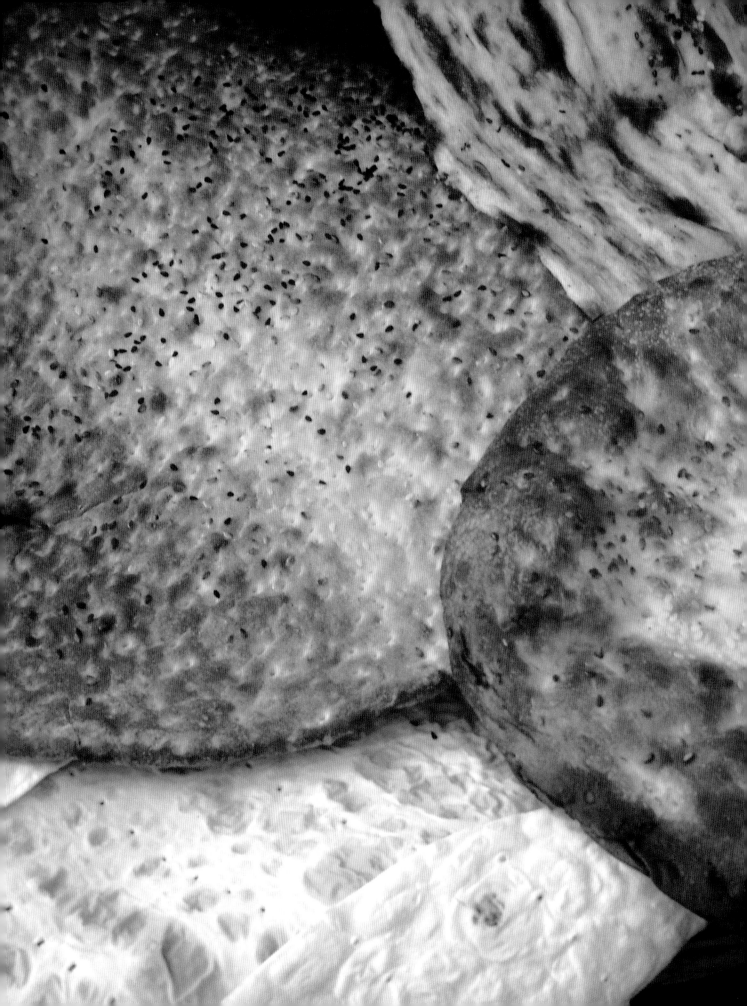

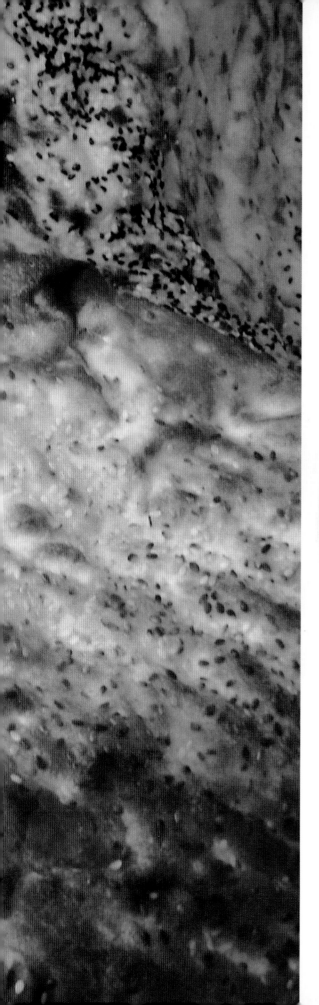

# Breads
## (Nan)

Although rice may be the main Iranian staple, bread is the one food no Iranian will want to do without. On nearly every street in every neighborhood of every city, there are several bread bakeries, often a short distance from one another. Bakeries usually specialize in one particular type of bread, for instance, a *sangak* bakery, a *lavash* bakery, etc. Bread is usually bought fresh before every meal; however, the breads suggested in this book can be made ahead of time, kept refrigerated in an airtight container (to keep their freshness and prevent them from drying out), and simply toasted on a very low setting just before serving. Bread can be kept this way for at least a week.

In addition to the breads commonly sold throughout Iran in bread bakeries, there are varieties of bread from various cities, towns, villages, and tribes. In many villages and tribes, individual families bake their own breads and, naturally, each family adds herbs, seeds, and spices to the bread to suit its own tastes. You may enjoy experimenting with various flavors by simply sprinkling different spices, herbs, and seeds on flattened dough or mixing them in the dough before baking.

About sandwiches: Western-style sandwiches introduced into Iran have often been changed to suit Iranian tastes and have become popular, especially in large cities. Among the most common sandwiches are *Sandevich-e Kotlet* (cutlet patty sandwich), *Sandevich-e Kuku* (green vegetable 'soufflé' sandwich), and *Sandevich-e Kalbas* (keilbasa), a favorite among many younger Iranians. These sandwiches are generally served on French-style bread with saltwater cucumber pickles.

# Taftun

(round flat bread)

*8 to 10 loaves*

**Ingredients:**
*2 Tbs. active dry yeast*
*1 Tbs. olive oil*
*5 cups all-purpose white flour*
**Spices:**
*1½ tsp salt*

### DIRECTIONS FOR PREPARATION

**1.** Dissolve yeast in 2 cups warm water.
**2.** Add salt and mix well. Mix in oil and flour and knead for 10 minutes. Cover with a damp cloth and let dough rise for 2 hours.
**3.** Preheat oven to 500°.
**4.** Warm up a cookie sheet in the oven.
**5.** Separate dough into 8 to 10 pieces. Shape each into a ball. Sprinkle a board or counter with flour to prevent sticking. One at a time, flatten each ball of dough on the counter or board by hand; sprinkle flour on top to prevent sticking to fingers. With a floured rolling pin, flatten the dough as you would for a pie crust into a round, approximately 1/8" thick, loaf. Take cookie sheet out of oven and gently lay the flattened dough on the ungreased cookie sheet. With fingertips, make a series of perforations into the dough to prevent the dough from bubbling.

**6.** Bake about 7 minutes for the first loaf, or until lightly golden in color, and about 5 minutes for each additional loaf.

Serve hot, or cool for a few minutes and store in an airtight container. Can be easily reheated in a toaster at low setting.

# Lavash

(wafer thin bread)

*about 20 loaves*

**Ingredients:**
*2 Tbs. active dry yeast*
*1 Tbs. olive oil*
*5 cups all-purpose white flour*
**Spices:**
*1½ tsp salt*

### DIRECTIONS FOR PREPARATION

**1.** Dissolve yeast in 2 cups warm water.
**2.** Add salt and mix well. Mix in oil and flour and knead for 10 minutes. Cover with a damp cloth and let dough rise for 2 hours.
**3.** Preheat oven to 500°.
**4.** Warm up a cookie sheet in the oven.
**5.** Separate dough into 20 pieces. Shape each into a ball. Sprinkle a board or counter with flour to prevent sticking. One at a time, flatten each ball of dough on the counter or board by hand; sprinkle flour on top to prevent sticking to fingers. With a floured rolling pin, flatten the dough as you would for a pie crust into an oblong, very thin loaf. Take cookie sheet out of oven and gently lay the

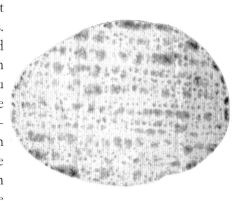

flattened dough on the ungreased cookie sheet. With fingertips, make a series of perforations into the dough to prevent the dough from bubbling.

**6.** Bake about 4 minutes for the first loaf, or until lightly golden in color, and about 2½ minutes for each additional loaf.

Serve hot, or cool for a few minutes and store in an airtight container. Can be easily reheated in a toaster at low setting.

# Barbari
(thick flat bread)

2 to 3 loaves

Ingredients:
2 Tbs. active dry yeast
1 Tbs. olive oil
5 cups stone-ground unbleached flour
Spices:
1½ tsp salt

Baking barbari bread in a traditional oven in Tabriz.
Photo by Susan Sprachman.

## DIRECTIONS FOR PREPARATION

1. Dissolve yeast in 2 cups warm water.
2. Add salt and mix well. Mix in oil and flour and knead for 10 minutes. Cover with a damp cloth and let dough rise for 2 hours.
3. Preheat oven to 500°.
4. Warm up a cookie sheet in the oven.
5. Separate dough into 2 to 3 pieces. Shape each into a ball. Sprinkle a board or counter with flour to prevent sticking. One at a time, flatten each ball of dough on the counter or board by hand; sprinkle flour on top to prevent sticking to fingers. With a floured rolling pin, roll out each ball, one at a time, in an oblong shape large enough to fit a cookie sheet. Perforate in the form of deep grooves with the fingertips.
6. If desired, spray with a little water and sprinkle with sesame, caraway, or cumin seeds. Bake for 7 to 10 minutes or until golden brown; repeat for each remaining loaf.
Serve hot, or cool for a few minutes and store in an airtight container. Can be easily reheated in a toaster at low setting.

# Sangak
(bread baked over pebbles)

*8 to 10 loaves*

**Ingredients:**
*2 Tbs. active dry yeast*
*2 Tbs. olive oil*
*3 cups unbleached wheat flour*
*1¼ cups white flour*
*cooking oil spray*
*sesame seeds*
**Spices:**
*2 tsp salt*

A sangak bakery in Tehran.

### DIRECTIONS FOR PREPARATION

**1.** Dissolve yeast and salt in 3 cups warm water.  Add olive oil.

**2.** Mix in flour; mix well (dough should be rather thin, more like a very thick pancake batter); add more water if necessary.  Let rise in a bowl covered with a damp cloth for 2 hours.

**3.** Preheat oven to 500°.  Separate dough into 8 to 10 equal pieces.  Lightly spray a cookie sheet with cooking oil spray.  Place one piece of the dough on the cookie sheet and spread out and flatten by hand to cover cookie sheet.  To spread the dough, dip hands in water frequently to help facilitate spreading and prevent dough sticking to fingers.

**4.** Perforate the dough with fingertips; sprinkle with sesame seeds.  Bake for about 10 minutes or until lightly golden in color.  Serve hot.

This bread is prepared in special bakeries in Iran in kilns with smooth pebbles on the bottom, and the dough is baked on top of these pebbles.

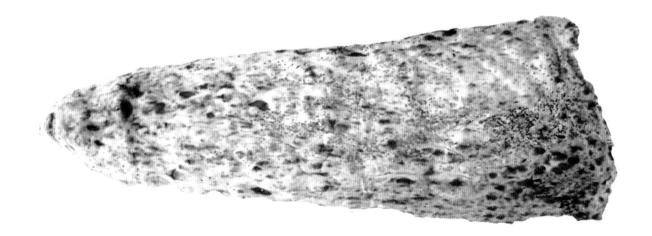

## Easy Persian-Style Bread

*8 to 10 loaves*

**Ingredients:**
*2 Tbs. active dry yeast*
*2 Tbs. olive oil*
*2 cups whole wheat flour*
*2 cups all-purpose flour*
*cooking oil spray*
*sesame, caraway, or poppy seeds*
**Spices:**
*2 tsp salt*

### DIRECTIONS FOR PREPARATION

**1.** Dissolve yeast and salt in 4 cups warm water in a large mixing bowl. Add olive oil.
**2.** Add flour and mix well with a spatula for several minutes (dough should be the consistency of pancake batter; add more water if necessary). Let rise in a bowl covered with a damp cloth for 2 hours.
**3.** Preheat oven to 450°. Lightly spray a cookie sheet with cooking oil spray. With a spatula or ladle, transfer some of the dough to the cookie sheet and flatten with the bottom of the spatula to the thickness of a pancake.
**4.** Sprinkle with seeds. Bake for about 10 minutes or until lightly golden in color. Serve hot.

## Nan-e Rowghani
(sweet bread smothered with sesame seeds)

*5 to 6 loaves / servings*

**Ingredients:**
*2 Tbs. active dry yeast*
*1 cup powdered sugar*
*3 cups all-purpose flour*
*½ cup olive oil*
*½ cup sesame seeds*
**Spices:**
*1 tsp salt*

### DIRECTIONS FOR PREPARATION

**1.** Dissolve yeast in 2 cups warm water.
**2.** Add salt and powdered sugar and mix well. Mix in flour and 2 Tbs. of the oil and kneed for 10 minutes; let rise for 2 hours.
**3.** Preheat oven to 450°. Grease a cookie sheet with some of the remaining olive oil.
**4.** Separate dough into 5 to 6 pieces, wet hands with a little water at a time, and flatten the dough by hand into ½" thick, round loaves. Use additional water, if necessary to flatten.
**5.** Cover each loaf generously with sesame seeds, brush with olive oil, and bake on the greased cookie sheet for about 10 minutes, or until a golden color.

# Nan-e Saji

(pan-baked bread, Bakhtiari style)

*8 to 10 loaves*

Ingredients:
*1½ Tbs. active dry yeast*
*2½ cups wheat flour*
*3 Tbs. olive oil*
*2 Tbs. sweet fennel seeds*
Spices:
*¾ tsp salt*

### DIRECTIONS FOR PREPARATION

**1.** Dissolve yeast in 1 cup warm water. Add salt; mix well.
**2.** Mix in 1 Tbs. of the olive oil and the flour; knead for 10 minutes. Cover with a damp cloth and let dough rise in a warm place for at least 2 hours.
**3.** Separate dough into 8 to10 sections. Flatten each piece by hand or with a rolling pin as thin as possible, large enough in diameter to just fit into a large skillet, using flour to prevent sticking to hands or rolling pin. Sprinkle with fennel seeds.
**4.** Lightly grease a large, heavy skillet and preheat over medium heat.
**5.** Place flattened dough one at a time in the greased skillet, cover and bake on top of the stove for 3 to 4 minutes. Turn bread over with a spatula and bake second side for 1 to 2 minutes, just until golden.

NOTE: This bread is usually baked on a large flat copper baking pan over an open fire.

# Nan-e Kamaji

(breakfast bread with poppy seeds, Isfahan style)

*8 to 10 loaves*

Ingredients:
*2 Tbs. active dry yeast*
*1 cup warm milk*
*2 Tbs. sugar*
*½ cup olive oil*
*5 cups wheat flour*
*¼ cup poppy seeds*
Spices:
*1½ tsp salt*

### DIRECTIONS FOR PREPARAIION

**1.** Dissolve yeast in 1 cup warm water.
**2.** Stir in milk, salt, and sugar.
**3.** Mix in ¼ cup of the oil; add flour and poppy seeds and knead well for 10 minutes. Cover with a damp cloth and set dough aside in a warm place to rise for about 2 hours.
**4.** Punch the dough down once and allow to rise again for 1 hour more.
**5.** Preheat oven to 500°.
**6.** Divide the dough into 8 to 10 portions.
**7.** Grease a large iron skillet with some of the remaining olive oil. Dip fingers in oil and flatten one portion of dough to cover the skillet, making an evenly smooth loaf. Perforate the dough with the fingertips. Bake in preheated oven for 10 minutes or until lightly golden in color.
**8.** Repeat above step until all dough is used up.

NOTE: This bread is particularly tasty served with feta cheese accompanied by butter and jelly for breakfast or mint or melon for a light supper.

# Nan-e Khoshkeh Do Atasheh
(Persian double-baked cracker-bread)

*4 or 5 loaves*

**Ingredients:**
*2 Tbs. active dry yeast*
*1 Tbs. olive oil*
*5 cups all-purpose white flour*
**Spices:**
*1½ tsp salt*

## DIRECTIONS FOR PREPARATION

**1.** Dissolve yeast in 2 cups warm water.
**2.** Add salt and mix well.  Mix in oil and flour and knead for 10 minutes.  Cover with a damp cloth and let dough rise for 2 hours.
**3.** Preheat oven to 500°.
**4.** Warm up a cookie sheet in the oven.
**5.** Separate dough into 4 to 5 pieces; shape each into a ball.  Sprinkle a board or counter with flour to prevent sticking.  One at a time, flatten each ball of dough on the counter or board by hand; sprinkle flour on top to prevent sticking to fingers.  With a floured rolling pin, flatten the dough as you would for a pie crust into a round, approximately ¼" thick, loaf.  Take cookie sheet out of oven (make sure it is not too hot, just warm, before continuing) and gently lay the flattened dough on the ungreased cookie sheet.  With fingertips, make a series of perforations into the dough to prevent the dough from bubbling.
**6.** Bake for 7 to 10 minutes.  Repeat for each loaf.
**7.** After all loaves are baked, reduce heat in oven to low *(150° – 200°)*.
**8.** Wait 10 minutes or until oven temperature has lowered, then, arrange the loaves on the oven racks and bake again for 15 more minutes.
**9.** Then, turn oven off, but leave bread on racks in the oven for a few hours, until the oven is cool.

NOTE:This cracker-bread should be very crispy and can be stored in a cool, dry place for long periods of time.
To serve, break loaves into smaller pieces and use as you would crackers, as snacks with feta cheese and fresh mint or walnuts or dipped in yogurt.

# Nan-e Khoshkeh-ye Qandi

(sweet Persian cracker-bread)

*2 to 3 loaves*

### Ingredients:
*2 Tbs. active dry yeast*
*2 Tbs. olive oil*
*1 cup powdered sugar*
*3 cups unbleached flour*
*3 Tbs. sesame seeds*
*2 Tbs. granulated sugar*
### Spices:
*1 tsp salt*

### DIRECTIONS FOR PREPARATION

**1.** Dissolve yeast in 2 cups warm water.

**2.** Add salt and powdered sugar and mix well. Mix in 1 Tbs. of the olive oil and the flour and kneed; let rise for 2 hours.

**3.** Preheat oven to 450°.

**4.** Lightly grease a cookie sheet with some of the remaining oil and warm in the oven a few minutes.

**5.** Separate dough into 2 or 3 parts. Shape each into a ball. Sprinkle a board, pastry cloth, or counter with flour to prevent dough from sticking. One at a time, flatten each ball by hand. With a floured rolling pin, roll the dough flat into a round or oblong, ¼" thick loaf.

**6.** Place one loaf on the cookie sheet. Sprinkle with some of the sesame seeds and sugar. Brush bread lightly with some of the remaining oil. Make a few indentations in the bread with the finger tips.

**7.** Bake loaf for about 7 to 10 minutes, until golden. Repeat steps until all loaves are baked.

**8.** After all loaves are baked, remove from oven; reduce heat to low (150° – 200°).

**9.** Wait for 10 minutes or until temperature has lowered. Then, arrange the loaves on the oven racks and bake again for 15 more minutes.

**10.** Turn oven off, but leave bread on rack in the oven for a few hours, until the oven cools.

NOTE: This bread keeps best in an airtight container. It is especially good for breakfast spread with feta cheese or butter.

A pastry shop in Tehran.
*Photo by Shabnam Rezaei,*
*persianmirror.com*

# Desserts, Sweets and Confections
## *(Shirini and Deser)*

The most common dessert, as such, in Iran is fresh fruit, particularly varieties of melons, oranges, pears, apples, grapes, cherries, etc., in season. Sweets such as those in the recipes presented here are generally served to guests—especially during *Noruz,* the Persian New Year, when visiting friends and relatives is a must—accompanied by hot tea. In titling this chapter "Desserts, Sweets and Confections" I have the American audience in mind.

Numerous European cakes and pastries have been introduced into Persian cuisine. Many Iranian bakeries devote entire sections to *Shirini-ye Danmarki,* or Danish pastry.

Some of the most important traditional Iranian confections included in this chapter, such as *baqlava* from Yazd and *sohan* from Qom, have become popular throughout Iran, and Isfahan's *gaz* (nougats made of manna) has become a cherished souvenir which travelers bring back from that city. Two of the items in this section, *Zanjebil-e Parvardeh-ye Shekari* and *Zanjebil-e Parvardeh-ye Khorma'i,* are believed to be remedies for rheumatic illnesses.

# Kachi I
## (sweet pudding)

*4 to 5 servings*

**Ingredients:**
*1½ cups butter*
*2 cups flour*
*1½ cups sugar*
**Spices:**
*½ tsp saffron, dissolved in 2 Tbs. hot water*

### DIRECTIONS FOR PREPARATION

**1.** In a deep, heavy skillet, melt butter over medium-low heat.
**2.** Turn heat down to low and add flour, stirring to mix well with butter; lightly brown, stirring constantly to prevent burning and to ensure that flour is evenly cooked, for about 10 minutes.
**3.** Add 1½ cups water and sugar and continue stirring until well mixed and the sugar is completely dissolved.
**4.** Add saffron solution to mixture. Cook for another 5 minutes.
**5.** Place on a platter and decorate using the back of a fork. *Kachi* should be the consistency of a thick paste.

NOTE: *Kachi* is usually served warm on certain religious holidays. However, it may also be served cold at any time for a snack or a heavy dessert.

# Kachi II
## (flour pudding, Khosbijan style)

*4 to 6 servings*

**Ingredients:**
*2 cups flour*
*2 Tbs. unsalted butter*
*3 Tbs. sugar*
**Spices:**
*½ tsp salt*
*1 tsp turmeric*

### DIRECTIONS FOR PREPARATION

**1.** Lightly brown flour by stirring constantly in a heavy skillet until it turns a golden color.
**2.** Stir in butter for 2 to 3 minutes more.
**3.** Dissolve salt and turmeric in 1 cup warm water and mix in with flour; stir for 5 minutes, or until mixture thickens.
**4.** Transfer pudding to platter and sprinkle with sugar.

NOTE: Khosbijan is a village near the city of Arak in central Iran.

# Samanu

(wheat sprout paste)

*about 4 cups*

Ingredients:
*1 lb whole wheat grains*
*1 cup whole wheat flour*

### DIRCTIONS FOR PREPARATION

**1.** Soak whole wheat grains in 4 cups water in a glass bowl for 24 hours.

**2.** Drain the water, spread a piece of wet cotton cloth in the bowl, place the wheat grains in the cloth, cover with edges and allow to sprout in room temperature for several days. Soak and drain two or three times a day.

**3.** Spread the sprouted wheat grains on a large platter or tray. Cover with a damp cloth and allow the sprouts to grow for two or three days, until they are about 1" to 1½" long. Keep moist by spraying several times a day.

**4.** Rinse wheat sprouts and roots in water, then place in a blender with 1½ cups water and pulverize.

**5.** Pour the contents of the blender into a pot; add 5 cups water and bring to a boil, then reduce heat and simmer for about 4 hours.

**6.** Mix in flour and simmer for another 30 minutes. Stir occasionally. The end product should be a sweet brown paste.

*Samanu* is usually prepared in early spring, and is one of the items placed on the *Haft Sin* for Persian New Year, *Noruz*.

A *samanu* vendor in Tehran

# Tar Halva

(sweet saffron-flavored paste)

*3 to 4 servings*

Ingredients:
*½ cup rice flour*
*¼ cup sugar*
*2 Tbs. butter*
Spices:
*¼ tsp saffron, dissolved in 2 Tbs. hot water*

### DIRECTIONS FOR PREPARATION

**1.** Dissolve rice flour in 1 cup water.

**2.** Simmer over medium heat in a medium-size saucepan for 5 minutes, stirring constantly to prevent sticking.

**3.** Add sugar and stir until it dissolves.

**4.** Add saffron, mix well.

**5.** Add butter; stir and let simmer for 5 more minutes. The mixture will be the consistency of a pudding while hot. Pour onto a medium-size platter. Garnish with finely ground pistachios.

Serve hot or cold to be scooped up with flat bread, generally as a snack, but can also be served as a dessert.

Prepared by Mehrangiz K.

# Masqati

(colorful sweet pudding)

*6 to 8 servings*

**Ingredients:**
*1 cup cornstarch*
*a few drops of rose extract or 4 Tbs. rosewater*
*1¼ cup sugar*
*a few drops of red, yellow, or green food coloring*
*4 Tbs. lemon juice*
*3 Tbs. butter*
*½ cup almonds or pistachios, finely chopped*
**Spices:**
*1 tsp cinnamon*

### DIRECTIONS FOR PREPARATION

**1.** Thoroughly dissolve cornstarch in 4½ cups water.
**2.** Bring to a boil, reduce heat, and add rose flavoring, sugar, food coloring, lemon juice, and cinnamon, stirring constantly to avoid sticking. Cook a few minutes more to make sure that sugar is completely dissolved.
**3.** Add butter and mix well; remove from heat.
**4.** Pour into serving bowls or individual dessert cups. Sprinkle with nuts. Serve chilled.

# Yakh Dar Behesht

(chilled pudding with rosewater and pistachios)

*5 to 6 servings*

**Ingredients:**
*4 cups milk*
*1 cup cornstarch*
*1½ cup sugar*
*¼ cup butter*
*1 tsp rose extract*
*¼ cup finely chopped pistachio nuts*

### DIRECTIONS FOR PREPARATION

**1.** Dissolve cornstarch in milk.
**2.** Add sugar, butter, rose extract, and 2 cups water; simmer, stirring constantly over low heat for 10 to 15 minutes, or until the mixture thickens.
**3.** Pour into an oblong glass cake pan and refrigerate for half an hour.
**4.** Sprinkle with pistachios and refrigerate for 1 hour. Cut diagonally to form 2-inch long diamond shapes and serve.

Prepared by Mina G.

# Fereni
(milk pudding with date syrup)

*4 to 6 servings*

Ingredients:
*½ cup cornstarch*
*2 cups cold milk*
*sugar, date, or maple syrup*
Spices:
*dash of salt*

### DIRECTIONS FOR PREPARATION

**1.** Dissolve cornstarch in cold milk.
**2.** Bring to a boil over medium heat, stirring constantly.
**3.** Stir in salt.
**4.** Pour onto a shallow serving dish and allow to cool; refrigerate. A thin crust will form on the top. Serve chilled, sprinkled with sugar or with amount desired of date or maple syrup.

# Shir Berenj
(thick rice pudding with date syrup)

*4 to 5 Servings*

Ingredients:
*½ cup rice*
*3 cups milk*
*date juice or sugar, to taste*
*(can be substituted with maple syrup)*
*½ tsp salt*

### DIRECTIONS FOR PREPARATION

**1.** Place rice, 2 cups water, and salt in a medium size pot over medium heat and simmer for 15-20 minutes or until rice is soft.
**2.** Add milk and simmer for 20-30 minutes more. Stir occasionally to prevent sticking.
**3.** Sprinkle with sugar or drizzle date juice over the top. Can be served warm or cold.

# Sholezard
(saffron-flavored rice pudding)

*6 to 8 servings*

Ingredients:
*1 cup rice*
*2 Tbs. butter*
*1 cup sugar*
*1 tsp. lemon juice*
*2 Tbs. slivered almonds*
*2 Tbs. chopped pistachio nuts*
Spices:
*½ tsp salt*
*¼ tsp cardamom*
*1 tsp saffron, dissolved in ¼ cup hot water*
*1 tsp cinnamon*

### DIRECTIONS FOR PREPARATION

**1.** Bring rice, butter, and salt to a boil in 5 cups water; cover and simmer gently until rice is soft and swollen, stirring occasionally to prevent sticking, about 45 minutes.
**2.** Add sugar and lemon juice to rice mixture and mash with potato masher.
**3.** Add cardamom and saffron solution to rice mixture. Mix well.
**4.** Pour pudding in large serving bowl. Decorate top with cinnamon and slivered nuts. Serve chilled.

Prepared by Shamsi F.

## Bastani-ye Zafarani ba Khameh
(saffron-flavored ice cream with frozen cream chunks)

*10 servings*

**Ingredients:**
*2 Tbs. gelatin*
*3 cups whole milk*
*2 cups cream*
*¾ cup sugar*
*rosewater syrup (optional; see recipe in "Drinks" section)*
**Spices:**
*1 tsp saffron*

### DIRECTIONS FOR PREPARATION

**1.** Soak gelatin in ¼ cup cold water.
**2.** Take ½ cup of the milk and ½ cup of the cream, mix well and pour out on a flat dish to form about 1/8" thick layer. Place in freezer until ready to serve.
**3.** Scald the remaining milk, but do not boil.
**4.** Dissolve the sugar in the hot milk; add to soaked gelatin and saffron mixture and beat vigorously. Chill in ice cream maker or freezer, but do not freeze.
**5.** Fold in the remaining cream and churn in the ice cream maker or return to freezer. As the ice cream thickens, break off thickened parts from sides and mix with the soft parts. When all of the mixture has thickened, place in bowls.
**6.** Remove frozen milk-cream mixture from freezer; break into chunks. Decorate the tops of ice cream with the chunks.
**7.** If desired, sprinkle rosewater syrup on top before serving.

Akbar Mashti, the first ice cream vendor in Persia (Iran).
Photo *circa* 1891(?).

## Saffron-Flavored Ice Cream
(made easy)

*makes ½ gallon*

**Ingredients:**
*½ cup whole milk*
*½ cup cream*
*½ gallon vanilla ice cream*
*¼ cup chopped pistachios (optional)*
**Spices:**
*1 tsp saffron, dissolved in 1 Tbs. hot water*

### DIRECTIONS FOR PREPARATION

**1.** Mix together well milk and cream; pour out on a dinner plate to form about 1/8" thick layer. Place in freezer until ready to serve.
**2.** Place ice cream in a mixing bowl; set container aside.
**3.** Add hot saffron solution to ice cream and mix in well with a potato masher; stir in pistachios (if desired).
**4.** Return softened ice cream to original container and freeze for 3 to 4 hours before serving.
**5.** Remove frozen milk-cream mixture from freezer; break into chunks. Decorate the tops of ice cream with the chunks.

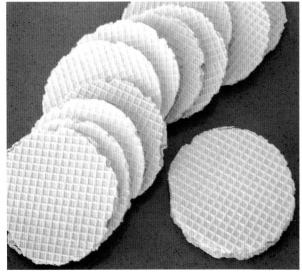

Ice cream wafers.

Ice cream served inside of a floral ice bowl.

*Paludeh-ye Shirazi* served inside of a floral ice bowl.

# Paludeh-ye Shirazi
## (frozen dessert, Shiraz style)

*6 to 8 servings*

**Ingredients:**
*about ¼ lb thin rice noodles, or rice sticks,*
*    the size of angel hair pasta*
*1 cup heavy cream*
*1 cup powdered sugar*
*2 tsp rosewater extract (optional)*
*1 cup lime juice*

### DIRECTIONS FOR PREPARATION

**1.** Separate and break noodles into smaller pieces, about 1" or 2" long.

**2.** Bring 2 quarts water to a boil in a large pot; add noodles and cook for 10 minutes, or until fairly soft, but not falling apart. Drain and rinse for several minutes in cold water; set aside to thoroughly drain in colander.

**3.** In a bowl, mix together cream, sugar, and extract (if desired).

**4.** Add noodles and mix together well; place in a freezer-safe dish and place in freezer for 1 hour. Remove from freezer, loosen, and replace in freezer for 1 more hour, or until the noodles are frozen and crisp.

*Paludeh* should be crunchy when ready for serving. To serve, place in sherbet or ice cream dishes; pour about 2 Tbs. of lime juice (to taste) or 1 Tbs. of sour cherry syrup over each serving.

NOTE: This dessert is generally not made at home, but only found in special ice cream shops.

## Shirini-ye Tar I
(layered cake)

*about 20 pieces*

Ingredients:
*2 medium apples*
*1 cup sugar*
*1 Tbs. lemon juice*
*1 plain pound cake*
Spices:
*½ tsp cardamom*

### DIRECTIONS FOR PREPARATION
**1.** Core, peel, and dice apples.
**2.** Bring ¼ cup water to a boil in a small pot.
**3.** Add sugar gradually and stir until it dissolves.
**4.** Add apples to boiling syrup; reduce heat and simmer over medium-low heat for 20 minutes.
**5.** Remove from heat and stir in lemon juice and cardamom; mash with potato masher; allow to cool.
**6.** Trim browned edges from pound cake and cut into an even number of slices approximately ½"- ¾" thick.
**7.** Spread a thick layer of the apple filling on half the slices of cake; place remaining slices on top.
**8.** Cut into squares of about 2".

NOTE: For variety, other fruits (about 1½ cups diced) can be substituted for apples. For a quick dessert, a ready-made preserve can be used as a filling.

## Shirini-ye Tar II
(Jello-filled cake)

*about 20 pieces*

Ingredients:
*1 3-oz package fruit Jello*
*1 plain pound cake*

### DIRECTIONS FOR PREPARATION

**1.** Follow package instructions for fruit Jello; place in refrigerator about 10 minutes or until cooled but not yet beginning to set.
**2.** Meanwhile, trim the browned edges from pound cake and cut into an even number of ½" - ¾" slices.
**3.** Place half the slices of cake in an oblong cake pan.
**4.** Pour cooled Jello over the cake.
**5.** Cool in refrigerator for 10 minutes, or until Jello begins to set, but is not quite firm.
**6.** Place remaining slices of cake on top of the Jello, making sure to match edges.
**7.** Return cake to refrigerator until Jello is firmly set.
**8.** Remove from refrigerator and cut into squares. Return to refrigerator until ready to serve.

## Floral Ice Bowl

This decorative bowl, made of ice and decorated with backyard flowers, adds a distinctive look for any type of food that needs to be served chilled, such as ice cream, caviar, shrimp, or *paludeh*. Take two stainless steel bowls, one smaller to fit inside the larger one with about an inch and a half of space between them. Partially fill the large bowl with water; place the small bowl inside the large bowl and place a weight of some sort inside the middle bowl that is heavy enough to stop it from floating. Arrange (sink) various flower petals and herbs in the water around the outside edge of the smaller bowl. Carefully place the two bowls in the freezer section of your refrigerator and allow the mixture to freeze over night. Remove both stainless steel bowls from the frozen bowl. You should now have an ice bowl the top edge of which is decorated with flowers. Place this bowl on a plate or platter, add your chilled food inside it, and bring it to the table to serve. (*See pages 221 and 222.*)

## Keyk-e Sadeh
### (plain pound cake)

*4 servings*

Ingredients:
*5 eggs*
*1½ cups sugar*
*1½ cups flour*
*¼ pound butter*

**DIRECTIONS FOR PREPARATION**

**1.** Break eggs into a small pot with a handle; add sugar and mix.
**2.** Bring 3 cups of water to a boil; place egg and sugar mixture in pot over the steam and beat well.
**3.** Remove egg and sugar mixture from steam and beat well until cooled.
**4.** Set aside two tablespoons of the butter. Melt remaining butter and stir in flour; add to the egg and sugar mixture and beat well. Preheat oven to 350°.
**5.** Grease a small baking dish; pour in mixture and bake for 15 to 20 minutes.

## Ranginak
### (date and walnut confection)

*25 to 30 pieces*

Ingredients:
*2 lbs pitted dates, chopped*
*2 lb walnuts, chopped*
*4 cups flour*
*1 cup unsalted butter*
*sugar*
Spices:
*2 Tbs. cinnamon*

**DIRECTIONS FOR PREPARATION**

**1.** Mix together dates and walnuts.
**2.** Heat and stir until well mixed in skillet over low heat.
**3.** Sprinkle cinnamon on a flat dish or cookie sheet. Spread the date mixture on it. Smooth the surface with a spatula.
**4.** Put the flour in a pot over medium heat. Stir until light brown.
**5.** Add butter, stir until flour is well browned and is about to separate from the fat.
**6.** Spread this mixture over the dates. Smooth the surface with a spatula.
**7.** Sprinkle lightly with sugar; allow to cool.
**8.** When cool, cut into squares or diamond shapes.

# Baqlava

## (Iranian baklava)

*About 30 pieces*

### Ingredients:
*1 lb fillo dough*
*1 lb unsalted butter, melted*
*3½ finely cups chopped almonds*
*½ cups sugar*
*2 cups rosewater syrup (see recipe in*
*    "Drinks" section)*
*½ cup chopped pistachio nuts*
### Spices:
*1 tsp cardamom*

### DIRECTIONS FOR PREPARATION

**1.** Place 3 or 4 sheets of fillo dough evenly over the bottom of a well-greased oblong cake pan, brushing each sheet on both sides with melted butter before placing another sheet on top.

**2.** Thoroughly mix together almonds, cardamom, and ½ cup of the sugar and spread evenly over pastry sheets in the pan.

**3.** Place 3 to 4 buttered sheets of fillo dough on top of the nut and sugar mixture.

**4.** Cut into square or diamond-shaped pieces (about 2" x 2").

**5.** Preheat oven to 350°. Bake for 25 to 30 minutes, then increase temperature to 450° and bake an additional 10 to 15 minutes or until top crust is golden brown.

**6.** Remove the baking dish from the oven and pour rosewater syrup evenly over the top of the baklava.

**7.** Sprinkle with pistachio nuts. Allow to cool.

**8.** Before serving, run a knife along the grooves where the baklava had previously been cut. Keep refrigerated until serving time.

Prepared by Jaleh P.

# Sowhan-e Asali
## (honey and almond confection)

### DIRECTIONS FOR PREPARATION

*About 10 pieces*

**Ingredients:**
*1 cup granulated sugar*
*2 Tbs. honey*
*3 Tbs. butter*
*½ cup slivered almonds*
*1 Tbs. crushed pistachios*
**Spices:**
*¼ tsp saffron, dissolved in 2 Tbs. hot water*

**1.** Melt sugar slowly in heavy skillet, stirring constantly to prevent burning.
**2.** Add honey, butter, and two-thirds of the almonds to sugar, stirring gently over low heat.
**3.** Add saffron mixture, mixing gently but quickly. Remove from heat.
**4.** Drop by tablespoonfuls on ungreased cookie sheet.
**5.** Press several pieces of remaining nuts on each piece.
**6.** Allow to cool. Gently remove from cookie sheet to prevent breaking. Store in cool, dry place in airtight container. Sprinkle with crushed pistachios.

# Lowz-e Badam
## (almond confection)

*about 10 to 15 pieces*

Ingredients:
*1 ½ cups almonds*
*½ cup butter*
*½ cup sugar*
*½ cup flour*
Spices:
*¼ tsp saffron, dissolved in 2 Tbs. hot water*

### DIRECTION FOR PREPARATION

**1.** Place almonds in 3 cups hot water for 5 to 10 minutes, drain, remove dark membrane. Allow to air dry. Pulverize in a food processor. Set aside.
**2.** Melt butter in heavy skillet over medium high heat.
**3.** Add sugar and stir constantly until it dissolves.
**4.** Add flour and almonds to form a thick paste. Stir constantly for 3 to 4 minutes.
**5.** Sit saffron solution well into mixture in skillet.
**6.** Remove skillet from heat and spread out contents evenly on a cookie sheet, using a spatula, to a thickness of about ½".
**7.** Cut diagonally into diamond-shaped pieces about 1½" from edge to edge. Allow to cool and serve.

# Lowz-e Nargil
## (coconut confection)

*about 10 to 15 pieces*

Ingredients:
*½ cup unsalted butter*
*½ cup sugar*
*5/8 cup flour*
*¾ cup shredded coconut*

### DIRECTIONS FOR PREPARATION

**1.** Melt butter in heavy skillet over medium-high heat.
**2.** Add sugar stirring constantly until it dissolves.
**3.** Add flour and ½ cup of the coconut and mix into a thick paste. Reduce heat to medium and cook an additional 3 to 4 minutes, stirring constantly.
**4.** Remove from heat and spread out evenly on a cookie sheet to a thickness of about ½".
**5.** Sprinkle remaining coconut evenly over top and press gently with the back of a spatula until it adheres to the mixture.
**6.** Cut diagonally into diamond-shaped pieces about 1½" from edge to edge. Allow to cool and serve.

# Bamiyeh
(saffron-flavored fried pastry)

*about 15 pieces*

Ingredients:
*5 Tbs. butter*
*1¼ cup flour*
*1 egg, beaten*
*2-3 cups vegetable oil*
*2 cups rosewater syrup*
    *(see recipe in "Drinks" section)*
Spices:
*¼ tsp saffron*

## DIRECTIONS FOR PREPARATION

**1.** Bring 1 cup water to a boil in a saucepan.
**2.** Add saffron and stir.
**3.** Add butter and stir until it melts.
**4.** Add flour and mix well with a fork until the mixture becomes a firm but manageable dough. Allow to cool.
**5.** Add egg and mix well with a fork, making sure the egg is mixed in completely with the dough and no lumps remain.
**6.** Heat vegetable oil in a deep fryer or deep pot on medium or medium-high heat. (Adjust the temperature if necessary after trying the first piece.)
**7.** Force dough through a snowflake-designed disc of a cake decorator (to make the grooves which are the distinctive design of this pastry) and separate from tool with a knife at about 2" and drop into the hot oil; fry a few pieces at a time until golden brown.
**8.** Remove from oil with a slotted spoon and place on a paper towel to drain. Repeat Steps 7 and 8 until all the dough has been used.
**9.** Allow to cool. Dip in rosewater syrup, then place on serving dish.

# Zulbiya
(pretzel-shaped sweet fritters)

*about 20 pieces*

Ingredients:
*2 cups sugar*
*1 tsp lemon juice*
*1 Tbs. rose extract*
*1 Tbs. dry yeast*
*2 cups flour*
*1 Tbs. plain yogurt*
*2 cups vegetable oil*

## DIRECTIONS FOR PREPARATION

**1.** Dissolve sugar in 1 cup hot water; simmer for 1 to 2 minutes, until sugar is completely dissolved.
**2.** Stir in lemon juice and rose extract. Set aside to cool.
**3.** Dissolve yeast in 1½ cups warm water.
**4.** Add flour and yogurt and mix well. Let mixture rise for 1 hour.
**5.** Heat oil in a heavy skillet over medium-high heat.
**6.** Put the flour mixture in a cake decorator or a pastry tube with a small round opening. Press through the opening into the hot oil in pretzel-shaped and sized figures. Fry for 40 to 60 seconds or until lightly browned. Carefully remove from oil with a spatula, slotted spoon, or tongs and place on paper towels to discard excess oil. Then dip into syrup.
**7.** Gently remove from syrup and place on a plate. The finished product will be firm, not quite crispy, but rather delicate.

# Qottab
### (nut-filled pastry)

*about 30 pieces*

**Ingredients:**
*½ lb unsalted butter, softened to room temperature*
*5 cups flour*
*2 Tbs. baking powder*
*1 egg, well beaten*
*1 cup milk*
*a few drops of rose extract*
*2 cups vegetable oil*
*1 cup ground walnuts*
*1 cup pulverized almonds*
*1¼ cup powdered sugar*

**Spices:**
*1 tsp cardamom*

### DIRECTIONS FOR PREPARATION

**1.** Beat butter for several minutes until it becomes creamy. Gradually fold in flour, baking powder, and cardamom and mix well.

**2.** Add egg and mix well. Then gradually add milk and rose extract; knead well. Let dough rise for 3 hours.

**3.** Make balls the size of walnuts; press flat to form round pieces about 2" in diameter.

**4.** Mix together filling of nuts and 1 cup of the powdered sugar. Place 2 to 3 tsp. of the filling on top of each flattened ball, fold in half to form semicircles. Press edges together.

**5.** With a knife, make a series of small indentations on the rounded edge of each piece of pastry, making sure not to poke a hole in the pastry. Continue Steps 3 and 4 until dough and filling are used up.

**6.** Heat oil in a heavy skillet and brown pastries on each side. Allow to cool.

**7.** Sprinkle on both sides with remaining powdered sugar; serve.

# Qorabiyyeh

(almond confection, Tabriz style)

*10 to 15 pieces*

Ingredients:
*3 egg whites*
*2/3 cup powdered sugar*
*1 cup powdered almonds*
*¼ cup butter, softened to room temperature*

### DIRECTIONS FOR PREPATATION

**1.** Mix together all ingredients.
**2.** Make walnut-size balls, place on cookie sheet about 2" apart. Bake in 350° oven for 20 minutes.
**3.** Remove gently with a spatula, place on newspaper and allow to cool.

# Nan Berenji

(rice flour cookies)

*about 30 pieces*

Ingredients:
*1 lb unsalted butter, softened to room temperature*
*4 cups rice flour*
*1½ cups powdered sugar*
*1 tsp baking powder*
*poppy seeds to garnish*
*2 eggs, well beaten*
Spices:
*2 tsp ground cardamom*

### DIRECTIONS FOR PREPARATION

**1.** Preheat oven to 350°. Beat butter for several minutes until it becomes creamy. Gradually add rice flour and mix together well.
**2.** Gradually add sugar and cardamom and beat for a few more minutes.
**3.** Add baking powder and eggs and mix together well.
**4.** Make balls the size of small walnuts. Arrange 2½" apart on an ungreased cookie sheet. Flatten lightly with the tip of your finger. Sprinkle with poppy seeds.
**5.** Bake cookies for 15 to 20 minutes, or until they become a golden color.
**6.** Remove gently with a spatula and let cool on wax paper or newspaper.

## Nan Nokhodchi
(roasted chickpea flour cookies)

*about 25 to 30 pieces*

**Ingredients:**
*1½ cups roasted chickpea flour*
*¾ cup unsalted butter, softened to room temperature*
*¾ cup powdered sugar*
**Spices:**
*½ tsp cardamom*

### DIRECTIONS FOR PREPARATION

**1.** Mix together all ingredients along with 4 Tbs. warm water in a mixing bowl to form a smooth paste. Make sure no lumps of flour remain in the mixture.
**2.** Take spoonfuls of the dough and role into balls the size of walnuts.
**3.** Arrange on a lightly greased cookie sheet about 2" apart. Press each ball lightly with a fork or potato masher to flatten slightly and imprint a design. Bake for 20 minutes in moderate preheated oven, 350°.

NOTE: *Nan nokhodchi* is very delicate and should be handled with care, but well worth the effort.

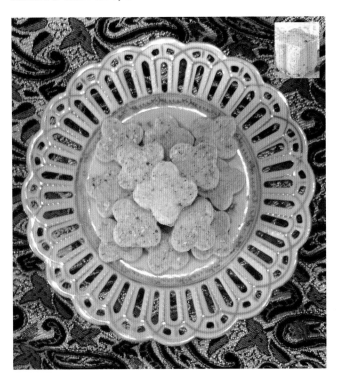

## Nan-e Panjereh'i
(latticework 'window bread': a crispy delicacy dusted with confectioner's sugar)

*25 to 30 pieces*

**Ingredients:**
*5 eggs*
*1 cup flour*
*1 tsp wheat starch*
*1 cup milk*
*2 cups vegetable oil*
*½ cup powdered sugar*
**Spices:**
*1 tsp cardamom*

### DIRECTIONS FOR PREPARATION

**1.** Beat eggs with an electric beater or vigorously with a wire whisk until light in color and texture.
**2.** Thoroughly dissolve flour, wheat starch, and cardamom in milk; fold into eggs.
**3.** Heat vegetable oil in a small, deep saucepan over medium heat.
**4.** Heat a rosette iron by dipping it into the hot oil; shake off excess oil; dip immediately into the batter. Quickly dip into the hot oil until batter becomes golden; shake iron to loosen rosette. Remove from oil and place on newspaper to drain. Repeat until all batter is used up. If batter sticks to the iron, the oil is too hot. Allow to cool.
**5.** Sprinkle with confectioners sugar. Store in an airtight container in a cool, dry place.

## Bereshtuk-e Kaka'o

### (cocoa confection)

*about 25 pieces*

**Ingredients:**
*1 cup unsalted butter*
*2 ½ cups white flour*
*½ cup finely chopped walnuts*
*1 cup powdered sugar*
*2 Tbs. cocoa powder*
*¼ cup finely chopped pistachio nuts*
**Spices:**
*1 tsp powdered cardamom*

### DIRECTIONS FOR PREPARATION

**1.** Melt butter in a skillet. Add flour and stir over low heat until the mixture turns a golden color.
**2.** Add walnuts and stir for 5 minutes.
**3.** Stir in powdered sugar and cardamom; remove from heat. Divide mixture in half.
**4.** Spread half the mixture evenly on a cookie sheet about ½" thick.
**5.** Add cocoa to second half of flour and nut mixture; mix well. Spread evenly over the previous layer.
**6.** Sprinkle with pistachio nuts; refrigerate for 1 hour. Cut into diamond shape pieces (2" x 1½"). Serve.

## Bereshtuk-e Ard-e Nokhodchi

### (roasted chickpea flour confection)

*about 25 pieces*

**Ingredients:**
*1 cup unsalted butter*
*2 cups roasted chickpea flour*
*1 cup powdered sugar*
*¼ cup finely chopped pistachio nuts*
**Spices:**
*2 tsp cardamom*

### DIRECTIONS FOR PREPARATION

**1.** Melt butter in a skillet. Add roasted chickpea flour and stir over low heat until golden brown.
**2.** Remove from heat and add sugar and cardamom. Mix well.
**3.** Spread on a small cookie sheet evenly to a thickness of about 3/4". Sprinkle with pistachio nuts.
**4.** Refrigerate for 1 hour before serving; cut into diamond shape pieces (2" x 1½"). Store in an airtight container in the refrigerator.

## Shirini-ye Zanjebili
(ginger and nut confection, Azerbaijan style)

*10 to 12 pieces*

**Ingredients:**
*1 cup flour*
*¼ cup ground walnuts*
*¼ cup ground almonds*
*½ cup unsalted butter*
*1¼ cup powdered sugar*
*2 Tbs. chopped pistachios*
**Spices:**
*1 Tbs. powdered ginger*

### DIRECTIONS FOR PREPARATION

**1.** Lightly brown flour in a skillet over medium heat, stirring constantly. Set aside.
**2.** Lightly brown ground walnuts and almonds in a skillet over medium heat; add to flour.
**3.** Melt butter; add ginger and sugar, stirring until sugar dissolves. Add to flour-nut mixture.
**4.** Spread out mixture on a cookie sheet to a thickness of about 3/4" and sprinkle with pistachios and sugar.
**5.** Cut into 2" squares. Cool before serving.

## Zanjebil-e Parvardeh-ye Shekari
(date confection with ginger and sugar)

*15 to 20 pieces*

**Ingredients:**
*¼ lb pitted dates*
*1 cup granulated sugar*
**Spices:**
*2 Tbs. powdered ginger*

### DIRECTIONS FOR PREPARATION

**1.** Grind dates in a meat grinder or food processor. Add 1 Tbs. hot water if dates are very dry.
**2.** Mix together sugar and ginger and set 4 Tbs. of this mixture aside.
**3.** Add remaining sugar and ginger mixture to dates to make a very thick paste. If dry, add 1 to 2 Tbs. hot water.
**4.** Sprinkle half the ginger and sugar mixture on a flat surface and flatten date mixture into a rectangle about 1" thick. Sprinkle surface evenly with remaining ginger and sugar and cut into 1" cubes.

## Zanjebil-e Parvardeh-ye Khorma'i
(date confection with ginger, Isfahan style)

*15 to 20 pieces*

Ingredients:
*1 lb pitted dates*
*¼ cup granulated sugar*
**Spices:**
*1 Tbs. powdered ginger*

### DIRECTIONS FOR PREPARATION

**1.** Grind dates several times in a meat grinder or food processor. If dates are too dry, sprinkle with 1 or 2 Tbs. hot water.
**2.** Mix together ginger and sugar, then divide in half.
**3.** Thoroughly mix together half the ginger-sugar mixture with dates to make a very thick paste.
**4.** Sprinkle some of the ginger and sugar mixture on a flat surface, then spread date mixture on top into a rectangle (about 6" x 4").
**5.** Cut the date mixture into 1" squares with a spatula or knife. Sprinkle remaining ginger and sugar mixture evenly over top.

## Gush-e Fil
(elephant's ear)

*about 20 pieces*

Ingredients:
*2 1/2 cups sugar*
*1 Tbs. white vinegar*
*1 cup rosewater*
*2 ½ cup vegetable oil*
*1 egg*
*4 egg yolks*
*1 Tbs. baking powder*
*1 cup milk*
*2 cups white flour*
*powdered sugar*
*½ cup pulverized pistachio nuts*

### DIRECTIONS FOR PREPARATION

**1.** Add 1 cup water to sugar in a small pot, bring to a boil. Add the vinegar and boil for one more minute.
**2.** Stir in rosewater; set the syrup aside to cool.
**3.** Combine vegetable oil with the egg and the egg yolks and beat until smooth.
**4.** Add baking powder and milk to the egg mixture along with ½ cup of the oil and beat well.
**5.** Gradually mix in flour mix. Cover with plastic wrap and let rise for 2-3 hours.
**6.** Place dough on a flat surface; roll out into a sheet 1/8 inch thick. Cut into 1½-inch squares.
**7.** Take two adjacent corners of each square and bring them together to make a fan shape.
**8.** Deep fry each pastry in hot oil until golden brown. Remove from oil with a slotted spoon. Place pastry on a paper towel to absorb excess oil.
**9.** Drop elephant ears in the syrup for an hour until syrup is absorbed. Remove from syrup.
**10.** Sprinkle with powdered sugar and pistachio.

Prepared by Fahimeh Z.

## Tut

### (boysenberry-shaped almond sweet)

*about 30 pieces*

**Ingredients:**
*2 cups unroasted skinless almonds (if unavailable, use slivered almonds), pulverized*
*½ cup powdered sugar*
*2 Tbs. rosewater*
*red and green food coloring*
*30 pieces of slivered almonds*
**Spices:**
*1 Tbs. finely ground cardamom*

**DIRECTIONS FOR PREPARATION**

**1.** Mix all ingredients except 30 pieces slivered almonds together into a paste.
**2.** Divide the mixture into three equal parts. Separately add red and green food coloring to two of the parts.
**3.** Take small portions of each mixture, roll into the size and shape of boysenberries. Stick a piece of slivered almond to one end of each as a stem (for added color, you can dip the pieces in green food coloring); arrange on a dish.

   This confection is usually prepared during the Persian New Year and served along with other sweets.

Shirini-ye Gerdu'i

## (walnut cookies)

*about 30 pieces*

**Ingredients:**
*1 lb unsalted butter, softened to room temperature*
*4 cups finely ground walnuts*
*1½ cups powdered sugar*
*1 tsp baking powder*
*2 eggs, well beaten*
**Spices:**
*2 tsp ground cardamom*

### DIRECTIONS FOR PREPARATION

**1.** Preheat oven to 350°. Beat butter for several minutes until it becomes creamy. Gradually add ground walnuts and mix together well.
**2.** Gradually add sugar and cardamom and beat for a few more minutes.
**3.** Add baking powder and eggs and mix together well.

**4.** Make balls the size of small walnuts. Arrange 2½" apart on an ungreased cookie sheet. Flatten lightly with the tip of your finger.
**5.** Bake cookies for 15 to 20 minutes, or until they become golden brown.
**6.** Remove gently with a spatula and let cool on wax paper or newspaper.

# Kolucheh Yazdi
## (cookies, Yazd style)

*about 15 pieces*

### Ingredients:
*4 eggs, well beaten*
*¾ cup unsalted butter, melted*
*1 cup sugar*
*2 cups flour*
*1 cup plain yogurt*
*1 tsp baking powder*
*1 tsp baking soda*
*a few drops rose extract*
*1 cup seedless raisins*
*½ cup blanched almonds*
*3 Tbs. chopped pistachios*
### Spices:
*½ tsp cardamom*

### DIRECTIONS FOR PREPARATION

**1.** Combine eggs, sugar and melted butter; mix well.
**2.** Gradually add flour and mix. Add yogurt and mix well.
**3.** Add rose extract, baking soda, baking powder, and cardamom to egg-flour mixture; mix well; let rise for 1 hour.
**4.** Stir in raisins and almonds.
**5.** Pour the mixture onto a cookie pan to a depth of ½". Sprinkle with pistachios. Bake at 325° for 15 to 20 minutes until golden brown. Let cool and cut into serving pieces.
Serve with hot tea or coffee.

Pastery section of an Iranian supermarket in California.
*Photo by Kamron.*

# Tea and Other Drinks
## (Chay and Sharbat)

The following drinks are generally served as refreshments, with the exception of *dugh*, which is usually served with meals.

By far the most common Iranian drink before meals, while shopping, when visiting friends, after dinner, and so on, is tea, which is served piping hot in small, transparent glasses and sipped over cubes of sugar held in the mouth.

Despite the fact that wines have almost always been made in Iran (some experts even claim that wine was invented in Shiraz, which is known as the city of wine, roses, and poets), alcoholic beverages are not commonly served, particularly in more traditional families. However, a seemingly endless variety of drinks with the delicate essence of fruit or blossoms, known as *sharbat*, and fruit juices are most common.

A Traditional Teahouse in Tehran.
*Photo by Jamshid Bayrami*

# Tea

Tea is by far Iran's national drink. One could almost say that serving and drinking piping hot tea are a national pastime. Hot tea is served at virtually all times: at breakfast, after lunch and dinner, for a midday break, after waking from an afternoon nap, when company comes to call, and even in shops over bargaining transactions. It is served in religious mourning ceremonies and national celebrations, at times of sorrow and at times of joy, at weddings, on picnics, in teahouses, at home, in the bazaars, in offices, and even in mosques. It is served at official functions and friendly gatherings. It is served in winter to keep you warm and in summer to cool you off, in spring to rejoice in nature and in fall to meditate on the season's change. One can always find an excuse to drink tea. You invite a friend over to drink tea or you invite yourself over to a friend's for tea. You drink tea to perk up and you drink tea to calm down. In fact, it might be said that tea is more than a national drink or even a national pastime in Iran; it is a national obsession, a national addiction.

Often the quality of the tea is the basis for judgment of a business establishment's esteem or the success of a party. After having left a dinner party, friends or family members can be heard to comment on the tea. People have even been heard to say they enjoy coming to a particular home because they know they will always have a good glass of tea.

Therefore, one of the most important household necessities for an Iranian family is a samovar. The magic of a samovar is that it enables one to continue serving piping hot tea of variable strengths to innumerable guests with only one relatively small teapot.

Iranians enjoy the act of drinking tea almost as

much as they do the tea itself. And there is an art to both serving the tea and appreciating it.

First of all, attention must be paid to the tea itself. For the Iranian, both color and temperature are of vital importance. The tea is appreciated as much visually as it is through the palate, much as the connoisseur appreciates good wine. That is why tea generally is served in small, clear glasses *(estekan),* so that one may observe the color and to ensure that the tea remains hot to the last drop. Before serving, a good host or hostess may pour a small amount of tea in an *estekan* and hold it up to the light to judge whether it is too light *(kam rang),* indicating either that it

Whole Sugar Cones; Kerman, Iran.
*Photo by Susan Sprachman.*

has not steeped long enough or that not enough dried tea leaves have been added to the pot, or too dark *(por rang),* indicating that it must be topped with more hot water.

When the tea has steeped long enough, to ensure that it is served hot, each *estekan* is rinsed in boiling water from the samovar. Strong tea is poured into the glass to only partially fill it, and more boiling hot water is added. This method allows individual tastes to be taken into consideration, as some guests may request tea light in strength (color) while others may prefer it strong. The tea is then served accompanied by sugar cubes, rock candy, or caramelized sugar *(pulaki,* especially in the city of Isfahan, see recipe in this book). Sugar cubes or *pulaki* are placed in the mouth and the tea is sipped over them, while the rock candy is dissolved in the tea.

For anyone lucky enough to have a samovar, serving tea is made easy. The water is boiled in the samovar and when it is hot enough, water is swished around

the inside of the teapot to warm it and prepare it to receive the tea, several spoonfuls of loose tea are added, and the pot is filled with boiling water from the samovar. The water in the samovar is then replenished and the teapot placed on top of the samovar to steep. As soon as the first round of tea is served, more loose tea and boiling water are added to the pot and the heat of the samovar is turned down to keep the water just below a boil.

The samovar was originally heated with charcoal, later on remodeled to heat with kerosene, and most recently converted to electricity. In the past two decades, kettles with faucets similar to that of the samovar have become very common, in which the water is heated on top of the stove. This is an excellent substitute for the traditional samovar. However, in all varieties, the principle remains the same. A bit of ingenuity can reproduce this effect without a samovar. If you have a kettle with a wide opening, use it to boil the water; when you have rinsed the inside of the teapot and added the tea and boiling water, refill the kettle with water, place it back on the burner, and place the teapot on top of it. This also helps prevent the tea itself from boiling, as it may do if it is placed directly on the burner, which destroys the flavor of the tea.

In my own albeit biased opinion, good tea, no matter what the advertisers say, is never found in tea bags. In fact, most tea bags are filled with tea dust or what remains when the quality tea has been packed. There are many blends of tea that are tasty, and you may wish to experiment with them. (I should mention that to the Iranian, what we call "herbal tea" is not considered tea at all, but medicine.) In Iran, many families blend their own favorites by combining different kinds of loose tea sold in open bags in special shops. One blend of tea our family finds especially pleasing consists of the following:

2 parts Darjeeling tea
1 part Earl Grey tea
A small amount of Orange Pekoe tea
(about 1 to 1½ oz. per 12 oz. of the above tea mixture)

Tea is delicate, which is why the teapot should be warmed before the tea is added. It steeps in 5 to 10 minutes and should not sit more than half an hour before it is served. After this amount of time, a fresh pot should be made.

### Decorated Sugar Cubes

Using cake decorating utensilss, you can decorate ordinary sugar cubes with various designs to fit a special occasion. At right, cubes are decorated with colored icings used to decorate candies and cakes. Be creative!

## Paludeh-ye Sib
(apple and lemon punch)

*6 to 8 servings*

**Ingredients:**
*1 cup sugar*
*½ cup lemon juice*
*2 apples, cored, skinned and grated*

### DIRECTIONS FOR PREPARATION

**1.** Make a simple syrup by dissolving sugar in ½ cup hot water.
**2.** Add lemon juice; let cool.
**3.** Dilute syrup with 3 to 4 cups water, to taste.
**4.** Just before serving, add apples.
Serve over ice.

## Sharbat-e Beh-Limu
(quince and lemon syrup)

*about 3 cups*

**Ingredients:**
*2½ cups sugar*
*1 large ripe quince*
*3 Tbs. lemon juice*

### DIRECTIONS FOR PREPARATION

**1.** Bring 1 cup water to a boil; add sugar and stir to dissolve thoroughly.
**2.** Peel and grind the quince; place in a pot and simmer in 1½ cups water until fully cooked. By this time the cooked quince should be pink to medium-red in color. Pass the mixture through a sifter and then combine with the syrup and let simmer one hour. Mix in the lemon juice and simmer 2 minutes. Set aside to cool.
To serve, dilute a few spoonfuls, to taste, in water and serve over ice.

## Ab-e Hendavaneh
(watermelon juice)

**Ingredients:**
*watermelon*
*sugar*

### DIRECTIONS FOR PREPARATION

**1.** Remove watermelon from outer skin and cut into small pieces.
**2.** Turn watermelon through a juicer to separate the pulp from the seeds or place in a colander over a bowl and, with a potato masher, press watermelon juice into the bowl.
**3.** Add sugar to taste, stir, and serve over ice.

# Sekanjebin
(sweet and sour mint syrup)

*about 4 to 5 cups*

Ingredients:
*6 cups sugar*
*1 ½ cup vinegar*
*couple of stalks of spearmint, or a few drops*
*   of spearmint extract*

### DIRECTIONS FOR PREPARATION

**1.** Put 2 cups water in a pot, add sugar, and let boil over medium heat until the sugar is dissolved.
**2.** Add vinegar and boil 5 to 10 minutes more. Remove from heat, add mint, let cool. If using fresh mint, remove stalks after syrup has cooled.

**To serve as a drink**: Mix 1 part *sekanjebin* to 2 to 3 parts cold water; serve over ice. For a change, add diced or grated cucumber to the drink.
**To serve as a snack**: Dip leaves of romaine lettuce in a bowl of *sekanjebin*. Can also be drizzled over romaine lettuce as a salad dressing.

# Sharbat-e Albalu
(tart cherry syrup)

*about 3 cups*

Ingredients:
*1 cup fresh or 1 can tart cherries*
*2 cups sugar*

### DIRECTIONS FOR PREPARATION

**1.** Place cherries in a pot with 1¼ cup water and simmer over medium-low heat for 20 minutes.
**2.** Place a colander or a sieve over a bowl and drain cherries, collecting juice in bowl. Using a potato masher or a spatula, press cherries to extract remaining juice, collecting it in the bowl.
**3.** Place sugar and juice in a pot, bring to a boil, reduce heat, and let simmer for 5 more minutes. Let cool. Will make a rather thick syrup.

To serve, put about 2 to 3 tablespoons of syrup in a glass, add cold water, stir, and add ice.

# Paludeh-ye Talebi
(pureed cantaloupe drink)

*3 to 4 servings*

Ingredients:
*1 cantaloupe*
*2 Tbs. sugar*
**Spices:**
*¼ tsp cardamom*

### DIRECTION FOR PREPARATION

**1.** Remove skin and seeds from cantaloupe and cut into small pieces.
**2.** Puree in a blender with 1 cup crushed ice, a few pieces at a time.

**3.** Add sugar and cardamom, stir; and chill.
Serve in a glass with a spoon as a refreshment or as a dessert.

NOTE: For variety, substitute honeydew or any other type of melon.

## Sharbat-e Rivas
### (rhubarb syrup)

*about 6 cups*

Ingredients:
*1 lb fresh or frozen rhubarb*
*4 cups sugar*

#### DIRECTIONS FOR PREPARATION

**1.** Clean and cut rhubarb into chunks (if fresh) and place in a pot along with 2 cups water. Bring to a boil and simmer over medium heat for 20 to 30 minutes or until rhubarb can be easily mashed. (If using frozen rhubarb, cooking time is about 10 to 15 minutes.)
**2.** Put a colander over a bowl and pour the rhubarb and water into it. With a potato masher, press the rhubarb pieces to get as much of the juice out as possible. (The unused rhubarb pulp can be used to flavor various dishes such as *khoresh.*)
**3.** Return juice to pot, add sugar, bring to a boil; reduce heat to low and simmer for 5 more minutes. Remove from heat and allow to cool.

NOTE: To serve, mix desired amount of syrup (about 2 to 3 tablespoons) in a glass of cold water and add ice. Syrup should be stored in a covered bottle or jar and kept in a cool place.

## Sharbat-e Bahar Narenj
### (orange blossom flavored syrup)

*about 3 cups*

Ingredients:
*2½ cups sugar*
*2 Tbs. orange blossom extract, or 1 cup orange blossoms*
*2 Tbs. lemon juice*

#### DIRECTIONS FOR PREPARATION

**1.** Bring 1 cup water to a boil; add sugar and stir to dissolve thoroughly.
**2.** Add orange blossom extract or orange blossoms and let simmer for 5 minutes.
**3.** Add lemon juice and simmer for 5 more minutes.
**4.** Allow to cool. If using orange blossoms, drain in a colander to remove petals. Store in a bottle in a cool place.

To serve, dilute a few spoonfuls, to taste, in water and serve over ice.

## Sharbat-e Narenj
### (orange-flavored syrup)

*about 3 cups*

Ingredients:
*3 cups sugar*
*juice of 4 bitter oranges*

#### DIRECTIONS FOR PREPARATION

**1.** Bring 1 cup water to a boil. Add sugar and let simmer until completely dissolved.
**2.** Add bitter orange juice and let simmer another 3 to 5 minutes.
**3.** Let cool; store in a sealed bottle in a cool place.

To serve, dilute several spoonfuls, to taste, in water and serve over ice.

# Dugh
(yogurt drink)

*2 to 3 servings*

Ingredients:
*1 cup plain yogurt*
*1½ cups carbonated water (optional)*
Spices:
*½ tsp salt*
*¼ tsp savory*
*¼ tsp celery salt*
*½ tsp powdered crushed mint*
*¼ tsp powdered rose petals (optional)*

### DIRECTIONS FOR PREPARATION

**1.** Place yogurt in pitcher and beat well.
**2.** Add 1½ cups water or carbonated water and seasonings and stir well. Serve over ice.

# Sharbat-e Gol-e Sorkh
(rosewater syrup)

*about 3½ cups*

Ingredients:
*2½ cups sugar*
*¼ cup lemon juice*
*2 tsp rosewater extract*

### DIRECTIONS FOR PREPARATION

**1.** Bring 1 cup water to a boil and add sugar, stirring until it is dissolved.
**2.** Add lemon juice and rosewater extract; stir.
**3.** Boil gently for 1 to 2 minutes.
**4.** Remove from heat; allow to cool.

Can be mixed with water and additional lemon juice to taste and served over ice as a refreshing drink or, as syrup, poured over vanilla ice cream or *Paludeh-ye Shirazi* (see recipe in the "Desserts" section of this book).

# Snacks & Sandwiches
## *(Tanaqolat)*

By far, the most popular forms of snacks in Iran are fresh fruits in season, dried fruits and nuts, and confections. Western-style sandwiches introduced in Iran have often been changed to suit Iranian tastes and have become popular, especially in large cities. Among the most common sandwiches are *Sandovich-e Kotlet* (see *Kotlet* recipes), *Sandovich-e Kuku* (see *Kuku* recipes), and *Sandovich-e Kalbas* (see recipe below), which is a favorite among the younger gen-

eration. These sandwiches are generally served

on French- or Italian-style bread or *lavash* bread with saltwater cucumber pickles.

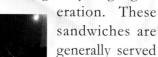

Fresh Iranian pistachios.
Photo by Jassem Ghazbanpour.

# Ajil
(mixed nuts, seeds and dried fruits)

Various mixtures of nuts, seeds, and dried fruits have been traditional favorites among Iranians, served primarily as snacks and to guests. There are, in fact, shops in Iran that specialize in preparing and selling various kinds of roasted nuts, melon seeds, pumpkin seeds, dried figs, raisins, almonds, pistachios, etc.

You can use your imagination in combining your own mixture of *ajil.* Here are some suggestions:

**Ingredients:**
*roasted pistachio nuts*
*roasted hazelnuts*
*walnuts*
*whole toasted almonds*
*roasted chickpeas*
*roasted watermelon seeds*
*roasted pumpkin seeds*

# Ajil Moshkel Gosha
(literally, "the nut mixture that solves problems")

Fresh walnuts in water.

**Ingredients:**
*whole almonds*
*walnuts*
*hazelnuts*
*roasted chickpeas*
*dried figs*
*dried apricots*
*dried peaches*
*red raisins*
*golden raisins*

In the region of Azerbaijan (in northwestern Iran), a variety of this *ajil,* called *Ajil-e Chaharshanbeh Suri,* named after the last Wednesday Eve of the Persian calendar year, is served while preparations are being made for the coming of *Noruz* (Persian New Year, which corresponds with the first day of spring). Symbolically to help one leave behind one's problems at the advent of the new year.

# Nokhodchi va Keshmesh
(roasted chickpeas with raisins)

**Ingredients:**
*2 parts roasted chickpeas*
*1 part red or golden raisins*

# Gandom Shahdaneh
(roasted wheat and hemp seed)

**Ingredients:**
*2 parts roasted wheat*
*1 part lightly roasted hemp seed*

Before the days of packaged snack foods, Iranian school children often carried in their pockets either roasted chickpeas and raisins, or a mixture of roasted wheat and hemp seed

# Tokhmeh-ye Budadeh
(roasted melon seeds)

*about 2 cups*

**Ingredients:**
*2 cups watermelon, honeydew, or pumpkin seeds*
*2 Tbs. olive oil*
**Spices:**
*1 tsp salt*
*1 tsp turmeric*
*½ tsp black pepper*

### DIRECTIONS FOR PREPARATION

**1.** Rinse seeds in warm water and drain in a colander.
**2.** Sprinkle with seasonings and mix well.
**3.** Spread seasoned seeds out on several sheets of paper towel; allow to dry completely (may take a day or so).
**4.** Place seeds in a bowl; add oil and mix well.
**5.** Roast in heavy, ungreased iron skillet over medium heat, stirring constantly to avoid burning.

# Sandovich-e Kalbas
(kielbasa sandwich)

*3 sandwiches*

**Ingredients:**
*1 loaf thin French or Italian bread*
*6 slices kielbasa*
*2 saltwater cucumber pickles, thinly sliced lengthwise*
*2 tomatoes, sliced*
*¼ cup chopped parsley*
*2 Tbs. finely chopped onion*
*3 Tbs. olive oil*
*2 Tbs. lemon juice*

**DIRECTIONS FOR PREPARATION**

**1.** Cut bread into 3 equal portions and then slice each piece open lengthwise.
**2.** On the bottom piece of each bread, place 2 slices of meat, 1/3 of each, pickles, parsley, and onions; sprinkle with olive oil and lemon juice; top with second half of bread and serve.

# Dastpich-e Kalbas
(kielbasa wrap)

*10 to 12 pieces*

**Ingredients:**
*1 loaf* lavash *bread*
*½ cup cream cheese*
*½ cup finely-chopped parsley*
*½ cup finely-chopped green onions*
*2 large pickles sliced*
*2 tomatos sliced*
*12 slices kielbasa or mortadella*

**DIRECTIONS FOR PREPARATION**

**1.** Spread out *lavash* bread on a large cutting board; spread softened cream cheese on bread; and evenly place kielbasa or mortadella slices on top. Sprinkle parsley and green onions and arrange pickles and tomatos as shown.
**2.** Tightly roll the bread and ingredients from shortest width to make a longer roll.

**3.** Slice the roll into 10-12 pieces. Place toothpick in each piece to hold wrap together if necessary.
Serving suggestion: Great as a finger food for parties.
NOTE: Mayonnaise may be substituted for cream cheese.

Prepared by Fahimeh Z.

## Ard-e Nokhodchi
(roasted chickpea flour)

*about 1 cup*

**Ingredients:**
*1 cup dried chickpeas*
*2 tsp olive oil*

DIRECTIONS FOR PREPARATION

**1.** Lightly grease an iron skillet with olive oil and place over medium heat. Place chickpeas in skillet and stir constantly until a light golden color, about 5 to 10 minutes.
**2.** Remove immediately from skillet and allow to cool.
**3.** Powder chickpeas in a food processor, coffee grinder, or with a mortar and pestle and sift to a very fine consistency.

## Qavut
(sweet roasted chickpea powder)

*about 1½ cups*

**Ingredients:**
*1 cup roasted chickpea flour*
*½ cup powdered sugar*
**Spices:**
*½ tsp cardamom*

**DIRECTIONS FOR PREPARATION**

Mix together all ingredients and serve as a snack in small, individual saucers with a small spoon.

## Qaraqarut (Qara)
(tart concentrated seasoning)

**Ingredients:**
*4 cups liquid from drained yogurt (or whey)*

**DIRECTIONS FOR PREPARATION**

**1.** Place yogurt liquid (from *mast-e kiseh'i*; see previous recipe) or whey liquid in a pot and bring to a boil; boil 5-10 minutes.
**2.** Turn heat to low and let simmer slowly until the liquid thickens to the consistency of molasses.
**3.** Simmer for another 10-15 minutes, stirring regularly. Remove pot from heat and allow to cool.
**4.** Scrape with a spoon or spatula spreader from the bottom of the pot; place in a container or plastic bag and keep in a cool place. *Qaraqarut* should have the consistency of taffy.

NOTE: Traditionally, *qaraqarut* was made of whey liquid by nomadic tribes in Iran. It is used to season most thick soups, especially *omaj*, by stirring small pieces into the thick soup just before serving. It can be used as a substitute for lemon juice. Before the days of commercial snacks, teenage girls would often place small pieces of *qaraqarut* on their thumbnail and lick it throughout the day.

# Pulaki
(caramelized sugar wafers)

*about 20 to 25 pieces*

Ingredients:
*¾ cup sugar*
*¼ cup pistachio (optional)*

**DIRECTIONS FOR PREPARATION**

**1.** Heat a small, heavy skillet over high heat.
**2.** Add sugar and stir constantly with a teaspoon until it liquefies.
**3.** Remove from heat immediately and quickly (before the liquid hardens) drop spoonfuls of the liquid on an ungreased cookie sheet to make pieces about the size of a quarter. (If desired, place two or three pieces of nuts on each and press in place.)
**4.** Allow to cool and remove by slightly twisting the cookie sheet until they pop loose.

NOTE: *Pulaki* is dipped into piping hot tea, where it usually shatters, and then placed in the mouth, and tea is sipped over it.

# Baqala Pokhteh
(cooked fava beans)

6 servings

Ingredients:
2 lb fresh fava beans in pod
Spices:
1 Tbs. salt
1 Tbs. dried oregano

**DIRECTIONS FOR PREPARATION**

1. Rinse fava beans thoroughly, place in a large pot, add salt and 10 cups water, and bring to a boil.
2. Reduce heat and simmer for 30 to 40 minutes.
3. Sprinkle with oregano and serve

NOTE: Baqala Pokheh is usually sold by street vendors and is a favorite snack, especially during late afternoon walks through the city parks and streets. It is a finger food.

# Balal
(charcoal roasted corn on the cob)

*6 ears*

Ingredients:
*6 ears of corn*
Spices:
*2 Tbs. salt*

**DIRECTIONS FOR PREPARATION**
**1.** Prepare hot charcoal.
**2.** Dissolve salt in 4 cups water in a tall container.

**3.** Shuck corn and roast on all sides, turning frequently to avoid burning.
**4.** Dip corn in salted water before serving.

NOTE: *Balal* is usually sold by street vendors and is a favorite snack, especially during late afternoon walks through the city parks and streets.

# Wine

*"...a jug of wine, a loaf of bread—and thou"*
*Omar Khayyam*

Goblet with geometric pattern.
Qazvin, Iran, c. 3500 BC.
A.K. Jabbari collection

Wine has been an indispensable part of the Iranian culture. The reason may be that many varieties of grapes are indigenous to different parts of Iran, especially Fars province. Following the Islamic-Arab invasion of Iran in the seventh century, which eventually changed the religion of the Iranian people, the Islamic ban on intoxicants was enforced, and basically wine and wine drinking were relegated to secrecy and to the privacy of people's homes. Because of the abundance of grapes, other uses for this fruit were developed, including making raisins and vinegar. Since in ancient times many families made their own wines, the tradition was preserved, albeit from making wine into making homemade vinegar in large vats. Since vinegar is not used in large quantities in Iranian homes, except for making different pickles, the large amounts of vinegar produced at home by many families seems to suggest that the tradition of wine making continued in the production of homemade vinegar. Wine has been available in Iran in the course of all centuries since the country converted to Islam. There were of course periods in which making and drinking wine were prohibited by the rulers, especially public consumption of wine, but essentially wine has been an inseparable part of the Iranian culture and it has been used as a metaphor, not only in secular but also religious and spiritual poetry. In recent centuries, until the late 1970s when theocratic rule was established in Iran, traditionally Jews and Christians made wines and sold them to their Moslem customers.

Qajar painting showing two
lovers drinking wine.

The best wines known in the mid-20th-century were generally made in Shiraz, known as "the city of wine and roses," the most widely sold variety of which was a heavy red wine known as "1001." In the 1970s, the government itself became involved in the production of wines, when a company called Pakdis produced a variety of wines in uniform bottles for general consumption. Since the establishment of the Islamic government in 1979, however, wine production went underground, companies such as Pakdis were shut down, and most secular families have returned to the old tradition of wine making for their own consumption.

The following is an informative article on wine making and drinking in Iranian history by Rudie Matthee, an international authority on the subject, who teaches Iranian history at the University of Delaware.

A jug pottery double rhyton.
Ardebil, Iran, c. 1000 BC.
A.K. Jabbari collection

*Preceding:* Drinking wine in the court of Shah Abbas II, depicted in the mural that adorns the walls of the Chehel Sotun Palace in Isfahan.

# Wine and Wine Drinking in Iran (Persia)

## Rudie Matthee

An Iranian legend holds that the mythical king Jamshid was the first to experiment with the fermentation of grape juice. He tried the liquid that resulted, thought the taste acidic and took it for poison. One of his wives, however, who suffered from terrible headaches, ingested the liquid to put herself out of her misery. Yet, instead of killing her, the drink put her to sleep and cured her. Overjoyed by this result, King Jamshid ordered greater quantities to be prepared and had it called "happy poison," *zahr-i khush*.

The historical record indeed points to Iran as one of the world's earliest areas of wine cultivation and consumption. Jars from 5400 to 5000 BCE containing deposits that most likely are wine remnants have been found at Hajji Firuz Tepe in the northern Zagros Mountains.

A libation vessel in the form of a stylized male. Marlik, Iran, c. 1000 BC. A.K. Jabbari collection.

Herodotus noted that the Iranians were very much given to wine, with a special kind reserved for their king. Centuries later, the Sasanian banquet, *bazm*, featured wine and music and represents an enduring model in Iranian and wider Islamic history.

The advent of Islam formally made wine drinking illicit, but in fact did little to interrupt its long tradition in Iran. Famously celebrated in Sufi poetry, wine also remained central to court culture, with the ruler regularly holding a *majles*, a gathering with his boon companions enlivened by poets and storytellers. The Iranian *bazm*, held in conjunction with warfare, razm, remained virtually unchanged from Sasanian times until the days of Mahmud of Ghazna in the 11th century, and as such is celebrated as a three-day feast in Iran's national epic, Firdawsi's Shahnamah. Wine's pivotal place in elite society was further reinforced by an

Wine had powerfully symbolic significance in ancient Iranian tradition. A substitute for blood in a Zoroastrian libation ceremony that replaced the earlier ritual slaughter of a bull, it continued to symbolize the liquid gold and flowing fire of the radiant sun, and it played a role in the Zoroastrian sacrificial festival of Mehragan. Historical evidence confirms, moreover, that in Achaemenid times Iranians were well acquainted with wine and consumed it in great quantities. The modern Persian word for wine, *may*, is related to the word madu in Avestan, which means intoxication. Elamite tablets found at Persepolis refer to wine rations for functionaries and courtesans. Wine flowed freely at the banquets of the elite.

The architecture of Darioush winery in Napa Valley, California is modeled after Persepolis, one of the capitals of ancient Persia (Iran).

influx of mostly Turkic peoples from Central Asia with a reputation for hard drinking. The Mongols, who ruled Iran from about 1250 to 1350, in particular sanctioned drinking, though they mostly consumed enormous amounts of fermented mare's milk.

During the Safavid period, the practice of drinking wine received an additional impulse from the influx of large numbers of people inhabiting the Caucasus, Georgians and Armenians, who entered Iran as slave soldiers to reach high positions in the army and the administration, in the case of the men, and power and prestige in the harems of the elite, in the case of the women. Both groups were accustomed to wine and brought their drinking habits with them to Iran.

Iranian wine was considered quite good by the Frenchman Chardin, our best outside source on Safavid Iran, who called the wines of Shiraz and Georgia excellent. Shiraz wine had the best reputation, with much of its production reserved for the royal court. Some was also exported. The German physician Kaempfer called the effect of Shiraz wine remarkable, since a moderate intake produced a wonderful alacrity and enhanced the appetite. French wines, Chardin claimed, were more delicate than Iranian ones, but then delicacy was not what Iranians wanted from their wines, he asserted in an opinion echoed by countless others after him: they were only interested in strength and body, and tended to drink it undiluted, at times spicing it with additives for enhanced aroma and intoxicating power, or against hangovers. To get drunk was the purpose, and if a wine didn't achieve this state fast enough, the consumer would ask: "What kind of wine is this? It has no kick (*damagh nadareh*)."

It is important to note that water was the most common beverage for ordinary people. For the Safavid elite, however, wine remained part of a cultural idiom shared by the entire eastern half of the Muslim world. Both the Safavids and the Mughals inherited the *razm-o-bazm* tradition of hard fighting and hard drinking as the expected pursuits of warriors. The court chronicles of the period reflect this in alternating descriptions of the

### The Winery in Napa Valley

Darioush Winery, noted for its Bordeaux style estate wines, implements old world labor-intensive, micro-vineyard management and new world state of the art technology to craft fine wines from its estates located in the appellations of Napa Valley, Mt. Veeder, and Oak Knoll. Under the direction of proprietor Darioush Khaledi and winemaker Steve Devitt, precision and quality are of the utmost importance at the winery.

### The Property

Darioush welcomes guests to its new visitor center and winery. The new architectural building comes after five years in the making, and combines materials, castings, and furnishings from distant lands and exotic locations. The 22,000 square foot winery, the first in America to combine architecture, design and Persian culture, provides a unique and exhilarating experience in California's most renowned wine destination. Reminiscent of the great noble architecture that once existed, the imagery of the Darioush building evokes Persepolis, the illustrious capital of ancient Persia.

shah's victories on the battlefield with portrayals of celebrations and each spring's joyous Noruz festivities, which invariably included drinking.

Wine in the Safavid period retained its spiritual, even sacral dimension reminiscent of the ancient libation rite. The shah was not just allowed to drink but supposed to drink in large quantity, both as a sign of his stature as a "big man," and as a demonstration that he occupied his own autonomous moral space—beyond the strictures of Islam. Emblematic of this is the huge goblet, made of gold, that he often forced upon his guests and that was called *hezar pisheh* (a thousand vocations), referring to the belief that those who had emptied it two or three times were capable of speaking randomly about a whole array of arts and professions. Often, this was little more than a form of burlesque entertainment for a monarch who loved to see high officials being carried away like corpses. There was a political rationale as well, reminiscent of what Herodotus had said about ancient Iranian kings: drinking loosened the lips and enabled the shah to extract secrets from his courtiers which otherwise remained hidden.

Wine, moreover, marked the boundaries of inclusion and exclusion. Who was and who was not invited to join the shah in his drinking parties betokened royal favor and disfavor. That even Western visitors were often included in these assemblies and allowed to share the shah's own cup betrays the emphatically secular make-up of a court that was not just willing to transgress the general Islamic ban on drinking but the more specifically Shi'i one on ritual purity as well.

Like other high-ranking officials, the shah had his own wine caves. The royal cave was a square space with a little pond filled with water in the middle. Tapestries covered the floor and wine bottles made of crystal were ranged around the pond as well as in niches surrounding the cave. Natural light entered the cave through several windows, and the play of sunlight on the wine gave a brilliant effect. It was the task of the shah's sommelier, the *shirehchi-bashi*, to provide the royal table with vintages from all over Iran and to supply wines for the shah's drinking sessions, banquets, and diplomatic receptions.

Yet as much as alcohol permeated early modern Iranian society, wine drinking retained its dubious status as a custom at variance with religious prescriptions. Alcohol remained socially unintegrated. The manufacturing and sale of wine was officially and mainly the bailiwick of non-Muslims, Armenians and Jews. Wine was a social lubricant and had political connotations, but its ultimate fate was simultaneous furtive embrace and public disavowal.

Little of this was visible in early Safavid times, when the Qizilbash, the tribal warriors who formed the military mainstay of Safavid power, consumed wine in a quasi-ecstatic fashion. Yet over time, as the Safavid state moved toward greater conformity to professed orthodoxy, the approach to alcohol began to change.

Of crucial importance in this transformation is Shah Tahmasb's famous repentance of 1532-33 (repeated in 1556)—his decision to give up and outlaw wine as well as to ban other forms of un-Islamic behavior, which led to the closing of taverns, brothels and gambling parlors. Aside from striking a blow at the hard-drinking Qizilbash, this decision symbolized a switch in the shah's image from incarnation of the divine to that of trustee of the imam, and as such marked a phase in the loss of the shah's divine pretensions that had begun with the Safavid defeat against the Ottomans in 1514.

Wine drinking and other un-Islamic activities seem to have abated—though not vanished—for the remainder of Shah Tahmasb's reign, with people abstaining either out of conviction or out of fear of the draconian punishment that awaited offenders. Shah Tahmasb did not set a standard for royal behavior, though. Later shahs resumed drinking, even if they no longer consumed alcohol in an ambiance that validated drinking. The religious leaders played an important role in this. In early Safavid times, Shi'i scholars developed the idea that, in the absence of the Hidden Imam, a qualified jurist might undertake the task of leading the community of the faithful in its efforts to uphold the divinely ordained social order. Heeding religious pressure, all subsequent shahs issued bans on drinking. Yet invariably such bans were honored in the breach more than in the observation. Their intent was ostensibly to curtail religiously proscribed behavior but, as numerous examples suggest, they really reflected a preoccupation with the preservation of public order. Drinking in public rather than drinking per se was seen as a problem.

The reign of Shah Abbas I (1587-1629) exemplifies this. Although Shah Abbas enjoyed drinking (in moderation) in the company of others, including visitors from Christian lands, his reign did not represent a return to the days of Shah Isma'il. Drinking parties at the court continued, and the shah ordered one of the renowned physicians of the time, Qazi b. Kashef al-Din Mohammad, to compose a treatise for him on the benefits and effects of wine and the etiquette of consuming it, but the days of ritualized and orgiastic drinking reflecting Qizilbash customs were over, and guilt was never far from the surface. One observer claimed how Shah Abbas, while never forcing his guests to consume alcohol, liked them to join him in drinking wine, viewing those who did not as hypocrites who by abstaining meant to reproach him for not abiding by the law of Islam. In 1620 Shah Abbas even instituted a ban on drinking for Muslims, but exempted himself on the basis of an unspecified illness. Some high-ranking officials, using the excuse that they suffered from a similar illness, were also allowed to drink—surreptitiously and indoors. The province of Fars, the center of Iran's viniculture and a semi-autonomous region whose inhabitants never saw and hardly recognized the shah as their sovereign, refused to heed the ban as well.

Under Shah Safi (1629-42), unbridled drinking at the court became the norm again. After a brief moment of sobriety following the shah's enthronement, his physicians advised him to take up wine, with the argument that it would dispel the "cold" that his indulgence in opium had introduced into his system. The shah's hard drinking had a negative effect on his capacity to govern—he had his the capable governor of Fars, Imam Qoli Khan, murdered in a drunken rage—and even the court chroniclers blame alcoholism for the brevity of his life—he died at age thirty-one.

The reign of Safi's successor, Shah Abbas II (1642-66), began with a general ban on wine, possibly in reaction to the alcohol-drenched reputation of his father. As of 1649, when he first reneged on his commitment to a life without wine, Shah Abbas II resembled his father in his prodigious alcohol intake. Drinking also figured promi-

nently at official banquets and audiences, some of which are depicted in the murals that adorn the walls of the Chehel Sotun palace in Isfahan to this day.

After the alcoholic excesses of Shah Abbas II's successor, Shah Solayman (r. 1666-94), the abstemiousness of Shah Soltan Hosayn (r. 1694-1722) appears natural, a swing of the pendulum. Exceedingly pious and acting on the advice of the most prominent cleric of the day, the stern Mohammad Baqer Majlesi, Soltan Hosayn in fact established his credentials as the realm's new ruler in 1694 by solemnly banning wine drinking and a whole array of other pastimes deemed frivolous and un-Islamic. The 6,000 bottles found in the royal cellar were emptied and ostentatiously smashed on the royal square. Yet a few months later the shah himself resumed drinking, apparently urged to do so by his Georgian great-aunt, Maryam Begom, who was addicted to alcohol herself. The ban itself was never repealed. Having lost its public visibility, wine was now relegated to the privacy of the palace.

Neither the Afghans, who briefly ruled Iran after the demise of the Safavids in 1722, nor Nadir Shah and his direct successors are known to have engaged in drinking. Indeed, the chroniclers of the period following the fall of Isfahan castigate the Safavids for having squandered the nation with their profligacy and decadence, and justify their demise as punishment for their misdeeds. Especially the ephemeral Shah Tahmasb III (r. 1729-32) is portrayed as the frivolous ruler who neglected his duties as he quaffed wine and engaged in lustful behavior, while Nadir Shah emerges as the virile warrior, the savior of the realm who deservedly took power and used it to reestablish order.

Under Karim Khan Zand royal merry-making seems to have resumed. Karim Khan himself is known to have indulged in wine as well as drugs and his capital Shiraz lived up to its reputation as an easy-going place filled with numerous taverns and brothels. Karim Khan's death in 1779 ushered in a period of turmoil, with contenders for the throne, among them his sons, who were all given to wine in excess.

The Qajar period resumed the tendency toward less prodigious royal drinking that had begun with the Afsharids and that Nadir Shah had affirmed. Both Agha Muhammad Khan, the founder of the Qajar dynasty, and his successor, Fath Ali Shah, are known to have drunk quite freely in the period before they acceded to the throne. Once in power, they sobered up, however, or at least confined their drinking to the private sphere. Mohammad Shah, Fath Ali Shah's successor (r. 1834-48), is not known to have touched alcohol, and in fact may have been a teetotaler.

Ideology seems to have played an important role in the Qajar attitude toward wine. Unlike the Safavids, whose authority had been buttressed by a divine aura deriving from the dynasty's alleged descent from the seventh Shi'i Imam, the Qajars came to power without much in the way of religious credentials. They derived their legitimacy mostly from the fact that, as loyal defenders of the Safavid legacy, they had restored the power of Shi'i Islam by reestablishing control over of the territory that had been lost in the 18th century.

Under later Qajar shahs the tendency toward moderation continued. Nasir al-Din Shah (r. 1848-96) is known to have enjoyed French wine with dinner, but he did not indulge immoderately, although I'timad al-Saltaneh in his diary attributes the dizzy spells the shah sometimes suffered to an unhealthy life that included, among other things, the (excessive) consumption of Shiraz wine. The women of his harem are said to have enjoyed wine as well. Nasir al-Din Shah's son and successor Mozaffar al-Din Shah (r. 1896-1907) displayed some of the traditional behavior of Iranian kings by drinking in private while upholding the appearance of abstemious devoutness in public, apparently in the belief that such comportment would help him to have his sins forgiven.

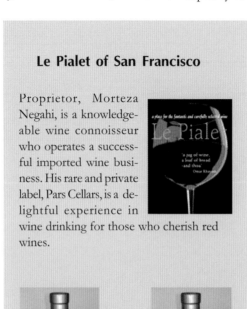

**Le Pialet of San Francisco**

Proprietor, Morteza Negahi, is a knowledgeable wine connoisseur who operates a successful imported wine business. His rare and private label, Pars Cellars, is a delightful experience in wine drinking for those who cherish red wines.

The court chroniclers followed suit. They continued to honor the razm o bazm tradition by paying lip service to it in their accounts, praising rulers for their fighting spirit and their capacity to engage in pleasurable activities, but their focus became hunting—a traditional royal pastime—and sumptuous food—an outdoor broth-making event now marked the highlight of the royal New Year ceremony.

As before, most Iranians, and especially those living in the countryside, did not drink, and the ambivalence remained, with imbibers attempting to reconcile their indulgence with a desire to be seen as good Muslims. Even in private people would drain their glass to the dregs, with their left hand under their chin to catch the drops of wine, lest they should be detected next morning in respectable society. Many high-ranking court officials, provincial governors, and members of the elite in general, on the other hand, continued to drink a good deal—out of sight and, anxious to uphold their reputation, behind the high walls of the andarun. And all cities had their drinking establishments, typically run by Armenians and Jews, and furtively patronized by Iranians of all ages, people of various class backgrounds, many of them lutis, urban ruffians, whose penchant for adultery and gambling was intertwined with their propensity to drink. Such taverns even seem to have taken the place of the traditional coffeehouse, which had largely disappeared during the turmoil of the 18th century.

Especially Shiraz, long known for its easy-going ways, was the scene of much drinking, by Muslims as well as Christians, though the former refrained from trafficking in wine for fear of too openly defying the bigotry of the local mullahs, who could stir up a riot at a moment's notice. As elsewhere, city officials punished only those drunks who caused a public nuisance and never bothered to intervene with indoor drinking parties.

Royal conduct notwithstanding, the consumption of alcohol, especially of hard liquor, may actually have increased in Qajar times following a more conspicuous Western presence and an attendant increase in imported European wines and liquors. Numerous instances of clerical agitation against the use of alcohol are on record in the 19th century, typically as part of outbursts against religious minorities. Complaining to chief minister Amir Kabir about an alleged increase in public drunkenness, the ulama in 1856 demanded a ban on the sale of intoxicating liquors. Amir Kabir, whose contempt for the ulama was well known, refused, insisting that the sale of alcohol was to remain permitted and that anyone should be free to drink as much as he wished. He warned, however, that the first person to be found drunk in public would learn the price of violating the law.

The 19th century appears to have produced a new consciousness about drinking. This manifested itself in an incipient medicalization of alcohol, with physicians referring to Western studies to warn about the negative health effects of drinking. The establishment of a society to combat drinking among the Armenians of Tabriz in the later part of the century must be seen in this light. In a different development, among the well-to-do many, having grown lax and skeptical in regard to the claims of their religion, openly began to flaunt their drinking habits. Much of this new outspokenness was in reaction to the growing intolerance and tyranny of the ulama in the face of a state with weak religious credentials. Members of the upper classes found in radical rationalism a tool to reject revelation and embrace individual judgment in matters of religion. Following a long-standing Iranian tradition of religious skepticism shading into deism, drinking became a means to express one's utter contempt for the clergy if not for revealed religion as such and a way to flaunt one's inner freedom. Though the circumstances had changed, wine thus retained its age-old function in Iranian culture as metaphor for the inner soul and the truth it pursues, free and unfettered, expressed as libertinism and freethinking, in contradistinction to the arid formalism of official religion.

# Special Occasions, Feasts and Banquets

Numerous occasions in Iran are observed and celebrated with banquets and special foods. Many of them that derived from a tradition as old as Iran itself stem from ancient Iranian customs and religions, and obviously have changed over the course of many centuries. Others concern Islamic Shiite ceremonies in which foods are served and which began a few centuries ago, but certainly have been influenced by ancient Iranian traditions.

Arrangement & photo by Noosheen Hashemi.

## Noruz

## Traditional Persian New Year

*Noruz*, Persian New Year, in harmony with the rebirth of nature, is celebrated on the first day of Spring as the most important of all Iranian holidays. A few weeks before the New Year, Iranians do a thorough house cleaning, buy new clothes for all members of the family, grow lentil or wheat sprouts in dishes, and buy or make various types of sweets and pastries. It is celebrated for thirteen days, during which families and friends exchange visits. As the hour of the Spring equinox approaches, everyone prepares for the coming new year freshly bathed, with new haircuts, and especially with new their clothes. On the thirteenth day, the celebrations end with picnicking (called *Sizdah Bedar*). On this day it is considered a bad omen to stay indoors.

Although *Sabzi Polo va Mahi* is the most common main dish served on the New Year, the menu can differ among different families and regions. The following is perhaps the most popular menu for Persian New Year in most parts of Iran:

Sabzi Polo va Mahi
Kuku Qandi
Mast
Salad-e Shirazi
Shirini-ye Tar I and II
Sharbat-e Bahar Narenj
Hot tea

## Haft Sin

For Persian New Year, every household in Iran sets a *Haft Sin*, a table of various items including seven ingredients the names of which start with the letter S in Persian.

These symbolic items typically include:

1. *Sabzeh* (lentil or wheat sprouts), representing the rebirth of nature
2. *Samanu,* a thick sweet paste made of slowly cooked wheat sprouts
3. *Sib* (apples)
4. *Senjed*, the fruit of a native Persian tree not found in the West
5. *Sir* (garlic), representing medicine
6. *Somaq* (sumac)
7. *Serkeh* (vinegar), representing age and patience

*Sekkeh* (coins) can also be substituted for one of the items on the *Haftseen*. Other items traditionally placed on a *Haftseen* table include, painted eggs, a goldfish in a bowl of water, a brazier for burning wild rue, a pot of flowering *sonbol* (hyacinth), which can also be substituted for one of the items starting with the letter "S," a mirror, and two candlesticks.

## Chaharshanbeh Suri
### Last Wednesday Eve Before
### New Year Celebrations

On the Tuesday evening before the last Wednesday before the Persian New Year, Iranians observe the ancient annual custom of all souls, similar to All Souls Day, or Halloween, the evening before All Saints Day. On that evening, they make bonfires to jump over, symbolic of the ancient belief that the fire will cleanse them, that they will give all sicknesses to the fire and receive health instead. They also disguise themselves: traditionally, women wear men's clothes and men disguise themselves in women's clothes, and they go to the houses in the neighborhood with a pot and a spoon, beating on the pot, and collecting rice and various beans  with which they make a thick soup, similar to what is known as "Stone Soup" in the West. They also serve a mixture of seven nuts and dried fruits, such as almonds, walnuts, and hazelnuts, and dried fruits such as apricots, peaches, and figs, called *Ajil-e Chaharshanbeh Suri.*

## Shab-e Yalda (Winter Solstice)

*Shab-e Yalda*, the winter solstice, is the longest night of the year. It marks the rebirth of the sun. This festival is traced to the Zoroastian concept of light and good against darkness and evil. On *Shab-e Yalda*, family and friends gather for a night-long vigil around the traditional winter heating apparatus called a *korsi*, a low, square table covered with a large quilt with people sitting on small mattresses around it. A brazier of glowing crushed charcoal is the heat source for this apparatus. In older times, when fresh fruits were not available in winter, families carefully saved all sorts of fruits, especially watermelons, to serve to guests on this night. Also, a variety of sweets and other foods are served to celebrate *Shab-e Yalda.*

# Persian Wedding Table
## Sofreh-ye Aqd

Arrangement by Afsaneh Sargordian
Photo by Sayeh Rashad.

Iranian weddings consist of two parts: the wedding ceremony (*Aqd*) in which the wedding vows are performed,
and the wedding celebration (*Arusi*), which occurs later,
sometimes within a year or two, after which the bride and
groom begin their lives together. Wedding celebrations were
traditionally often observed for seven days and nights with
the participation of large numbers of relatives and friends.
Wedding celebrations include elaborate dinner banquets and

are usually followed by music and entertainment. Wedding
ceremonies, on the other hand, are more simple.  An important feature of the wedding ceremonies is the *Sofreh
Aqd*, on which the following symbolic items are displayed:

*Ayeneh-ye Bakht* [Mirror of Luck], a mirror representing
light (an important symbol in the ancient Iranian religion,
Zoroastrianism) and good fortune.

Two candles or candelabras, symbolizing fire, another important element in Zoroastrianism, which represents a bright future for the couple.

A copy of the *Koran* or *The Divan of Hafez,* or *Avesta.*

Gold coins, a symbol of wealth.

Needle and thread, signifying sewing up the lips of the mother-in-law to prevent her from speaking ill of the bride.

Two cones of sugar to be grinded together over the heads of the bride and groom, and decorated rock sugar candy, *nabat*, representing a happy and sweet life for them.

A tray decorated with colorful herbs and spices, sectioned in square forms, and generally prepared by an herbalist, usually including the following items: turmeric, cinnamon, salt, black pepper, paprika, sumac, dried crushed mint, tarragon, oregano, thyme, and cloves. After the wedding, these spiced are mixed and used for good luck.

A tray decorated with various seeds, including caraway seeds, celery seeds, nigella seeds, poppy seeds, and sesame seeds.

A loaf of flat bread specially baked, decorated with various seeds and herbs and inscribed with *"Mobarak Bad"* [Congratulations] using a colorful spice such as saffron. This symbolizes prosperity for the feasts and for the couple's life thereafter.

Decorated eggs, a symbol of fertility.

To be shared with the wedding guests: a platter of feta cheese and fresh herbs.

Several platters of pastry and confections.

A basket of fruit.

Decorated almonds, walnuts, and hazelnuts.

# Religious *Sofreh* (Banquet)

The term, *sofreh*, which literally means "supper cloth," implies a dinner or luncheon party. Such a party is given on various occasions, such as celebrating a circumcision or a wedding, or for religious purposes. A religious *sofreh* is usually organized and attended by women. In every *sofreh*, candles are used for decoration and bread, water, and dates are served. Bread represents a blessing from God, while dates are important as they were one of the favorite foods of the Prophet Mohammad, and water is the source of life. It is also an important symbolic element in the Shi'i tradition, since it is associated with the Battle of Karbala in which the third imam of the Shi'ites, Hoseyn, and many members of his family were prevented from having access to water and were ultimately killed. Candles represent God, the Illuminator.

### Sofreh-ye Hazrat-e Khezr, or Prophet Elias
(a Shiraz tradition)

This *sofreh* is spread on the last Friday of the year and remains in place until the Persian New Year. This sofreh is an elaborate banquet in which the hostess usually has a wish that she hopes will be fulfilled. It contains numerous kinds of cooked food, such as meat dishes and a variety of rice dishes. It also contains all kinds of fruits in season as well as dried fruits. A typical *Sofreh-ye Hazrat-e Khezr* includes the following:

> A bowl of fresh water with floating green leaves
> Coins, which are usually concealed under the supper cloth
> Fruits, meat dishes, rice dishes, bread, and dates

Once the *sofreh* is set, the hostess and the guests of the household perform special prayers. Then they leave the room and close the door behind them. After New Year, an adult member of the family enters the room. If the participants conclude that some of the food has been consumed, they regard it as a good omen, that Elias has visited the house and has eaten some of the food on the *sofreh*. The food then is sent out to relatives and others.

Preceding: *Nakhl*, or shrine showing pieces of cloth fastened by the faithful to mark vows made in the hope of divine assistance in reaching a goal or fulfilling some special need. *Ethnological Museum, Tehran.*

### Sofreh-ye Hazrat-e Abbas (Abolfazl)

It is believed that hosting this *sofreh* wards off any danger, misfortune or sickness. A typical *Sofreh-ye Hazrat-e Abbas* includes:

> *Ajïl-e Moshkel Gosha,* mixed nuts made of seven kinds of nuts.
> *Kachi*
> Fruits in season.
> A variety of rice dishes, including *Adas Polo, Lubiya Polo, Baqali Polo, Kalam Polo, Shirin Polo,* and *Chelo.*
> Various kinds of *khoresh*
> Feta cheese
> *Halva* and variety of sweets.

Like other *sofreh*s, this *sofreh* is also concluded with special prayers. The food is then distributed among the guests.

### Sofreh-ye Hazrat-e Roqiyeh

This is among the least elaborate religious banquets. Normally it is hosted by a woman who is making a religious pledge to give this *sofreh* in order to have a wish fulfilled regarding a child. It is hosted on a Monday night and can be any Monday of the year. This simple *sofreh* usually includes bread and dates. Preferably, the ceremony takes place among ruins, as a reminder of the way Roqiyeh was captured and lived in ruins after the Battle of Karbala. The bread and dates are distributed among the poor.

## Sofreh-ye Ommolbanin, the Mother of Abolfazl

This banquet requires a specific thick soup called *Omaj* and a special bread called *Kamaj*. This *sofreh* is given for the fulfillment of various wishes, including recovery from disease, paying a debt, safe journey for a traveler, and the safe return of child or husband who is imprisoned. A requirement of this *sofreh* for the hostess is to identify in advance seven households in which live a female by the name of Fatemeh (named after the daughter of the Prophet Mohammad). On a Thursday, the hostess of the banquet carries an empty container, and walks with bare feet in the street. She goes to each of the previously identified houses. She knocks on the doors and "begs" for some of the ingredients for preparing *Omaj*.

When the stew is cooking on the fire, small pieces of *Kamaj* bread are added to the pot and cooked with the rest of the ingredients. During the cooking process, the women praise the Prophet Mohammad and his family. When the guests arrive, the *Omaj* is poured into small bowls and placed on the *sofreh*. Some of the *Omaj* is placed in a large bowl and placed on one corner of the *sofreh* along with an empty bowl and a spoon. While the guests are at the table, one of the young girls named Fatemeh, who must be under the age of puberty, is selected. As an important part of this banquet, she sits on the floor at the *sofreh* facing Mecca. The empty bowl and the spoon are placed before her. At this point, an elderly woman with religious learning recites from the Koran. This is followed by prayers and praise for Mohammad and his family. With each prayer and recitation, the young Fatemeh dishes out one spoon of *Omaj* from the large bowl into the empty bowl. At the end she dishes out seven large spoons of *Omaj* into her bowl. Then the content of this bowl is mixed with the rest of the *Omaj*

and is divided among the guests. Each guest can ask God to grant her wish while partaking in this banquet. Men and pregnant women are not allowed to eat from this meal. It is believed that any man who eats from this *Omaj* will end up in jail, and if a pregnant woman eats it, if her baby is a boy he will be jailed when he grows up.

## Sofreh-ye Bibi Zeynab

This *sofreh* is hosted during crises and emergencies. *Ash-e Reshteh* is served for this banquet, which must be cooked indoors. At all times, doors and windows are kept closed to prevent outsiders from seeing or touching the *ash*. The eldest woman among the guests (or if it happens to be the hostess) distributes the food. Before consuming the food, a prayer specific to Zeynab, the granddaughter of the Prophet Mohammad, is recited. Men and boys are not allowed to partake in this banquet. Pregnant women also are not allowed to consume this *ash*.

## Halva-ye- Fatemeh Zahra

Prepared to honor the daughter of the Prophet Mohammad, there is no elaborate ceremonial *sofreh* attached to this sweet dish. There is no need also to have any guest over. The halva is distributed among women only. If the wish of the hostess is granted, then she is obligated to prepare this sweet dish every year.

Facing: *Alam* or processional standard used during *Ashura*. Pahlavi steel crown, made in Isfahan in 1972, is visible in the center of this particular *alam*. Other parts variously date to 220 years old.
*Ethnological Museum, Tehran.*

Front row, from left to right, *Halim Badenjan, Kabab Shami, Khoresh-e Kadu.*
Middle row, *Kuku Sabzi, Adas Polo, Khoresh-e Karafs, Ash-e Reshteh.*
Back row, *Dolmeh-ye Kalam, Khorak-e Havij va Lubia Sabz, Rice with Tahdig.*

All dishes are prepared by the students at the author's cooking class in Austin, Texas.

# Menu Suggestions

T he following menus, presented in two different formats, are offered merely as suggestions for successful meals, taking in mind, for the most part, dishes that are traditionally served together. But, they should not be looked upon as limitations; the only limitation on the combinations of dishes should be one's own imagination. Various Persian dishes also combine quite well with many American foods.

The section on Vegetarian Dishes contains rice dishes, khoreshes, ashes, kukus, stuffed vegetables, and salads that do not contain meat. However, most dishes with the exception of kabob can be prepared without meat.

All foods, with the exception of desserts and tea, are generally served together as one complete course. Occasionally, a particular drink, such as dugh, is served with a meal, but most often no drink or merely water accompanies the meal.

Tea, however, is served at all times, after every meal and usually with breakfast, in between meals with fruit, and especially when guests come to call—either expectedly or unexpectedly.

As for desserts, to most Iranians, dessert means fruit, but fruit does not necessarily signify dessert, as fresh fruit in season is usually served after lunch and dinner, often with breakfast, as well as for midday or late evening snacks. Sweets, such as those found in the dessert section, are usually reserved for guests, but they have been included in the menus.

In the first section, foods are presented for general everyday use at home whereas in the second section the dishes are presented in a typical restaurant menu.

As your meals begin collecting rave reviews, you can reply, as the Iranians, do, **"Nush-e jan."**

## Suggested Menu For Home Use

### Breakfasts

Halim
Adasi
Taftun bread
Hot tea with Pulaki
\*\*\*
Omlet-e Khorma
Hot Barbari bread
Hot tea
\*\*\*
Khagineh
Hot Barbari bread
Hot tea
\*\*\*
Nan Khoshkeh
Butter
Panir-e Khanegi
Moraba-ye Sib or Albalu
Hot milk
\*\*\*
Barbari bread
Panir-e Khanegi
Fresh grapes, cantaloupe, or pears
Hot tea
\*\*\*
Sangak or Lavash bread
Butter
Panir-e Khanegi
Walnuts
Moraba-ye Kadu Tanbal
\*\*\*
Nan-e Kamaji
Butter
Moraba-ye Balang
\*\*\*
Nan Khoshkeh or Nan Khoshkeh Qandi
Hot milk

### Lunches

Kabab-e Kubideh
Sabzikhordan
Sangak bread
Dugh
\*\*\*
Beriyan
Taftun bread
Sabzikhordan
Dugh
\*\*\*
Kotlet-e Gusht-o Sibzamini
Barbari bread
Sabzikhordan
Mast-o Musir
\*\*\*
Ash-e Torsh
Hot Barbari bread
Panir-e Khanegi
Sekanjebin
\*\*\*
Abgusht-e Nokhod va Gusht-e Kubideh
Taftun bread
Torshi Liteh
\*\*\*
Dolmeh Kalam
Ash-e Mast
Tar Halva
\*\*\*
Sandovich-e Kalbas
Shirin Tareh
Soft drink
\*\*\*
Pirashki ba Gusht
Sabzikhordan
Mast
\*\*\*

Lavash Dolmasi
Torshi Bademjan
***
Salad-e Gowjeh Farangi ba Morgh
Barbari bread

## Luncheon Buffet Suggestions

Kotlet
Kuku Sabzi
Kuku Qandi
Halim Bademjan
Mast-e Kiseh'i
Hot Taftun bread
Fereni
Hot tea
***
Baqala Qateq
Seshandaz-e Havij
Dolmeh Kadu
Kufteh Kari
Salad-e Shirazi
Bereshtuk-e Kaka'o
Hot tea or soft drink

## Special Occasion Luncheon

Ash-e Reshteh
Qemeh
Kabab Shami
Taftun bread
Sabzikhordan
Mast
Torshi-ye Haft Bijar
Sholehzard
Hot tea

## Dinners

Fesenjan
Chelo
Kuku Bademjan
Mast-o Esfenaj
Ranginak
Hot tea
***
Baqali Polo
Kuku Sabzi
Khoresh-e Bademjan
Mast
Lowz-e Badam
Fruit in season
Hot tea
***
Dolmeh Bademjan
Adas Polo
Mast-o Khiyar
Cantaloupe
***
Kabab-e Soltani
Chelo
Mast-o Khiyar
Sabzikhordan
Dugh
Bastani ba Khameh
Hot tea
***
Tahchin-e Morgh
Khoresh-e Kadu
Mast-o Labu
Melon and grapes
Hot tea
***

Khoresh-e Rivas
Chelo
Qelyapiti
Mast
Sabzikhordan
Tar Halva
Fruit in season
Hot tea
***
Kalam Polo
Khoresh-e Bademjan
Salad-e Shirazi
Mast-e Kiseh'i
Lowz-e Nargil
Hot tea
***
Shirin Polo
Mast-o Esfenaj
Paludeh Shirazi
Hot tea
***
Kufteh-ye Shevid-o Baqala
Kabab Moshti
Mast
Shirini-ye Tar I
Hot tea
***
Khoresh-e Morgh-o Alu
Chelo
Dolmeh-ye Barg-e Mo
Mast-o Khiyar
Yakh dar Behesht
Hot tea
***
Khoresh-e Karafs
Chelo
Kuku Qandi
Burani-ye Kangar
Fruit in season
Hot tea
***

Kabab Hoseyni
Adas Polo
Khoresh-e Esfenaj
Sabzikhordan
Zulbiya
Hot tea
***
Abgusht-e Sabzi va Gusht-e Kubideh
Estamboli Polo
Taftun bread
Torshi
Melon
Hot tea
***
Morassa' Polo
Khoresh-e Anar Avij I
Kuku-ye Shevid va Baqala
Salad-e Karafs-o Gerdu
Nan-e Panjereh'i
Hot tea
***
Ash-e Kashk
Mahi-e Qobad ba Hashu
Kalam Shur
Qottab
Hot tea

## MAYKADEH RESTURANT
### A San Francisco Landmark

mutton, poultry and seafood, all blended with exotic herbs and spices. The proprietor, Mr. Mahmoud Khossoussi, established this restaurant in 1985. As *San Francisco Examiner* has observed, "Ancient Persia had its Xerxes, now San Francisco has its own Persian Restaurant fit for a King."

Located at the heart of the historic North Beach in San Francisco bay area, Maykadeh , literally meaning a tavern where poets, mystics and intelligentsia met to enjoy good food and wine in Persia ( Iran), offers a variety of delicious foods. Ingredients include basmati rice, saffron, pomegranate sauce, top choice of beef,

# APPETIZER
## [MAZEH]

# SALADS & RELISHES

# SOUP & POTTAGE

# RICE DISHES

## WITH BEEF OR LAMB

| | Page |
|---|---|
| **Adas Polo ba Gusht** | 12 |
| (rice and lentils with beef or lamb) | |
| **Baqali Polo ba Gusht** | 16 |
| (rice with fava beans, dill weed and beef or lamb) | |
| **Estamboli Polo** | 20 |
| (rice with beef or lamb, tomatoes, and green beans) | |
| **Kalam Polo** | 15 |
| (rice with beef or lamb and cabbage) | |
| **Reshteh Polo** | 20 |
| (rice with noodles and beef or lamb) | |
| **Tahchin-e Badenjan** | 33 |
| (eggplants and beef or lamb in a crust of saffron-flavored rice) | |
| **Tahchin-e Barreh** | 32 |
| (lamb and orange peel in a crust of saffron-flavored rice) | |

## WITH CHICKEN

| | Page |
|---|---|
| **Polo-ye Qalebi-ye Shirazi** | 26 |
| (rice with chicken, eggplants, and *zereshk*) | |
| **Shirin Polo** | 18 |
| (sweet, saffron-flavored rice with chicken) | |
| **Tahchin-e Morgh** | 30 |
| (chicken in a crust of saffron-flavored rice) | |

## WITH SHRIMP

| | Page |
|---|---|
| **Polo Meygu** | 27 |
| (rice with shrimp) | |

## VEGETARIAN RICE DISHES

| | Page |
|---|---|
| **Adas Polo** | 12 |
| (rice with lentils) | |
| **Albalu Polo** | 13 |
| (rice with tart cherries) | |
| **Baqali Polo** | 15 |
| (rice with fava beans and dill weed) | |
| **Zereshk Polo** | 14 |
| (rice with *zereshk*) | |

# STEWS
## SERVED OVER RICE

## WITH CHICKEN

| | Page |
|---|---|
| **Fesenjan** | 44 |
| (braised poultry in walnut and pomegranate sauce) | |
| **Khorak-e Morgh ba Khameh** | 64 |
| (chicken baked in cream) | |
| **Khoresh-e Morgh-o Alu** | 46 |
| (chicken and prune stew) | |

## WITH BEEF OR LAMB

| | Page |
|---|---|
| **Kabab Moshti** | 169 |
| (carrot and meatball stew) | |
| **Khoresh-e Badenjan ba Gusht** | 52 |
| (eggplant stew with beef or lamb) | |
| **Khoresh-e Bamiyeh** | 50 |
| (okra stew with beef or lamb) | |
| **Khoresh-e Kadu Tanbal** | 58 |
| (pumpkin stew with beef or lamb and yogurt) | |
| **Khoresh-e Karafs** | 47 |
| (celery stew with beef or lamb) | |
| **Khoresh-e Qarch** | 59 |
| (mushroom stew with beef or lamb) | |
| **Khoresh-e Qeymeh Badenjan** | 59 |
| (split pea and eggplant stew with beef or lamb) | |
| **Khoresh-e Rivas** | 50 |
| (rhubarb stew with beef or lamb) | |
| **Qeymeh** | 24 |
| (yellow split pea stew with beef or lamb) | |
| **Qormeh Sabzi** | 25 |
| (green herb stew with beef or lamb) | |

## VEGETARIAN STEWS

| | Page |
|---|---|
| **Khoresh-e Badenjan** | 53 |
| (eggplant stew) | |
| **Khoresh-e Kadu** | 47 |
| (zucchini stew) | |
| **Qelyeh-ye Kadu-ye Rashti** | 66 |
| (yellow squash and lentil fricassee) | |

# KABOBS

## BEEF OR LAMB

| | Page |
|---|---|
| **Kabab Digi** | 80 |
| (roasted beef with saffron) | |
| **Kabab Hoseyni** | 79 |
| (skillet beef or lamb kabob) | |
| **Kabab-e Barg** | 76 |
| (grilled skewered beef or lamb kabob) | |
| **Kabab-e Kubideh** | 74 |
| (grilled ground beef or lamb kabob) | |
| **Kabab-e Qafqazi** | 80 |
| (grilled kabob, Caucasian style) | |
| **Kabab-e Soltani** | 76 |
| (grilled skewered "royal" kabob of beef or lamb) | |
| **Kabab-e Tanuri** | 81 |
| (oven-baked kabob of beef or lamb) | |
| **Shish Kabab** | 79 |
| (beef or lamb grilled with vegetables) | |

## CHICKEN AND DUCK

| | Page |
|---|---|
| **Jujeh Kabab** | 72 |
| (broiled skewered chicken) | |
| **Kabab-e Morghabi** | 81 |
| (grilled duck) | |

## FISH AND SHRIMP

| | Page |
|---|---|
| **Mahi Kabab I** | 108 |
| (grilled fish kabob) | |
| **Mahi Kabab II** | 108 |
| (grilled fish kabob, Persian Gulf Coast style) | |
| **Meygu Kabab** | 116 |
| (shrimp kabob) | |

# MEATBALLS & STUFFED DISHES

| | Page |
|---|---|
| **Dolmeh Badenjan** | 161 |
| (stuffed eggplant) | |
| **Dolmeh Kalam** | 161 |
| (stuffed cabbage leaves) | |
| **Dolmeh-ye Barg-e Mo** | 156 |
| (stuffed grape leaves) | |
| **Dolmeh-ye Beh** | 159 |
| (stuffed quinces) | |
| **Dolmeh-ye Felfel-e Sabz** | 163 |
| (bell peppers stuffed with beef or lamb and rice) | |
| **Dolmeh-ye Gowjeh Farangi** | 163 |
| (tomato stuffed with ground beef or lamb and yellow split peas) | |
| **Kufteh Tabrizi** | 170 |
| (meatballs with split peas stuffed with boiled egg) | |
| **Kufteh-ye Shevid-o Baqala** | 174 |
| (meatballs with dill weed and lima or fava beans) | |

# MEAT PATTIES & CUTLETS

## WITH BEEF OR LAMB

| | Page |
|---|---|
| **Beryan** | 78 |
| (beef or lamb patty served on flat bread) | |
| **Kotlet-e Gusht-o Sibzamini** | 87 |
| (beef or lamb and potato patties) | |
| **Kotlet-e Tu Por** | 87 |
| (stuffed cutlet) | |
| **Shami Kabab** | 84 |
| (patties with chickpeas and beef or lamb) | |
| **Shami-ye Lapeh** | 84 |
| (patties with yellow split peas & beef or lamb) | |

## WITH FISH

| | Page |
|---|---|
| **Kotlet-e Mahi** | 112 |
| (fish patties) | |

# SEAFOOD

# SIDE DISHES

# DESSERTS

# BEVERAGES

# Conversion Table for Cooking

## U.S. to Metric

*Capacity*

1/5 teaspoon = 1 ml

1 teaspoon = 5 ml

1 tablespoon = 15 ml

1 fluid oz. = 30 ml

1/5 cup = 50 ml

1 cup = 240 ml

2 cups (1 pint) = 470 ml

4 cups (1 quart) = .95 liter

4 quarts (1 gal.) = 3.8 liters

*Weight*

1 oz. = 28 grams

1 pound = 454 grams

*Temperature*

100 F = 38 C

200 F = 93 C

300 F = 149 C

400 F = 204 C

## Metric to U.S.

*Capacity*

1 milliliters = 1/5 teaspoon

5 ml = 1 teaspoon

15 ml = 1 tablespoon

30 ml = 1 fluid oz.

100 ml = 3.4 fluid oz.

240 ml = 1 cup

1 liter = 34 fluid oz.

1 liter = 4.2 cups

1 liter = 2.1 pints

1 liter = 1.06 quarts

1 liter = .26 gallon

*Weight*

1 gram = .035 ounce

100 grams = 3.5 ounces

500 grams = 1.10 pounds

1 kilogram = 2.205 pounds

1 kilogram = 35 oz.

*Temperature*

100 C = 212 F

200 C = 392 F

300 C = 572 F

## Cooking Measurement Equivalents

16 tablespoons = 1 cup

12 tablespoons = 3/4 cup

10 tablespoons + 2 teaspoons = 2/3 cup

8 tablespoons = 1/2 cup

6 tablespoons = 3/8 cup

5 tablespoons + 1 teaspoon = 1/3 cup

4 tablespoons = 1/4 cup

2 tablespoons = 1/8 cup

2 tablespoons + 2 teaspoons = 1/6 cup

1 tablespoon = 1/16 cup

2 cups = 1 pint

2 pints = 1 quart

3 teaspoons = 1 tablespoon

48 teaspoons = 1 cup

All measurements are rounded to the nearest figure.

Traditional wooden spoons and ladles.

# INDEX

## About the Author

M. R. Ghanoonparvar is Professor of Persian and Comparative Literature at the University of Texas at Austin. He has published widely on Persian literature and culture in both English and Persian. Internationally recognized as an expert on Iranian culinary arts, he is the author of two best-selling books on Persian cuisine and numerous articles on the history of food and food preparation in Iran in various encyclopedias and journals, and he has taught Iranian culinary courses throughout the United States. His television cooking show, *Persian Cuisine*, was popular for several years in the 1980s in such major cities as Austin, Houston, Los Angeles, and Washington D.C.